FOLLOW
THE ROAR

....

FOLLOW THE ROAR

··

TAILING TIGER FOR ALL 604 HOLES
OF HIS MOST SPECTACULAR SEASON

BOB SMILEY

HARPER

An Imprint of HarperCollins*Publishers*
www.harpercollins.com

HarperCollins books may be purchased for educational, business, or sales promotional use. For information, please write: Special Markets Department, HarperCollins Publishers, 10 East 53rd Street, New York, NY 10022.

Portions of "Chez Tiger" reprinted courtesy of ESPN/Starwave Partners d/b/a ESPN Internet Venture, 2008.

FIRST EDITION

Designed by Jaime Putorti

Library of Congress Cataloging-in-Publication Data is available upon request.

ISBN: 978-0-06-169025-9

08   09   10   11   12   DIX/RRD   10   9   8   7   6   5   4   3   2   1

For Bruce Jenner.
You were right.

"Before starting out, however, I'd like to observe that experienced spectators realize that the least satisfactory way of watching a medal play tournament is to trek around the course with one particular pair of players. It's an accepted fact that walking 18 holes is more tiring than playing them."

—BOBBY JONES, AUGUSTA NATIONAL GOLF CLUB SPECTATOR GUIDE, 1949

CONTENTS

PREFACE

February 24, 2008 • 11:20 am • Marana, Arizona

Stewart Cink lines up an uphill, five-foot putt for par. His opponent, Tiger Woods, is already in the hole with a bogey. Tiger's 4 up on Stewart, halfway through the 36-hole final of the Accenture Match Play. But it's not over. In fact, if Cink makes this, he can stall Tiger's momentum and cut into the lead, starting the last 18 holes a very catchable 3 down. A big putt, to say the least. He takes a practice stroke with his belly putter, then carefully rests it behind the ball. I look around to see if everyone else shares my suspense and notice I'm the only person actually watching Stewart Cink. I follow the gallery's eyes to the far side of the green to see what's so distracting.

Tiger Woods is putting on his watch.

LONELY AT THE TOP

Somewhere just west of Orlando he was improving on perfection. On the driving range just steps from one of his many houses, he was shaping shots in the cool December afternoon. Left . . . right . . . high . . . low . . . The finishing touches in his preparation for yet another season as the undisputed best player in golf. And on his shoulders he seems happily to carry the weight of a million fans, of billion-dollar corporations, and of his own late father's expectations not just to be the greatest golfer ever, but to do more for humanity than any man before him.

On that same day, I'd been on the roof of our rented single-story house in the bowels of L.A.'s San Fernando Valley for forty-five minutes after having failed to fix the air conditioner, the poorly balanced aluminum ladder rocking back and forth in the breeze just out of reach of my right foot, while my wife, my two kids, and the collective universe were completely indifferent to the fact that I was both nowhere to be found and, in more ways than one, completely stuck. If you're ever feeling fragile about your life, I suggest you don't start by comparing yourself to Tiger Woods.

Yet I did. All the time. I couldn't help it. I'd been doing it since long before he ever showed up at the Greater Milwaukee Open in 1996 to utter his famous opening line, "I guess . . . hello, world." Tiger and I both played high school golf in Southern California—he in the city of Cypress, just south of L.A., and I in Ventura, just north of it. He was a grade older, and I specifically remember my sophomore year when my Buena High Bulldogs made it past the first round of regional playoffs. The question before our next tournament was not what the toughest team would be, but whether Tiger Woods would be there. Even then we knew he was special. And since we were high school boys, we hated him for it.

Tiger was a threat to everything all of us had decided went hand in hand with being a teenager—namely the overarching tenet to blend in with the crowd, a commitment threatened only by acne and grounded at all times in a general lack of self-confidence. When he made it to the U.S. Amateur in 1994, we followed him in the paper and on TV as he picked apart his opponents, famously saving the killing blow for the last few holes, when, at the precise moment that the little voice in his challengers' heads started to say, "You know, I could win this thing . . . ," Tiger would effectively tear out their souls with putts no kid is supposed to make, punctuating them with a fist pump that we read as pure aggression. And if you think those defeats don't leave scars, don't talk to Trip Kuehne, Tiger's victim in the finals in 1994. He never turned pro, and fourteen years after the loss, he still hasn't watched the highlights of the match. "I don't want to," he has said, with the same seriousness that someone who survived a plane crash might turn down the opportunity to listen to the last sounds from the cockpit voice recorder. Tiger wasn't just winning golf tournaments; he was crushing spirits.

So when Tiger's fame exploded two years later, a twelve-month span in which he won his third straight U.S. Amateur and sixth straight USGA title, dropped out of Stanford at the age of twenty, signed $60 million worth of endorsement deals, then proceeded to win the Masters by 12 shots, I had already staked out my lonely position as a golf fan who had no interest in watching Tiger Woods succeed. He was talented, but his path to greatness was so merciless and calculated—nothing resembling the country club gentility that typified the way I had been taught to play the game—that to me there would be nothing sweeter than spending my Sundays watching more amicable players challenge him shot for shot and then finish him off, leaving the great Tiger Woods to face the reality that even he can be beaten.

There was just one problem—in the eleven years of my golf watching since Tiger had turned pro, I'd never seen it happen. Never. I mean, I knew it *had* happened. In 1996, a journeyman named Ed Fiori had kept Tiger from winning his first PGA event at the Quad Cities Open. And at the Nissan Open in 1998, Billy Mayfair became (and remains) the only person to beat Tiger in a playoff. Just my luck, somehow I'd missed those Sundays. But I would never miss a major. Thirteen different times Tiger had entered the final round in the lead or tied for the lead, and do you know how many times he had won? Thirteen. Rooting against Tiger on Sunday was the equivalent of watching skeet shooting and rooting for the clay pigeons. Yet, inevitably as the sun set, there I'd be, watching Tiger once again raise a trophy in that obnoxious red shirt and flash that golf-ball white smile, a grin that translated in my head to three simple words: "Bob, you suck."

And so, as I sat on the roof of my house—unemployed, uninspired, out of shape, a once-dependable single-digit golf game in ruins—I finally had to embrace the idea that every person who'd ever taken on the number one player in the world (yes, even Ed Fiori and Billy Mayfair) had long ago reached: maybe Tiger Woods could teach me something.

Tiger himself has said that there's no better way to learn who someone is than by spending quality time in that person's presence. But considering his yacht is named *Privacy* and I didn't have much in the way of a journalistic pedigree (that is to say, I didn't have one), I felt fairly certain that I'd have to track Tiger the old-fashioned way, on foot, from the gallery.

When he arrived in Southern California later that month for his off-season invitational, the Target World Challenge, I was there—from the moment he stepped out of his courtesy car till the second he disappeared into the press tent. Tiger shot the lowest score I'd ever witnessed in person, a 62 and a tournament record. And what took place outside the ropes was just as entertaining. I was lectured by former Olympic Gold Medalist Bruce Jenner, who responded to one of my self-deprecating jokes with a stern, "Never underestimate yourself!" I overheard hysterical conversations, my favorite being the middle-aged guy who told anyone willing to listen that Tiger's ascent to stardom was a lot like Hannah Montana's and "you probably don't know this, but his real name is actually Elrod." By the end I found myself high-fiving grown men I'd never met and would never see again. I wasn't a Tiger fan, but I was struck by the impact he made on everyone else.

I wrote an article about the experience for ESPN.com, a minute-by-minute account of the day. Once it was posted on the site, e-mails flowed in. They ranged from jealous Tiger lovers who wished they had been there to righteous ones who thought I didn't realize that his real name is El*drick*, not Elrod. Mixed in was an e-mail from someone who posed a sincere and absurd question: "Are you going to be doing this all season?" *Yeah, right*, I thought. But over the next few weeks I couldn't shake the idea.

An entire season.

Every tournament.

Every round.

Every hole.

The proposition was intriguing because (1) I wasn't sure it was physically possible; (2) the 62 at the Target World Challenge had me wondering whether this was Tiger's year; and (3) I had no other marketable job skills. I'd spent the last four years writing sitcoms. I'd even had a little success, but every year there were fewer comedies on the air, and on December 14, 2005, the one for which I worked was canceled. I know the date because it was two days after my first child, Danny, was born. So every time someone asked me, "And how old is your son?" I wanted to answer, "Look, there just aren't any jobs right now!"

Coupled with this was the onset of the Hollywood writers' strike, which meant I wasn't allowed to work even if there were a job. When it wasn't resolved within the first few weeks, both sides agreed it was going to last months and possibly all the way to June. Danny would be two and a half.

The idea to follow Tiger for a year wasn't without its obstacles. My friend Andy, a corporate accountant with an admitted obsession with spreadsheets, ran the numbers in Excel and helped me see that even with some help, between traveling and supporting my family, we would run out of money sometime before the British Open in July. But I was convinced I could pull it off if I booked the cheapest flights, rented the smallest cars, and, whenever possible, stayed with friends, family, even strangers along the way.

Another problem was that despite having written a handful of golf pieces for ESPN.com, I had no special access, which meant that everything from getting into the events to keeping up with Tiger from the gallery was solely up to me. Success would require planning, self-discipline, and endurance. None of those was an adjective friends would ever insert in an acrostic of my name.

In the end I decided this was an adventure that needed to be taken. Not just for me, but for anyone who stood to gain something from following greatness. After all, how often does one have the chance to see a person do something better than perhaps it has ever been done before or will ever be done again?

At least that was how I pitched it to my wife.

And so, in the last week of January, I unearthed my work bag from the recesses of my trunk, bought a pedometer and a notebook, kissed my wife and kids, and hit the road. Tiger would tee off in less than twenty-four hours. I couldn't be late.

FOLLOW
THE ROAR

....

THE MACHINE

. . . .

The Buick Invitational

Torrey Pines Golf Course
La Jolla, California
January 24–27, 2008

When Torrey Pines Golf Course was refurbished back in 1999, workers discovered that rubble and pieces of old toilets had been used to build up the tees and greens, evidence to all that no matter how pretty the cameras make it look on TV, the home of the Buick Invitational and this year's U.S. Open is at its core a city-owned muni. My old boss Alan wasn't even that kind. "It's a dump," he had pronounced after a weekend trip to play it a few years back. I'd been to the Buick Invitational once before, back when my high school friend A.J. was in college just down the street at UC San Diego. At the time I hadn't been to a professional golf tournament in years, and A.J. had never been to one, a dangerous combination that led to me stupidly telling him that sure, he could go ahead and bring his camera. When A.J. tried to take a picture of Jeff Sluman (why he chose Jeff Sluman of all people remains a mystery) the marshals were all over him, forcing him to hand over his film as if he had just snapped a shot of Area 51.

Tiger Woods' memories of Torrey Pines were likely quite a bit fonder. For one thing, he'd won the Buick a total of five times, including the last three years. But his history there goes back a lot further than that. Every July when Tiger was growing up, his parents, Earl and Kultida, would pack Tiger in their car and head down the 405 freeway, eventually funneling into Interstate 5 in Orange County, then south past the double-boob-shaped nuclear power plant at San Onofre, through the coastal military expanse of Camp Pendleton, passing the bright yellow signs that warned them to watch out for illegal aliens crossing the highway, then finally west to Torrey Pines and the home of the Junior World Golf Championships, one of *the* premier events in junior golf. How premier? In 1984, David Toms won the 15- to 17-year-old division, a South African named "Ernest" Els won the 13- to 14-year-old division, and Eldrick Woods won the 9- to 10-year-old division. He was only eight. A few years later, he was old enough to play the big course and made the adjustment, winning his age group in 1988, '89, '90, and '91. It was safe to say that Tiger Woods had plenty of positive memories to keep him coming back to San Diego.

Despite the city being just two and a half hours south of L.A., I couldn't remember the last time I'd made the drive. With two little kids, any trip longer than about an hour means trouble. My friend A.J., on the other hand, had never left. Nine years removed from college, he'd risen in the ranks as a mechanical engineer and was working on defense projects that he claimed he couldn't discuss with anyone, including his wife. As a result, any visit with him would inevitably involve some version of this conversation:

"Does your work involve missiles?"

"I can't really talk about it."

"So it *does* involve missiles."

"Stop it."

Our friendship went back to the fourth grade but was cemented a few years later when his parents bought the house next door. He was the smallest kid in the class, and I wasn't much bigger. Nevertheless, that didn't stop us from spending almost every summer afternoon between eighth and ninth grade shooting hoops in my driveway, determined to make the freshman basketball team in the fall. On most afternoons, the sound of one of us bouncing the ball on the cement was enough to draw the other out of his room. We played one-on-one, HORSE, even ran drills we'd learned in basketball camp, anything to improve our game. In early September, the coach's decision was taped to his classroom door. Neither of us made the cut. For two smart kids who had worked hard, it was the first time in our lives that we learned the grown-up lesson that sometimes you can't accomplish everything you want just by trying.

There's not much worse than failing alone, so the fact that both of us fell short made the disappointment manageable, and we instead retreated to the athletic skills we already had. I tried out for and made the golf team in the spring, and A.J. did the same in tennis. After high school, I went east to college and he went south. And after graduation, the real world took over. I met my wife, Hillary, got married, had two kids. He had one dog, then two, then married a pharmacist with a dog of her own. We'd spent the last few years talking more about getting together than actually doing it, and you can keep that up for only so long before friends morph into acquaintances or eventually disappear altogether. So when I called A.J. a few days before the Buick Invitational to say I might need a place to stay, it was comforting to hear his answer: "Stay as long as you want." Theoretically, I could be going home Friday night if Tiger were to miss the cut. But Tiger doesn't miss cuts. Especially at Torrey Pines.

FIRST ROUND

It's 6:30 in the morning. Not many fans feel the need to arrive at Torrey Pines two and a half hours before Tiger's tee time. As I walk onto the property, the volunteer-to-spectator ratio is two to one, and workers compete over who can hand me the day's pairing sheet. On a grassy island in the parking lot, I sit and enjoy the quiet morning and the comings and goings of less famous golfers. Stewart Cink, six top tens last year but no wins, passes by in a pair of workout shorts carrying his own bag. Boo Weekley, a charmer from the Deep South, walks through security and has to show his ID, the camouflage shirt draped over his shoulder not doing much to scream PGA professional.

Tiger Woods, on the other hand, is nowhere to be found. An hour before his tee time, I move to the driving range where the photographers are antsy, so desperate for his whereabouts that one of them repeats the unhelpful rumor that his caddy had been seen going into the Lodge at Torrey Pines, but that he never came out, like one of the victims in Willy Wonka's Chocolate Factory.

Tiger reenters our lives on a golf cart, edging around the outside of the players' parking lot at top speed, buffeted on one side by his swing coach Hank Haney and in front by Steve "Stevie" Williams, his forty-four-year-old camera-crunching caddy, who, thanks to Tiger, is one of the wealthiest men in his native New Zealand. Secured between his legs is the gray-and-blue Buick golf bag belonging to his boss. Tiger sits stoically, hands on his knees, staring straight ahead. I'd hoped to draw some great insight from his entrance, about the beginning of the new season, but he goes by so quickly that all I can write down is: "Thursday: black shirt."

"Team Tiger" doesn't stop at the public bleacher end of the driving range, but continues up the cart path to the far end, behind security lines. It isn't just at tournaments that Tiger eschews the crowd's eyes. During practice rounds, Tiger always schedules his tee times at first light, knowing that he will be off the course before most fans have even found a parking spot. A marshal told me that they were out so early one day this week that Stevie spent the first few holes wearing an LED headlamp so he could read his yardage book. When fans eventually found Tiger, he didn't walk along the ropes and sign autographs like other players; he walked down the middle of the fairway, head down. I don't get it. Wouldn't the guy who had been trained to play through his own father's nutty intentional distractions (jingling change, toppling golf bags) benefit from playing under the microscope? And didn't he owe his loyal fans a lot more love than he gave? By comparison, the man of the people Phil Mickelson is with me on the close side of the range. When one father and son ask for an autograph, Phil turns and addresses them personally, saying, "I won't sign any right now, but I will after the round." Phil leaves people with hope. Tiger just leaves.

I can't lose him this quickly, not this early in the year. There are only two ways to get closer. One is to exit the tournament grounds altogether and watch Tiger from Torrey Pines Road, the main artery just east of the range that connects the northern town of Del Mar with La Jolla to the south. When I drove down it at 6:25 this morning, the lure of watching pro golfers beat balls for free had already attracted the attention of a handful of bicyclists and joggers who had decided that was a lot more fun than actual exercise. The other option is to somehow bypass security, find a back way to the far side of the range, and see Tiger up close. Chalk it up to early-season bravado, but I choose the latter. I stride down the empty 18th hole on Torrey Pines' North Course, keeping the range on my right up the hill. Near the tee box I cut back across, through the low-rent dirt lot where the caddies are forced to park, then up the embankment to the range. A second red-jacketed security guard is positioned directly in my way. Thankfully, he wants to see Tiger too and is facing the other direction. Head down, I steam right by.

I'm not the only one who has made it through. Two other random guys are there, standing between a couple of parked cars. I want to hear their story, how they got here, but their look says one thing: "Don't talk to us, and we won't talk to you." It's the same look guys exchange when they're shopping by themselves at Victoria's Secret. Thirty feet in front of us, Hank Haney is standing with his arms folded on his chest as Tiger hits majestic middle-iron after majestic middle-iron. No need for last-minute fixes here. If his coach has any critique, I can't imagine what it is. I mean, seriously, if you're Tiger Woods' coach, what could you say? "Good one." *Smack.* "Good one." *Smack.* "*Really* good one." His star student's swing is powerful but controlled, a big-block V8 cruising in third gear. The three of us are mesmerized, but not for long. We have been silent but not invisible, and another guard marches over to deliver the bad news: "No spectators." The other two guys skitter off, but I hold my ground and decide to ask a fair question: "What about press?" In my defense, I don't actually say I *am* press. If he wants to jump to that conclusion and allow me to stay, so be it. But all this question does is pull the string in his back. "No spectators," he repeats in the same tone. I nod and make the long walk back, knowing Tiger is indeed hitting the ball well, and that eventually he will have no choice but to come to us.

Tiger's arrival at Torrey Pines' putting green is completely different from his entrance at the range. Here, he is loose, carefree, all smiles. Even a great warm-up session with Haney would not have left Tiger this giddy. As he works his way around the putting green, more interested in chatting with other players than following the trail of his custom-made Nike Ones, the dynamic is obvious—it's Tiger's first day of school. He goes from the Swede Fredrik Jacobson to the Australian Rod Pampling, getting caught up on the last four months since he has crossed paths with most of them. No one goes to Tiger, of course; he comes to them. No one except George McNeill. And why not? Two years ago he was a club pro in Florida, having failed to find much success on the pro circuits. Deciding to give it one more shot, he not only made it to the final stage of the PGA Tour's qualifying school at the end of 2006, he won it. Before last year ended, he'd won the Frys.com Open and a two-year exemption on the Tour. And now today he arrives at the course knowing he will not only be seeing Tiger for the first time this season, he will also be playing with him, a fact that makes the moment all the more painful when McNeill stretches out his hand toward Tiger and it is obvious that Tiger has no idea who he is. To McNeill's credit, he stands his ground and keeps talking. Eventually, he fills in the blanks, reminding Tiger that they played against each other in college, and

Tiger shakes back. After a few more words, McNeill wanders off, and the Big Man on Campus resumes his reunion tour around the putting green.

8:59 AM • The first hole at Torrey Pines South heads due west, away from the clubhouse and toward the Pacific. A 452-yard slight dogleg right par 4 with bunkers on both sides of the fairway, it doesn't ease a player into his round; it pushes him. Standing off to the right side of the tee is the 9 a.m. pairing of Tiger, McNeill, and, rounding out the group, the loopy-swinging Jim Furyk. They swap scorecards, grab their drivers, and then stand, in silence, waiting for the official starter's watch to strike nine. Punctuating the moment, a pair of fighter jets roars out of Miramar Marine Corps Air Station five miles to the east. Three tournaments have already been played this season, and I watched all three of them. But most golf fans aren't like me—they have hobbies, a job, a life. And until they pop their heads out of their cubicles and see Tiger Woods, frankly, they'd rather just be left alone. As the clock strikes nine, the talking stops and a dozen photographers focus their cameras. The real season starts now.

"From Windermere, Florida, five-time defending champ . . . Tiger Woods." *Five-time defending champ.* If that number doesn't cause someone to pause, it should. To put that into perspective, the English golfer Luke Donald is ranked in the top 25 in the sport, and he has won four times. Worldwide. In his entire career.

Over the past few hours, I've been joined by a solid four hundred committed fans whose applause is mixed with a handful of hoots and whistles for good measure. Most people seem to be holding back, wanting to conserve their full range of emotions for the five hours in front of them.

Tiger tees up the ball, his left leg extended behind him as he leans down. Even the most grotesque of golfers does this, but Tiger makes it appear artistic. He stands behind the ball and stares down the fairway, visualizing his shot. At last Tiger is doing something I actually do. When I do it, I see everything. First the fairway. Then the rough. The traps. The trees. Eventually my eyes float way right to some fancy house with new windows that if I were to really block a shot, I just might reach. It's safe to assume that Tiger's visualization skills far exceed mine.

Tiger returns from the trance, addresses the ball, and gives one final look down the fairway. That glance is his trigger, and when it's over, he immediately draws his arms back, his yellow-soled driver orbiting around him before stopping just short of parallel above his head. The unique element of Tiger's swing is what happens next. As the club reverses direction, he appears to almost sit down, using his own weight along with his strength to pull the club face back to the ball with as much speed as possible. From this point comes The Great Unraveling—his wrists, his hips, his back, his shoulders . . . everything uncoiling through impact and turning toward his target in unison. For as squatty as he was at the beginning on his downswing, by the end of it he is tall and light.

Tiger has hit the drive hard, like he always does, but it catches the left fairway bunker, 290 yards away. As he retrieves his tee and heads down the fairway, his fans set off with him. Up ahead, another few hundred are waiting around the green. It's Thursday, round one, hole 1. Everything is possible.

9:47 AM • Tiger stands on the 4th green, sizing up a ten-foot birdie putt. You'd never pick the 488-yard, ocean-hugging 4th as the place Tiger might make his first birdie of the year. But he couldn't make his twenty-foot birdie putt on number 1, missed a twelve-footer on number 2, and was happy with par on number 3 after pulling his approach way left. Yet, here Tiger is, just ten feet away from a tricky left hole position after ripping a drive down the middle and sticking a long-iron just inside Jim Furyk's ball. Furyk makes his, which in turns shows Tiger the exact line for his putt. He can't possibly miss now. He doesn't. Tiger Woods makes his first birdie of 2008 and is into red numbers.

9:55 AM • I catch up with XM radio announcer Mark Carnevale, who is inside the ropes and describing the par-4 5th hole to his invisible audience. ". . . 314 yards to clear the fairway bunkers," he says. This quickly becomes irrelevant when Tiger pulls his drive into some thick grass at the base of a crooked Torrey pine. It's Tiger's first foray outside the ropes this year, and I can't miss it. The problem is, I'm on the opposite side of the fairway. And so, for the first time this year—I'm running—on a golf course, of all places. The only way to get there is to traverse the 275 yards back to the tee box and then around the other side. Along the way I sprint past Tiger's twenty-eight-year-old Swedish wife, Elin, who without ever swinging a club attracts plenty of attention of her own. I arrive at my destination just ahead of her husband and join the seventy-five other people who happened to be in the right place at the right time.

The ball sits nestled on the grassy upslope with the pine looming above it. Tiger walks, takes one look, and pronounces it, in his best deadpan, "perfect." Without any options, he grabs a wedge, puts one leg on top of the grass mound, and bunts the ball down the fairway about eighty yards. He's walking before the divot hits the ground. And what a divot. A squirrel could have been buried alive by the thing. Fans gather around the crater he has left behind and stare down in awe. Mind you, this wasn't even a shot that made it to the green, just a pitch out. One lanky teenager decides to step into Tiger's stance and see what it feels like, then smiles and nods. It feels good. Golf has a deserved reputation of being a rich man's sport, but for a fan it is anything but that. The cheapest ticket you can buy just put us within two feet of the game's biggest star.

10:30 AM • Tiger arrives at the par-3 8th, an uphill 175-yard par 3 that is defended by a three-leaf clover of a bunker short of the green if you don't play enough club. Tiger avoids that mistake but misses left, hole high. It's his first chip of the round. He finished his warm-up this morning with a few just like it. He made the last one, so that positive image has to be bouncing around his brain somewhere.

And just as he did about an hour and a half earlier, he casually chips it in for a birdie. The cheer of eight hundred people is delayed by a split second as our collective brains are jolted out of the malaise into which we'd slipped after three straight pars. I try to move out of the crowd to get to the next hole, but I'm boxed in by those who feel compelled to stand around and discuss what just happened. "How demoralizing is that when you're playing with him?" one man asks. A woman adds, "It doesn't matter where he hits the ball, he always comes out all right." This is another reason that I've rooted against him for so long. When Tiger Woods is playing well, he makes the world's hardest game appear easy. It's unfair.

11:01 AM • There can't be a stranger dichotomy in golf than the west and east borders of Torrey Pines South. On one side there is the coast— unobstructed, 180-degree vistas of the Pacific, a backdrop that is usually filled by hang gliders and catamarans. To the east are business parks, research facilities, and, here at the 9th, the Scripps Green Hospital. As Tiger arrives, dozens of employees in green and blue scrubs line the hospital's chain link fence for a closer look. I close my eyes, listen, and can almost hear abandoned patients calling out, "Nurse? Nurse? . . ." Tiger doesn't make his four but still makes the turn in 34, a good start on the South Course.

11:25 AM • After adding another birdie on the 10th, Tiger passes through a gauntlet of fans as he walks to the 11th tee. There's no one type of person following Tiger Woods. The gallery has the same diversity as the pictures on Girl Scout cookie boxes. It's no wonder every corporation would love a piece of him.

Halfway through the shoot, a shaggy-haired kid sticks out his hand to get a low-five. He's clearly delusional. But as Tiger walks by, he gives it to him. Tiger doesn't smile, doesn't even make eye contact, but he puts out his hand to slap the youngster's before pulling it safely back to his side. The kid's eyes go wide, but not as wide as mine. What I just witnessed was basically the equivalent of Phil Mickelson taking off his shirt and spinning it over his head like a pinwheel. Up to this point I was pretty sure Tiger was a robot built in Earl Woods' basement using secret Army technology. I'm officially upgrading him to Darth Vader— part machine, part man.

The 11th at the south course is the second-longest par 3 on the course, 221 yards played all the way back. Tiger hits a solid shot to twenty feet. As he walks to the green, a group of thirty-something women on the balcony of a nearby office building scream out in unison, "Go, Tiger!" It's so loud that we all, Tiger included, reflexively turn and look. And again Tiger lifts his mask to return the call with a wave. His season is only two hours old, and it's starting to feel like a coronation. That feeling only grows when Tiger makes his putt and gets to 4 under.

11:49 AM • Tiger could only be thinking birdie on 13. A 541-yard par 5, it's the easiest hole on the back nine. *Thinking birdie.* Even when I was a good golfer, I don't think I ever thought birdie. I sometimes didn't even think par. One time I set the bar even lower.

A few years ago, I stumbled into the chance to play in some corporate golf event where Annika Sorenstam was making an appearance. As we piled into our carts, they made the announcement that Annika herself would be playing three holes with every group. Most of the guys applauded. My mind went in another direction.

Oh, crap.

With every passing year, my ability to play golf or do much of anything else under pressure has crumbled. When I was fifteen, a senior

Tour event was coming to town, and to promote it, the tournament held "closest to the pin" contests at courses all over town. I beat out everyone at my dad's course and earned the chance to go to the resort and compete in a second contest against the other qualifiers in town. We met on the 18th fairway. It was a one-shot deal. 160 yards, a little uphill. A 5-iron. I remember being nervous, but had no reason to think those nerves would actually affect the shot, and they didn't. I stuck it to ten feet, won a hundred dollars to spend in the pro shop, and free tickets to the tournament for the week.

Back to Annika. The corporate tournament was a shotgun start, and my group was set to begin on the 10th. As we stepped to the tee, she pulled up in her cart, and waved. I wouldn't just be playing any three holes with Annika, I'd be playing my *first* three holes with Annika. The cocky guy in our group had already hit one down the middle. I was next. With the best female golfer in the game standing off to the side, a content smile on her face, I went through my normal preshot routine. As I set the club behind the ball, I had one goal: don't whiff. I made contact and off it flew. Long. And right. Like seventy yards right. I think I said something like "Ahhh . . . ," but that was just to cover the fact I was so relieved it had gone anywhere. Somewhere between the ages of fifteen and thirty, I hadn't lost just my mental fortitude; I'd lowered my own definition of excellence. As Annika stepped in behind me to tee it up, she waited until my ball had come to a rest on the 12th hole and said, "Well, it's in *a* fairway."

Tiger is in a fairway, too. The correct one. His iron to the green safely clears the five bunkers leading up to the green and he has a chip for eagle. The chip is a good eighty feet long and matches the topography of the hole he just traversed. It starts out flat, then goes steeply downhill before turning back uphill at the end, all the while drifting right. It rolls out to eight feet away. He makes the birdie putt. Five under. And after finally finding a leaderboard, it's official. For the first time in 2008, Tiger Woods is tied for the lead.

12:53 PM • Tiger doesn't slow down, draining a long putt on 15 to get to 6 under. While Tiger and the rest of his group walk the short distance to the next tee, the guy next to me turns and asks: "Furyk—black hat? Tiger—white hat?" I don't know how to respond. It's forgivable not to be sure whether a hole is a long par 4 or a short par 5, but not to be able to differentiate between Jim Furyk and Tiger Woods is something that should get a spectator banned from all professional golf tournaments for life.

I bury what I want to say and confirm that yes, the person in the white hat is Tiger Woods, and move down 16, a 220-yard par 3 with a canyon both left and long of the hole. Down at the green I find myself standing next to Hank Haney. In golf, coaches aren't allowed to give advice once a round starts, but with his student all the way to 6 under, he at least wants to enjoy his work. Maybe Tiger feels Haney watching: after missing the green short, he hits his worst shot of the day, chunking a simple uphill chip that stops ten feet short of the hole. He shakes his head as he goes to mark. How can a guy be 6 under and then do that? Haney winces, and some idiot leans over to him and says, "You need to give him a chipping lesson," then laughs despite the deafening silence. Haney gives the man a sympathy smile, which is generous. Tiger misses his par putt, his first bogey of the year. Furyk and McNeill aren't done yet, but Haney walks away and I do the same.

1:20 PM • Tiger pars 17 and arrives at the 18th 5 under. The 18th hole at the South course plays to 572 yards when the tees are all the way back. More than the other holes, the 18th demands a drive in the fairway, because in front of the green is the course's only water hazard, a broad round lake out of which Bruce Devlin once tried to hit his ball in 1975. He didn't "once" try to do it. He tried seven times and ultimately made a 10. Torrey Pines would later rename it Devlin's Billabong and place a plaque at the bottom of it, a piece of golf history covered most of the year by a layer of muck and forgotten golf balls.

Tiger misses his drive left and it jumps into a bunker. He'll have no choice but to lay up. He walks to the side of the tee box and slams his driver to the ground, then mutters to himself, "Come on . . ." I have seen this enough times to know how it will play out from here. Tiger will par the hole instead of birdie but still post one of the low rounds of the day. Then he will get in front of the cameras and complain about all the shots he left on the course. A reporter will ask him specifically what he needs to work on, and he'll probably say something absurd like, "Everything." And because reporters are professionals, they will nod rather than roll their eyes. Bobby Jones once said, "It would seem that if a person has hit a golf ball correctly a thousand times, he should be able to duplicate the performance at will." Tiger Woods believes this to be true more than anyone else in the history of the sport.

He indeed makes par, an opening-round 67 to put him one shot off the lead. As I shuffle along with the thousand people who are following him by the end of the day, not a single one seems disappointed.

FLAG HUNTING • Beyond the massive bleachers of the 18th green, a thick line of fans armed with Sharpies awaits the players as they leave the scoring trailer and head for the exit. Tiger has a different route in mind. He finishes his postround interviews and slips through a hole underneath the bleachers. He emerges a few seconds later through another hole on the far side, skips across a cart path, and disappears into the Torrey Pines Lodge without ever facing the mob.

Back in the line, my new acquaintance Margaret has just heard the bad news. "He's gone . . ." she says, sounding like a bride who's been left at the altar. Margaret and Tiger would make an interesting couple. Somewhere between fifty and seventy, Margaret's actual age is hidden beneath an enormous pair of Jackie O. sunglasses and an odd brown wig. Beehive on top and long in back. I wasn't alive in the 1960s, but I don't think it's a hairdo that was ever actually in style.

She's the most unlikely of Tiger fans I've come across today, so of course I have to ask her why she likes him so much. "His dad told him to shoot for the stars," she says. "He hit the stars and the sun and the moon." Margaret's been here every day since Tuesday but rarely ventures onto the course, preferring to stay near the clubhouse and get as many autographs for her souvenir flag as possible.

I ask her who some of her prized signatures are. "Oh, I don't know," she says. "I don't like golf." I laugh, but she's not joking. For Margaret, all the other names on that flag are just there to fill in the empty space around the sacred spot she has reserved right in the middle for Tiger.

I notice Jim Furyk pass behind her and tell her she's missing her chance to grab some more window dressing. She can't catch Jim, but she does snag McNeill, who actually held his own today, shooting an even par 72. She turns back around with a smile, "I don't know who that was, but I got him!" In not knowing McNeill, she and Tiger are not that different after all. I tell her who he is, and then, to my horror, I see that McNeill has signed right in the very middle—Tiger's spot. "Oh no. Margaret?" I say, slowly pointing to it. She's quiet for a moment and then reassigns the still empty top-left corner as Tiger's new spot, vowing to get him to sign it before the week is through.

SECOND ROUND

4:45 AM • I just had a dream about him. I mean, honestly, this is sad. Sure, I'm devoting a year to tailing Tiger, but to have him enter my dreams after just one day is a little creepy. I wonder if this is how seemingly healthy people become stalkers. It starts with a general interest. Then slowly over time it morphs into an obsession that consumes their conscious thoughts and eventually takes over their subconscious. I assume that normally takes months or years. Apparently not.

In the dream, Tiger has invited me to a postround dinner with some of his close friends. On my way, I meet my wife, Hillary, and her parents, who attempt to take me to Pinkberry, a trendy yogurt place that I've never been to and whose allure completely baffles me. Its main draw is that the stuff is made with *real* yogurt that is then frozen, versus "frozen yogurt," which—who knew?—is frozen but not real. People line up outside the store for it, then readily admit it's not as good as the fake stuff. All of which has nothing to do with Tiger.

So in my dream I show up at Tiger's restaurant. I'm in a collared shirt, a casual brown jacket, dress shoes, and no pants. I walk up to him and say hello. His greeting is warmer than the one he gave George McNeill but only slightly. "Hey," he says with a slight head nod. After a few awkward seconds, I have nothing more to say and tell him I should probably take off. He thanks me for coming and then calls out to his wife, Elin, whom he calls "Ulna." Tiger asks her when they're going to come to church with me. She hems and haws about it. Before they can decide, I wake up. It's not even worth trying to interpret. It's insane.

5:00 AM • I can't go back to sleep, but that's okay. Perhaps even more pathetic than having a dream about Tiger Woods is the fact that I've got a doctor's appointment at Torrey Pines this morning. You see, since my family lost our Writers' Guild health insurance at the end of the year, we've been under a Blue Cross plan that has an almost unreachable deductible in exchange for a semireasonable monthly premium. It's pretty much scared us off from getting regular checkups and has us, instead, saving our money for when the kids get sick. So when I spotted an RV offering spectators free skin exams from a real dermatologist near the 9th fairway on Thursday, it was as if they were giving away hundred-dollar bills.

9:52 AM • As Vijay Singh, the mighty Fijian, leaves the tee box, vacating it for Tiger's group, a fan leans in to his buddy and says, "Hell, yeah. Here we go." I want to feel the same way, but I'm still thinking about that appointment I just had. As a fair-skinned blond guy who loves golf, I'm a dermatologist's dream patient. But that's only half of it. I also have a red birthmark on one side of my neck and a brown one on my right arm. The last time I went to a new dermatologist, she called in one of her medical interns, who looked at my different marks and exclaimed gleefully, "I've read about these in class!" The doctor tried to make me feel less like a freak by mentioning that Richard Gere actually has the same thing on his arm that I do. But then she called in a nurse who circled my spots with a pen and took Polaroids of them. "For our records," she insisted.

Today's appointment was awkward from the very beginning. The nurse led me into the exam room/converted RV bedroom and asked, "Do you want upper body only, or would you like a gown?" I went with only upper body. Just because I'm willing to see a doctor practicing out of a motor home on a golf course doesn't mean I've lost all dignity. Even just the top half of me left the female doctor reeling. "You have a lot of moles," she said, as if I'd flown in from some country without mirrors. In the past, doctors would follow that statement by reassuring me that nothing really looked serious. Instead, she picked up a carbon-copy outline of a body and started to note everything that looked suspicious, eventually having to draw arrows to spots when she ran out of space inside the lines. The RV was hot and was listing at a twenty-degree angle, but what really made me uncomfortable was that while watching her scribble, I was reminded of the fact that had been hammering me more and more over the last few years: I'm not a kid anymore. When you hit your thirties, checkups don't end with a pat on the head and a lollipop. They end with warnings. "You promise you'll go see a doctor in Los Angeles?" she said as I put my shirt on. "I promise," I said, grabbing a handful of free sunscreen samples and making for the tee.

11:20 AM • Tiger played his first five holes on the North 1 under par. Not bad but not exactly lighting it up. The North is by far the easier course of the two, and players tend to go low here and hang on for dear life on the South. It looks as if Tiger is doing the opposite.

His group started on the back nine, and his one problem, as it was yesterday, is his driver. He missed left on 10 and right on 11, the dreaded two-way miss off the tee that has always appeared to frustrate Tiger more than any other part of his game. The "two-way miss" is a good golfer's way of describing a bad golfer's problem, that essentially he has no idea which way his ball's going. Walking down the 15th, a simple, downhill 394-yard par 4, I don't know which way it's going either, but I guess right. Give me five spins on the roulette wheel and I'll be wrong five times, but this call is perfect. Tiger's drive isn't as far right as my first shot with Annika, but it's bad. And since the 15th green is about the farthest point away from civilization on the already vacant North Course, only thirty or forty fans are gathered around his ball. As expected, Tiger is in no mood to socialize.

When Tiger arrives, he's still holding his driver and fuming, his jawbones jutting out beneath his cheeks. He takes one look at his ball and the eucalyptus tree that is blocking his next shot and says, loud enough for us to hear, "Stupid f*****."

Tiger's propensity for swearing on the course is not something of which he is proud and may be the only flaw he routinely fails to keep under wraps. This can mean only that bad language is either the one thing in life Tiger Woods can't beat or he's not really trying to control it at all. His dad, Earl, said that early on he tried to teach Tiger to bottle up his emotions on the course, but in time Tiger proved that his outbursts could spur him on to better results. It's a theory that completely goes against the conventional wisdom of most every sports psychologist. Bob Rotella, golf's most famous guru, goes so far as to make *not* getting angry one of his ten commandments of mental golf, drilling home the mantra that "nothing will bother or upset you on the golf course, and you will be in a great state of mind on every shot." I've read a few of his books myself and have always admired the idea of peace at all costs on the golf course, mostly because as a teenager it was the easiest place to find it.

My father moved out near the end of my freshman year in high school, a public rift in a small town. During that following summer, I was at the course six days a week. If it had been open on Mondays, it would have been seven. My mom dropped me off in the morning, and my dad joined me in the late afternoon for a few holes, a Cherry Coke, and a ride home. His exit hurt everything except my golf game, and by the time school started again in September my handicap was down to 4. During those early-evening drives with Dad, the reasons why he did it never came up. He believed, as a judge and the son of a lawyer, that conflict was best handled calmly, with reason, behind closed doors. Or even better, not at all.

My wife, on the other hand, was raised completely the opposite. As a teenager, Hillary's parents went so far as to remove her bedroom door so she couldn't slam it in their faces. Five years into our marriage, she often said there was nothing so frustrating as when she would have a meltdown and I would just sit in silence, digesting the problem and eventually talking through a solution with only slightly more emotion than a mannequin. From my point of view, there wasn't much to be gained by getting upset. I mean, I had; it just never ended very well. As a kid, I remember being so hacked off that I threw a club fifteen yards down the fairway, walked to get it, and then threw it another fifteen yards. I did this the entire length of a par 5. That night my dad received a call from the man I'd been paired with, who told him he'd never play golf with me again. Another time, I was so angry about a muffed shot that I stepped on the cart's gas pedal before my dad had finished sitting down. The movement slammed him into his seat and wrenched his back for the rest of the round. I had learned my lesson.

Back in the 15th fairway, Tiger is still swinging his driver, another big Rotella no-no—"the only shot you think about is the one at hand!" He finally stuffs it back in the bag, but he doesn't pull out another club yet; rather, he stands behind the ball and places his hands behind his back. And then he closes his eyes. Call it meditating, exorcising demons, I don't know. But the séance lasts a good five or six seconds as some of us in the crowd shoot one another a quick glance to ask, "Um, what's going on?" When Tiger opens his eyes, his mood is different. Lighter. He shakes out both hands and says, "Okay." Stevie has been waiting patiently, as if this happens a lot, and is ready when Tiger casually asks, "How far?" "Eighty-seven hole, eighty-two front," he shoots back. Tiger nods, then grabs a wedge and punches it under the tree. It comes hotter than he expected, hops the green, and then disappears back down the other side. Tiger doesn't swear about this one but reacts as if it went exactly where he wanted it to and starts walking.

I run the 87-plus-10 yards to the ball, wondering if perhaps he had painted such a positive mental picture of the shot that he was physically unable to see what really happened. Before he was in trouble, but now he's in jail. His third shot has to go under some pine trees, then up a steep bank of thick rough, then back downhill to a pin that is cut close to the back of the green. Tiger looks at the shot, unconcerned and clearly still feeling residual warm fuzzies from his astral planing, pitches the ball up the hill. It appears perfect from our point of view, but once on top we see it never made it to the green, getting snagged by the rough. A bogey would be a gift at this point. Meanwhile, McNeill and Furyk just stand there, putters under their arms, for once waiting for a hack named Tiger Woods.

Tiger gets up to the ball, takes a brief look at the hole, and then, calmly, chips it in for par. Perhaps feeling liberated enough to express real emotion, I open my mouth and out come two words I almost never use: "Holy s***." Tiger picks the ball out of the cup and moves off to the side of the green, where he coolly starts to reapply some lip balm. He's a monster. Or at least a monster with lips that dry out easily. We're still cheering, but he doesn't appear to hear us. Stevie's laughing, but Tiger doesn't notice him. He's still somewhere else. Furyk putts out for a conventional par, then sidles over to Tiger, shaking his head and smirking. Finally, Tiger snaps awake and laughs. It is the deepest and scariest focus I've ever seen.

1:09 PM • After that mystical par on 15, Tiger Woods steps on the gas. He promptly birdies the 16th, an uphill 336-yard par 4, using a 3-wood off the tee for one of the first times all week. *Seven under.* He birdies the 18th, the boring 520-yard par 5 that I sneaked across the day before to get to the range. *Eight under.* On the par-5 1st, he blocks one into the right trees, and when the marshal asked us all to take ten steps back, Tiger tells us to stay put, adding "I'm not playing that badly, am I?" Up and down for birdie. *Nine under.* On the short 326-yard 2nd, Tiger short-sides himself but makes the putt for three anyway. *Ten under.* And for good measure, he birdies the 4th. *Eleven under.* I add them up as I walk. Five birdies in seven holes?!

I go out of my way to catch a glimpse of the only leaderboard on the North Course. At 11 under par, Tiger Woods is in the lead. By four. A fan next to me notices Furyk's total and says, "Four under, that's good," then thinks for a second and adds, "unless you're Tiger, in which case that's crap." In a matter of less than two hours on a Friday morning, and ignited by something that on paper will look like a "nothing special" par, Tiger Woods has put away a tournament that won't officially be over for two more days.

PHOTO OP • Who knew that all this week I'd been trying to get close to Tiger and all I needed to do was head to the Buick Clubhouse along the 18th fairway. You may remember the commercial in which Tiger opens the front door in a nice sweater and says some version of "Hi. Welcome to the Buick Clubhouse. Come on in . . ." What doesn't quite come through in that ad is that the actual Buick Clubhouse isn't a clubhouse at all but an enormous big-rig trailer with fake wood paneling. To get in, all I have to do is fill out a form, which "just takes a second," yet I assume will mean I'll be receiving e-mails from Buick for the next ten years. The cool thing about the "clubhouse" is that after posing for a photo in front of a greenscreen, a computer lays in a picture of Tiger, so it looks as if he and I really had our picture taken together. The finished product is pretty impressive. Oliver Stone would peg it for a fake right away, but most of my golfing buddies would never suspect a thing. It's marketing genius. By only having to smile once, Tiger has found a way of appeasing hundreds of thousands of fans.

THIRD ROUND

Tiger has a four-shot lead entering Saturday and is paired with Stewart Cink and Kevin Streelman, the world's 1,354th-ranked player. Streelman is the perfect example of the no-name pro I would love to see topple Tiger. He has spent the last seven years bouncing around minitours, the low point coming a few years back when he was deserted by a group of disillusioned investors who had promised to pay his tournament entrance fees. This week he was only an alternate into the field and found out just five minutes before his tee time that a spot had opened up. Now, after two solid rounds, he has his chance to take on Tiger and see if he can keep things close.

But I know he probably won't. For years the cakewalk has always been my least favorite of the Tiger wins, because after spending all week looking forward to seeing a gripping tournament, I'd make a sandwich, turn on the TV right at twelve o'clock on Saturday, and discover it was already over. At least with the nail-biters I could get through the majority of a weekend before Tiger ruined it. Hillary could always tell what had happened by the droll look on my face.

"Tiger's winning?"

I'd nod.

"Is it close?"

I'd shake my head. "I'm sorry," she would always say, secretly happy that Tiger's dominance had won her another six hours of quality time with me before I returned to work on Monday morning.

The only person who is refusing to admit this week's event is over is Tiger himself. And ironically, it is that refusal that makes his winning all the more inevitable. "They're not handing out the trophy today," he said yesterday to the press. "Anything can happen." It's a nice thought, but no, anything can't. Tiger doesn't lose tournaments when he has a four-shot lead. All his comment does is safeguard himself against some catastrophic, one-in-a-billion scenario—that either a La Jolla hang glider wipes him out on the 12th hole or he incorrectly signs his scorecard and is disqualified, but even in the case of the latter, I have to imagine that the official in the scorer's trailer would look at Tiger's card, then slowly slide it back to the biggest name in sports and say, "Are you *sure* you want to turn this in?"

10:54 AM • Tiger has cruised through the first three holes as expected, par-par-par, then adds a birdie on the hard 4th for the second time in two tries this week. Streelman actually had a chance to make himself known on the first hole after knocking it inside Tiger to just five feet, but he missed. Now evidence of a blowout is everywhere. Back at the tee, I passed two twenty-something girls having what they surely considered their first deep discussion about Tiger.

"It's amazing how good you can get at golf so quickly."

"Didn't he start when he was three?"

"I guess that is kind of a long time when you think about it."

Further down the fairway, a dad watches only half-interestedly as Tiger passes by, instead helping his sons collect pinecones to take home. Even I can't keep my focus and start talking to a fellow spectator, Dwayne, and his wife, who are sporting the most high-tech periscopes I've ever seen. About an inch thick and made of hard metal, they put the '80s cardboard ones to shame. They not only extend, they focus and even zoom. "It's even got a hook for your pants," Dwayne's wife boasts. Turns out the devices are for sale in the Torrey Pines pro shop. But what's really odd is that they are made and distributed by none other than Phil Mickelson's father. "Don't you feel guilty about watching Tiger and not Phil?" I ask. "We watch enough of him too," Dwayne says, slightly insulted at the insinuation, then quickly turns back to Tiger. At eighty bucks a pop, his wife warns me not to buy one unless I'm planning on seeing more than one golf tournament this year. I laugh and know I have just found my strangest tax write-off for 2008.

11:01 AM • There haven't been as many sportswriters tracking Tiger from inside the ropes as I'd imagined. The only one I have seen walking a few holes every day is a writer I've nicknamed Luau Larry. I don't know his real name or for whom he writes, but he is always wearing a Hawaiian shirt tucked into shorts, a look that exposes a pair of tan legs of which he seems rather proud. It has been downright cold some mornings this week and pants are never an option. I've also never seen him actually write anything down. He just tromps along inside the ropes, occasionally using his collapsible metal monopod seat to time and again nab the best seat in golf. I'll admit it, I'm jealous.

11:10 AM • Matt Kuchar has experience playing around Tiger's gallery, just not like this. While Tiger is busy nearly holing his approach into number 5, up on number 2 Kuchar has just blown his approach long and left, a bad miss that hits the cart path and then careens an extra twenty yards down the hill and right into the middle of Tiger's throng. Faced with a ridiculous flop shot over a camera tower and a couple of pine trees, the always grinning 1998 U.S. Amateur champ can only laugh at the fact that his gallery has instantly gone from literally seven people to about a thousand. And since Tiger is on the verge of going to 14 under, the crowd is delighted to turn its attention to a player whose round is actually in jeopardy. Matt surveys the shot, then opens up his lob wedge as much as he can and swings. Somehow, the shot clears the trees and lands short of the flag, leaving him just eight feet for par. He receives a Tiger-size cheer as he strides up the hill, high-fiving fans the entire way. Within thirty seconds, his gallery is back to seven.

12:25 PM • I don't know how the San Diego Police Department decided which cop should walk along with Tiger Woods' group this week, but clearly height was a factor. Officer Brian Freymueller is big. Six-feet-five and solid. He doesn't need a billy club; he looks as if he could do just as much damage with a paper towel roll. And for the first two days, he's been a tough guy to crack. On Thursday, I mustered the courage to ask him if he's allowed to enjoy this. He wouldn't answer. On Friday, he laid into a college kid who ran under a marshal's ropes, nearly melting him with his Ray-Bans. But as I lean around the corner of 10 to see where Tiger's approach has landed, Freymueller is suddenly next to me giving color commentary, "He's about fifteen feet hole high. Probably not going to be happy with that." Glad to see he's loosening up, I tell him I guess this beats waiting for someone to roll through a stop sign. As he thinks of a reason to arrest me, I slink back into the crowd.

12:34 PM • Tiger hits his best shot of the day on the downhill, 220-yard 11th. I'm positioned perfectly behind the ball as he zones in on the back-left pin. It's a high laser that starts one yard left of the flag, then corrects its course about halfway to the hole. It looks as if it might go in and ends up just six feet past the cup. Kevin Streelman's caddy can only shake his head in silence. When Tiger makes the putt, which at this point I can only assume he will, he'll be at 15 under par. For perspective, 15 under par was Tiger's winning score last year and he still has twenty-five holes left. Streelman, of course, is going the other way. With a double on 9 and a bogey here, he's nine shots back.

2:36 PM • Tiger adds two more birdies before he is done, one at 15 and the other a tap-in at 18 for a round of 66. In five hours, he has doubled his lead from four shots to eight. Streelman could muster only a 75. *Another crushed spirit*, I think. But for some reason Streelman is beaming as he shakes Tiger's hand. He's acting as if he just received a medal from the president.

Back at my buddy A.J.'s house, I go online and find the transcript of Streelman's postround interview. "What was it like?" he was asked. "Man, that was one of the coolest things ever, no doubt about it. [Tiger] was fun to watch but just kind of fun to compare myself against him, as well. It's inspiring and very educational." Huh. Tiger apparently wasn't going to be the star in any of Kevin Streelman's recurring nightmares.

When Tiger came on the Tour in the mid-1990s, his approach to the sport was thoroughly different from the status quo and therefore totally offensive. During his first week back in 1996, Tiger said his goal was not to finish second or third but to win. His interviewer, two-time U.S. Open champ Curtis Strange, chuckled and said, "You'll learn." Actually, Strange learned. Tiger won his first Tour event five weeks after that and his second just two weeks later.

Twelve years later, there's a new generation of players arriving on Tour who, like Streelman, has never questioned Tiger's superiority. Getting whooped by him doesn't make them dry heave, it makes them want to improve. At thirty-two years old, Tiger has become a mentor—whether he wants to be one or not.

FINAL ROUND

For most of Saturday night, it looked as if there might not be any tournament taking place today. Southern California typically only has one stretch of bad weather every year, and it happens to be when the Tour schedules its annual West Coast swing. Back in 2005, the rain farther north was so heavy that it shortened the Nissan Open in Los Angeles to just 36 holes. At the same event a year later, rain caught Tiger and Stevie without umbrellas, and Tiger would later withdraw with the flu, the first time in his professional career he had ever withdrawn. None of that sounds as bad as the weather forecast that I caught Saturday night. It wasn't "heavy rains" that caught my attention but "cyclones and tornadoes." When the rain and wind start to beat against A.J.'s house early this morning, I figure that's it: despite having a giant lead, Tiger will have no choice but to hang out in La Jolla for one more day until Mother Nature lets him make it official.

Nevertheless, by 8 a.m., the storm of the century has slowed a bit, so I put on my rain pants and head for the course.

10:40 AM • A real golf fan has to be ready for anything, and at nine o'clock this morning, my outfit makes a lot of sense. Wool socks, jeans, rain pants, a thermal shirt, a sweater, a rain jacket, a beanie, and an umbrella. No storm is going to slow me down, not this early in the year. There's just one problem. It is a problem that has been developing for the last hour and has come to fruition just as Tiger stripes his drive down the middle of the first fairway. The last remaining cloud in Southern California has just blown past Torrey Pines. The only thing for which I'm not prepared is the sun.

The jacket can be wrapped around my waist along with the sweater. The beanie would probably fit in my pocket, and the umbrella might go through a belt loop. None of this really matters, of course, since the end result is that I look like a complete fool. Until I meet Nelson, a fit-looking fifty-three-year-old who is somehow wearing even more layers than I. "How'd you place in the Iditarod?" I want to ask. Instead I just go with the safer "Beautiful day." He rolls his eyes, and for the first time this season, I've found a kindred spirit. Nelson woke up early, drove an hour, and overreacted to the weather for one reason—to follow Tiger Woods. He didn't bring a friend or his wife, just himself, knowing that no matter how bad the tempest was, he would see something amazing. He receives that gift early when Tiger drains a 35-foot putt on the 1st for birdie. Nineteen under. Tiger waves as he walks to the cup. "He's been like this all week," I say, as if I were describing a great-uncle who hasn't taken his medicine. When Nelson finds out how I'm spending my year, he asks the question I've started to get a lot: "Do you know him?" "Yeah, right," I say.

When two random guys meet on a golf course, the information about each other usually trickles out slowly, and only just between tee shots and approaches. One of my favorite lines is from *Golf Digest*'s David Owen, who joked that after years of playing golf with his friends, he knew most of their spouses' names and even what some of them did for a living. Nelson operates a little faster. And so had his parents. When his dad turned eighteen, he asked Nelson's mom to marry him. She was fourteen. So why should I be surprised that within two holes, I have heard most of Nelson's life story? His job, his wife, his kids.

One of his stories is about his oldest son, Jesse, who four years ago was a Major League Baseball prospect at just seventeen, throwing 95 mph, batting .605, and running a 5.0 to first base as a freshman in high school. One day Jesse came home complaining of soreness in his throwing arm. It took a year of tests before doctors finally discovered cancer. With specialists unable to tell how much of the cancer was in the soft tissue and how much was in the bone, he started chemotherapy the very next day. After six months, they took a break to do a month of radiation, then gave the humerus two to three weeks to rest before they removed it altogether, saving his life but ending his dream of playing in the pros.

Nelson's faith is no great secret. You don't name your kids Jesse, Samuel, Hannah, and Gabriel unless you've taken a few spins through the Bible. And no doubt seeing your son go through so much pain and loss is either going to push you away from God or draw you closer. For

Nelson, it was the latter. "It's sometimes hard to see how God orchestrates things in life, but you have to believe he is, even if you don't understand it," he says as we charge up the hill from 5 to 6, having seen Tiger make pars on the last four holes. There's not a bit of resentment in his voice and certainly no looking back, just a peace about life's dead ends that can only be supernatural.

12:15 PM • Walking down number 6, I predict that Tiger will birdie it. "You think so?" Nelson asks. First off, I tell him I'm insulted that he'd even question me, considering I've watched all fifty-nine of the holes Tiger has played this season. I explain that the 6th is one of the only holes out here that Tiger has not played well this week. He's parred it twice, but since it's a downwind, 560-yard par 5, that's bad. This time around, Tiger puts his third shot to four feet, sinks the putt for a birdie 4, and Nelson promises never to doubt me again. Twenty under par. And a ten-shot lead.

1:45 PM • After his first bogey in forty-five holes at the 7th, Tiger cruises till he reaches the 11th, where he leaves his shot on the par 3 in the back-right corner. Unfortunately, the pin is in the front left, leaving him a terror of a putt, a good fifty feet long. Tiger isn't reading it all at once. He's reading it in sections, dissecting it from beginning to end, then piecing it back together little by little to decide exactly what his line should be. This is the longest he has taken reading any putt all week. He walks to the side of the putt, judging its steepness. He reads it from behind the cup, looking back to his ball. He spends so much time on it that I start to think maybe it's not even his turn. But his fellow players Stewart Cink and Joe Durant are watching Tiger, too. To have any chance, he has to putt across the side of the tier the first forty feet, then get the ball to die a good ten feet above the hole, where it will take a seventy-degree turn back toward the front of the green and pick up speed. The only thing that can stop it at that point is the hole itself.

Believing he has the putt decoded, he hits it, then straightens up to see how he did. The ball rides the tier like a surfer, then slows and cuts left down the hill. It's racing now, nearing the cup. As impossible as it seemed, it falls in the right side for birdie. Tiger is the only real show in town today and five thousand eyes are there to scream an "Ohhhhh!" when it drops. Even I have to join in this time.

When a football team calls a play, you don't know which one it has chosen until the ball has been hiked and the players go into motion. But here at the 11th we were able to watch Tiger at work and knew exactly what he was attempting to do before he ever drew the putter back. But that still doesn't mean anyone believed he could make it.

With the ball safely in the cup, Tiger raises the grip end of his putter above his head and pumps his right arm. Stevie picks it out and tosses the ball back, where he casually slips it into his pocket and heads to the 12th tee.

2:50 PM • Nelson returns, having disappeared for a few holes to buy one of the Mickelson periscopes. And now that he has an unobstructed view on the 14th, he suddenly believes he can see things no one else can see.

"Tiger looks tired," he says, pulling away from the eyepiece.

"You're nuts."

"Here, look." I begrudgingly put it up to my eye.

"He's not tired," I say. "Besides, he's drinking Tigerade. He'll be fine."

Nelson's not buying it and takes the periscope back. "I don't know. I think he's struggling. I can see his slumped shoulders. I'm worried about him." I tell him those aren't slumps; those are muscles. But Tiger indeed bogeys the 14th, 15th, and 16th, dropping to 17 under. "Something's wrong," Nelson says, in case I'd forgotten his earlier pronouncement. "Fine," I say, "he's tired. *I'm* tired!"

I had e-mailed my old boss Alan earlier in the week to tell him the pedometer I'm wearing says I'm walking close to six miles a day, to which he responded that I was the only member of the striking Writers Guild of America whose walking distance went up once I stopped picketing.

As a member in good standing with the Writers Guild ("good standing" meaning I don't currently owe the union any money), I am expected to picket four hours a day, five days a week. Best I could see, the only immediate benefit of this strike was that rather than referring to myself as an unemployed writer, I could now tell people I was a *striking* writer, which makes me sound much more important.

I wasn't able to picket the first day of the strike. I will neither confirm nor deny that I may or may not have been playing golf with a friend. Driving home from the place I may or may not have been, I called an old coworker to tell him what I had shot and to see how the picketing was going. He said it was so painful that after just one day on the lines, he had already called the Guild and asked if there was anything he could do instead. *Way to be tough, Norma Rae*, I thought.

The next day, I showed up to picket at CBS along with a couple hundred other energized writers. As a car drove by and honked, a friend raised his fist and yelled, optimistically, "We're winning!" A little later two eighty-something writers who probably hadn't worked in thirty years anyway began smashing their signs against a teamster's truck and then attempted to open his passenger door to challenge him to fisticuffs. The whole thing was actually a lot of fun. For about forty-five minutes. I spent the next hour realizing what a waste of life this was. Then, at the two-hour mark, I decided I was ready to give in to the studios' demands. You don't want to pay us for running shows on the Internet? Fine. You want to get rid of residuals altogether? I'm listening. Just please don't make me walk in circles while pretending to talk on the phone with my agent again. So much for not wanting to walk.

3:10 PM ● Tiger rights the ship on the 17th with a par and plays down the 18th hole with a seven-shot lead. The smiles he has buried all week are coming easily now, the finish line in sight. The crowd cheers as Tiger hits his third shot in close to the back-right pin. Nelson says good-bye as he heads for the merchandise tent, and I find myself enjoying the walk up 18. I understand why Tiger enjoys winning so much. It's hard to feel bad about yourself when a few thousand people are on their feet applauding you. I know I never took one swing this week, but as I reach the 72nd green, I secretly pretend that some of the accolades are for me.

Tiger makes the twelve-footer at the last hole for a round of 71, a four-day total of 19 under and the largest margin of victory in the history of the tournament. It's the sixth time he has started the year with a victory and his 62nd win on the PGA Tour, tying him with Arnold Palmer.

It's impossible to walk away from this first tournament and not appreciate the things Tiger can do that no one else can. Even the most hardened golf fan couldn't deny that. But I understand even less why so many people consider him beloved. He's too good. Too intimidating. At least to me—and the other 153 players in the field.

After picking up my new periscope, I make for my car and spot Margaret (with the beehive wig) waiting at the city bus stop on Torrey Pines Road. "Margaret!" I say. "Did you ever get Tiger's autograph?" "Yes!" she says, then pulls it out to show me. He wouldn't sign the flag, but he signed her Buick Clubhouse picture with faux Tiger that she'd had taken earlier in the week. "He signed it and then he gave me this little smile." She does her best Tiger half smile to help me visualize the moment. As for the flag, Margaret says she'll bring it back next year. Forget next year. He'll be back in June for the U.S. Open.

ELDRICK OF ARABIA

The Dubai Desert Classic

The Majlis Course—Emirates Golf Club
Dubai, United Arab Emirates
January 31–February 2, 2008

If you pick up a globe, put your finger on Los Angeles, then run it up to the North Pole and back down the other side of the planet, you will hit Dubai, the biggest city in the United Arab Emirates. In other words, after going to the tournament that couldn't be closer to home, I am now traveling as far as I possibly can. I stumble upon this fact during my one full day between Tiger's tournaments when I look at the itinerary Hillary is printing out and ask, "Where is Dubai, anyway?" Most Americans who travel there undoubtedly ask that question, but they probably don't ask it twenty-four hours before they board the plane.

The whole adventure of this year had caught me a little off guard. Until the Writers Guild went on strike, I was busy trying to sell a TV pilot I had written called *Viva Doug*. It was about an American loser who at the low point of his life discovers that his childhood pen pal has risen to power as a dictator in a South American country and is giving Doug all the credit for making him the ruthless monster he has become. In total honesty, I started writing it as a movie but couldn't get past the first thirty pages, so I chopped off the end and told people it was meant to be a TV pilot the whole time. I had gone in to pitch it to Fox, a meeting that I thought went well, until the end of the meeting when the V.P. to whom I was pitching thanked me and then asked if I had opened the Fiji Water she had given me.

"Yeah, actually I did."

"Oh. That's okay. If you hadn't, I was just going to ask if I could have it back."

Writing and trying to sell that script was one of the two moments of levity in an otherwise dim two-year career stretch. The other was a brief stint writing for *The ½ Hour News Hour,* a sort of a Republican version of *The Daily Show* for the Fox News Channel. As with most new shows, some elements really worked, some didn't. But the concept was a home run, enough to make me announce during my second week there, "This show will run forever!" Two days later we were canceled.

Dubai is certainly not the first place one thinks of going when running low on money, but since Tiger's going, I have no choice. I will fly on Delta from L.A. to Atlanta, then take a direct flight from Atlanta all the way into Dubai. Tiger will travel on his private jet, of course, and said earlier in the week that to pass time on the plane he usually spends the whole flight eating. I don't have that luxury. Despite the second leg of my flight clocking in at just under fourteen hours, the reservation states that my flight includes dinner only.

Leaving the family for the Buick was easy. This one's tough. Hillary inadvertently lightens the mood at the curb when she tells me to make sure I drink a lot of water and walk around a lot during the flight so I don't have a stroke. "How old do you think I am?" I ask before giving her a hug. I lean in and kiss my daughter, Katie, who is still too young to know how far away I'm really going, and then do the same to my son, Danny. As I wheel my bag away, I turn back one last time, and through the tinted glass I can make out his little hand, waving good-bye.

L.A. TO ATLANTA • Thankfully the woman with the forty pounds of frozen raw meat at her feet is near me for only the three-and-a-half-hour leg of my journey. "They don't have Trader Joe's in Myrtle Beach," she explains to the poor couple sitting next to her. Every seat on the flight has its own mini-TV, but until further notice this lady is the in-flight entertainment. Within twenty minutes of takeoff, she is watching *Just Shoot Me* on her TV and the first *Lord of the Rings* movie on her portable DVD player, a strange combination that has her snickering one second and completely entranced the next. When *Just Shoot Me* ends, I notice that an episode of the sitcom *Yes, Dear* comes on. An episode I wrote. Writing for TV, it is always hard to get an accurate idea of what people really think of your work. Family and friends reflexively say they loved it. The next day the ratings come in and tell you a few million people were watching, but you never know if they actually enjoyed it. Frozen Meat Girl is temporarily distracted by Gandalf and Frodo, so I wait. After a few minutes she looks back up at the TV, scrunches up her nose, realizes what she's watching (or, perhaps even worse, isn't), and, for the first time in the flight, turns the TV off.

Tiger Woods never rests on past accomplishments. He makes new goals, looks ahead. I'm not that secure, which explains why I put down my book, flip on my episode, and begin laughing out loud at jokes I wrote three years ago. I watch the whole thing, then turn it off, but only after my name flashes in the credits, almost too small to see on the four-by-six-inch screen. When I wrote that episode, I thought I knew exactly how life was going to play out; the new house by twenty-eight, the country club membership by thirty-five, the flying car by forty. I might even have achieved some of it if I had actually made any effort to put the plan into motion. Instead, I did nothing. And now I'm on a flight to the other side of the Earth, playing catch-up with the help of the world's greatest athlete.

ATLANTA TO DUBAI • I am curious to see what kind of people actually travel to Dubai. Our gate is about the farthest one from the center of the terminal, and the collection of people scattered about is comprised of some of the most intimidating men I've ever seen. Most of them are wearing khaki cargo pants and work boots. They're middle-aged, leathery, tattooed. Mixed in with them is a smattering of women who aren't scary at all, just scared. Once on the flight I find out that for most of them, the final destination isn't Dubai; it's Iraq. They've signed on for a tour of duty, so to speak, with KBR, a former subsidiary of Halliburton and the largest nonunion construction company in America.

Sitting next to me on the flight is Mary, a small, curly-haired former FedEx driver who pretends she's excited about the year ahead, but doesn't act like it. The lure of working in Iraq is simple: the pay is good, and as long as you stay out of the United States for 330 days, it's tax-free. "329 left," Mary says. She didn't even know she was going to Iraq until Friday and did her required weeklong training just this past week, the worst part of which was wearing "the banana suit," a claustrophobic yellow outfit that will protect her from chemical attacks. The man on the aisle, Bill, is just finishing his second year in Iraq and tells her not to worry about the suit. "I don't even know where mine is."

Bill is the poster boy for KBR, a beefy, sixty-year-old former concrete pourer from Illinois who cannot resist the lure of $1,800 a week. On his most recent trip home he was able to pay cash for a $30,000 truck. Next time he's buying a modular home. Mary knows what she'll do with the money, too. She recently bought a spot in an RV park near the water in Galveston. Her motor home is waiting for her to come back and fix it up.

I tune in to an episode of *Megastructures* about Dubai's famous palm-shaped island. The show gladly spits out over-the-top facts, figures that you just accept because you have no way of proving or disproving any of them. The nuttiest is that so much earth was moved to build the island, it's "enough sand and rock to build a twenty-five meter wall . . . around the entire world." Really? This is how Dubai operates and survives—hype.

I wake up from a long stretch of sleep and tune my TV to the map that shows our progress. A few hours ago, we were off the coast of Ireland. Now I see we're about to fly right over Iraq. On cue, the plane banks smoothly to the right, then straightens course. I pull up my shade and see miles and miles of fog. When my eyes adjust, I see it's not fog at all but sand. We're flying down the east coast of Saudi Arabia. After an hour the plane banks back to the left, Iraq no longer below us, and descends over the Persian Gulf and into the bright lights of Dubai.

As the plane taxis to the runway, the interior lights come on and so does the welcome music. It takes me a second to place the song, but then it's unmistakable—"The Little Drummer Boy." Not the musical accompaniment I would have guessed for my first moments in a Muslim country. The song is shut off abruptly, and we roll the rest of the way in silence.

I collect my bag and jump into a taxi whose cabbie, Mahmut from India, asks where I'm staying. Dubai is home to the world's most lavish hotels, none more famous than the sail-shaped Burj Al Arab, Tiger's home for the week and the tallest hotel in the world. I'm staying on the first floor of the Golden Sands Hotel Apartments, a low-price option that is still costing me $200 a night. But when I say "Golden Sands," Mahmut asks me a debilitating question:

"Which one?"

Apparently saying Golden Sands is the equivalent of arriving in Chicago and saying you're staying at the Best Western. Mahmut decides to take me to the closest Golden Sands, where they can look up my reservation on their computer. While driving, he asks me why I'm in Dubai. "To see Tiger Woods," I say.

"Who?"

I had to fly halfway around the world, but I've done it. I've met the first person who doesn't know who Tiger Woods is.

"Tiger Woods?"

No response.

"The golfer?" I mimic a golf swing as Mahmut looks in the rearview mirror. "Oh yes," Mahmut says, now clearly knowing exactly the man in question.

FIRST ROUND

Though I have no real pull in the world of sportswriting, one night while I was in San Diego, I went to the Dubai Desert Classic Web site to see how much tickets cost and found a tab marked "Media Accreditation." I clicked, and it opened to an online form to apply for official credentials for the week. *It can't be this easy,* I thought. I filled in my name, e-mail address, and phone number. The only question that tripped me up was "media type." Not liking any of the choices they gave me, I put in "other," then hit send. Some part of me wondered whether it was wise to mess with the system in an Arab country, but two seconds later an e-mail popped up in my inbox: "Your application was successful and you have been approved to receive media accreditation for the 2008 Dubai Desert Classic."

This morning I take a cab across town to the Emirates Golf Course, passing minivan after minivan packed with workers heading to construction sites, and climb the steps to the white media tent. Behind the main desk is a well-dressed employee of Pakistani descent speaking perfect English. "Good morning," she says as I tentatively slide the e-mail across the desk. She picks it up, looks at it briefly, and then hands me my pass. The credential won't get in me inside the ropes, but it will get me closer to Tiger than I will probably get all year.

The Dubai Desert Classic is officially a European Tour event, but looking at where it has been playing, you'd never know it. Last week the Euro Tour was in Qatar. Three weeks ago it was in South Africa, and next week it is headed to India. At least it's not fighting the fact that no one really wants to play golf in Europe until spring. Tiger first played in the Dubai Desert Classic in 2001, took a few years off, and has now played every year since 2004. He finally won in 2006, defeating South Africa's Ernie Els in a playoff when Els dunked his ball in the water on the first extra hole. For someone who won't even show up for all the PGA events in his home state, there must be another reason Tiger's here, and it's not because he's doing some work on the side for KBR. The European Tour allows its sponsors to give players undisclosed appearance fee money in order to lure them to events. If the rumors are true, Tiger has already made $2–3 million by the time his jet touches the ground.

7:25 AM • Seven days and 8,338 miles from La Jolla, Tiger Woods and I are back on the range. I feel sorry for the chump warming up next to him. He doesn't even have a Tour bag; he has one of those walking bags with a stand. And not even a nice walking bag with a stand. As Tiger crushes a 3-wood, the player next to him duck-hooks his shot, and quickly looks away in shame. When Tiger enters the field, it's remarkable how many players automatically have no chance of winning. I'm sure this guy is a good golfer. He may have even won a tournament or two in his life. But never before have I seen such a stark contrast between a very good golfer and a great one.

8:15 AM • Tiger is starting this morning on the 10th tee and is paired with Scotland's Colin Montgomerie and Sweden's Niclas Fasth. Around me are only a hundred fans or so. The peppy British announcer kindly asks the gallery to put away cell phones and cameras, saying that there are plain-clothed officials in the crowd who will be monitoring us. This can't possibly be true, since the man next to me is using his video-camera and still camera at the same time. He's obviously a tourist, and a look around makes me think everyone else is, too: Brits, Germans, Africans, Indians, and most of them openly taking pictures.

With the empty warning out of the way, the announcer shifts gears to what really matters. "And now on the tee, the 2006 winner of the Dubai Desert Classic. . . . From the United States . . . Tiger Woods." There's no jet lag on his swing as his drive on the 550-yard 10th splits the fairway. While Monty and Fasth can't get any closer to the green in two shots than eighty-five yards, Tiger carries his second all the way to the rough just short of the green. His chip rolls out just short of the hole. A tap-in birdie to start his day.

8:30 AM • There are a lot of things you aren't allowed to do in Dubai, but exaggerating is certainly not one of them. According to the tournament Web site, the Emirates Golf Club was built when "His Highness General Sheik Mohammed bin Rashid Al Maktoum, Vice-President, Prime Minister of the UAE, Ruler of Dubai and Minister of Defense gave his approval for the innovative concept of developing a grass golf course in the desert." Tacking five different titles onto just one man is pretty bold, but pretending to be the first golf course ever built in a desert is over the line. It's certainly pretty, with lush green fairways separated occasionally by dark brown bunkers and bright blue lakes. There are no pastels here. Everything's bold. Even more striking are the skyscrapers of various shapes and sizes that surround us. Some are finished, others are still being built, but there's no real organization to their layout, as if the city planners don't really know which way they're going to expand next.

Tiger's iron to the straightforward 169-yard 11th starts right and stays right. He yells to himself in the third person, "Tiger!" then adds an expletive. Down at the green the Indian man next to me sees Tiger's ball just twenty feet from the hole and says, "That's a *bad* shot for Tiger?"

9:06 AM • Compared to the Buick, the crowds here are sparse. It would make following Tiger relatively easy except for the marshals. They may not care about cameras, but they are passionate about there being absolutely no movement while a player hits a shot. It doesn't matter if Niclas Fasth has his back to us and is a hundred yards away; the marshals hold up their hands, yell "Stand, please!" and we all resign ourselves to the fact that we've just signed on for a four-and-a-half-hour game of Red Light/Green Light.

With Tiger going for the green in two on the 13th, I get a chance to catch up to him. He and Stevie lean against the bag and look around, pointing out the buildings that have sprouted up since they were here last February. The green clears, and Tiger pushes his 3-wood so far right that he drops his club on the follow-through. As I walk ahead, it's clear why he's upset—there's a lake to the right of the green, and he is in it. It's his first penalty stroke this year.

"In England, that's called 'taking a piss.'" That was my introduction to Ali, a hip, Kangol-wearing British expatriate who has spent the last twelve years working for one of the thousands of sheiks who essentially own and run the emirate. It doesn't make Ali a local, but almost. I ask him why I haven't seen any actual Arabs on the course. It's an easy answer. "Arabs hate golf," he says. Ali, on the other hand, loves it. He even credits Tiger's book *How I Play Golf* for his seven-handicap and *five* holes in one. I've never had a hole in one, and I've been playing since I was eight, but what makes me more jealous is that before the season started, Ali was able to find 33-1 odds on Tiger winning the Grand Slam and was smart enough to put a hundred pounds on it. In the United Kingdom. One of the few Muslim laws Dubai hasn't discarded is a ban on gambling. "It's just a matter of time," Ali insists, pointing out that it's hard to bill yourself as the Vegas of the Middle East without it.

Tiger takes a drop out of the water, then nestles his fourth shot to three feet to save par.

9:30 AM • The 14th at the Emirates is a downhill, dogleg left par 4 with desert on both sides. Even without wind, the safest shot for Tiger is a low stinger with his 3-wood to the center of the fairway. Without much fanfare, he hits his second shot to eight feet and makes the birdie to go to 2 under. Walking down 15, I spot a man in the traditional white *dishdasha* robe and Arab headdress, the first real local I've seen all day, and point him out to Ali. Ali notices the way the headdress is spun around his head and corrects me. "He's from Saudi Arabia."

11:41 AM ● Tiger is breezing through this round. He's birdied the 18th and the 1st, stuck it close on the par-3 4th to grab another shot, and arrives at the par-4 6th already 5 under par. The 6th is without a doubt the hardest hole on the course. It's uphill, 485 yards, with a waste bunker all down the left, a traditional bunker on the right, and deep rough everywhere else. You must hit driver, and even if you find the fairway, you're faced with a narrow, elevated green and another trap waiting to swallow any shots that come up short. He addresses the ball and, when he needs to most, hits his best drive of the day. It draws about three yards before landing and rolling out, 315 yards away. Colin Montgomerie, who is next to play, turns and says to the crowd, "This kid's got potential." The crowd laughs, and Tiger smirks.

Monty is always happiest on the European Tour, a place where he has won the Order of Merit (the Tour's top money earner) a record eight times. Yet he has never won a major championship. Even more remarkable is that he has never won *any* tournament on American soil. At age forty-four, the chances of either are starting to fade.

Monty's chummy relationship with Tiger has come a long way since they were paired together on Saturday at the 1997 Masters. Down by three shots, Monty said he considered himself the favorite. Eighteen holes later, and after shooting a not entirely embarrassing 74, Monty was down by nine. Asked if there were a chance Tiger could still lose, Monty snapped, "Have you just come in? Have you been away? Have you been on holiday? There is no chance. We're all human beings here. There's no chance humanly possible." That Saturday round was so dizzying for Monty that he went out the next day and shot an 81, finishing an unbelievable 24 shots behind Tiger. He's just one back of Tiger today, but after his joke he goes on to double-bogey the 6th, slipping out of contention.

12:11 PM • Dubai's hottest months are obviously during the summer, when 110 degrees and up isn't considered outrageous. But even in January the temp has climbed to the mid-80s. If I can just hold on for forty-five more minutes, there are free bottles of water in the media tent. And unlike in Hollywood, no one will be asking for them back.

But first Tiger has to negotiate the 8th. The par-4 6th is a tough hole, but the par-4 8th is a great hole. The tee shot is elevated and looks down on a fairway a good forty feet below it. In the distance, dozens of skyscrapers rise above the palm trees. From the landing area, the hole turns uphill and right, tempting players to cut off some of the corner from the tee. But missing right may lead you to the most penal place on the course, an open expanse covered in scrub brush where a ball will almost never be found. Tiger avoids all the potential mess, arrives at his ball in the fairway, and yawns. That would be the only evidence that he's tired. He knocks his second shot into birdie range and drops the putt, making a simple 3 on a hole that will humble most players before the week is through.

By the end of the day, eleven players shoot 67. None shoots 66. Tiger shoots 65. And after watching him walk away with a par on the last, I was about to experience my first Tiger Woods press conference.

12:51 PM • "Tiger Woods in the interview room," Michael Gibbons, the moderator, calls out quickly as he tries to keep pace with Tiger as he strides through the media tent. I grab a seat, assuming a stampede, but many of the reporters hang back by the entrance, anxious to get back to the stories they've already started writing.

The moment Tiger is seated, Gibbons begins by asking him to take us through his birdies and bogeys. Tiger didn't have any bogeys, but he's not rattled by the insult. Instead, he proceeds to fly through his round in a display of memory that is as impressive to me as the 65 he just shot:

"Started on ten. I hit driver and a five-wood just short. Chipped up to about an inch and made that. Fourteen, I hit a five-wood and a five-iron to about eight feet and made that. Eighteen, I hit three-wood and a three-wood and two-putted from about thirty-five feet. On number one, I hit a driver and a seven-iron to about twenty feet. Four, I hit a seven-iron to about two feet. Seven, I hit a six-iron to about eight feet and made that. Eight, I hit a driver and a seven-iron to again about eight feet and made that."

He can remember all that, and I'm not even sure which hat I am currently wearing on my own head. With the floor now open to questions, he is asked how his play today compared to last week. "Oh, definitely better. I had two good days of practice the last couple days and started to hit the ball a lot better than I did last week." A lot better than a week in which he won by eight? I stifle my amusement. This guy is unreal. A few more questions, and the reporters are already out of ammo. Tiger Woods is difficult to interview. In general, if a player is in the lead, he'll follow his round with a visit to the press tent. Because Tiger is in the lead so often, there aren't many golf-related questions he hasn't been asked after more than a decade. Outside of lobbing softball questions about the rewards of fatherhood, personal questions are typically off limits. Even what seems like the most banal of inquiries can be shot down without warning. After winning the 2006 British Open and talking candidly about the emotions of winning his first major since his father's death, Tiger was asked the seemingly less personal question of what he might put in the Claret Jug trophy to celebrate. "Beverage of my choice, and not just once." The press room laughed and a reporter naturally followed by saying, "May I ask what the beverage of your choice is?" "Yes, you can," Tiger answered. "You just asked. Will I answer? No."

What remains are the questions that are neither personal nor about golf, which are my favorite because of how tortured Tiger becomes when they're asked. During yesterday's press conference, while I was still at 30,000 feet, Tiger was asked what he thought about Barack Obama. "Oh God, here we go," Tiger said. His angst goes back to an understandable lack of trust with the press. In 1997, when he was only twenty-one, he famously told some inappropriate jokes to a *GQ* reporter and was dismayed when the writer put them into print. Since then, he says in public only what he wouldn't mind reading on the front page the next day. And because he says so little, that's usually where his comments land.

Which leads back to his Obama answer. "Well, I've seen him speak. He's extremely articulate, very thoughtful." Then, perhaps recognizing he was coming too close to an endorsement, he changes course. "I'm just impressed at how well, basically all politicians really do, how well they think on their feet." Ironically, it's exactly what Tiger just did.

Some writers have critiqued Tiger's press conferences as bland. I don't see that at all. I see calculation, the upshot of which is that he remains in complete control. In a room of thirty writers all hoping to convince their editors that sending them to Dubai was a worthwhile expense, shutting them up is pretty fun to watch.

After we sit in silence for a few beats, Tiger says, "Is that *it*?" After one more question, it is. Tiger says thanks and stands up, and I, thinking it appropriate after his round of 65, start to applaud. When no one else in the press tent follows my lead, I feel like an idiot. Only after the fact do I remember the famous maxim: no cheering in the press box. My cover nearly blown, I slip out the door and head for the taxis.

THE TIGER WOODS • It doesn't seem like such an outrageous idea. All I want to do is drive to Al Ruwaya, the golf course Tiger is designing, and see what it looks like. The announcement that Tiger's first foray into golf course architecture would be in Dubai came at the end of 2006. On Wednesday, Tiger told the press he hadn't made it out to the site yet this trip, but that they have two holes shaped and are working on a third. Two and a half holes in fourteen months? What are they using, Tonka trucks? Everything in Dubai happens quickly, except, for some reason, this. The course's Web site isn't much more helpful and provides no photos of the progress, just some rough sketches of what the holes will look like when they're completed. I want to see for myself and figure that when I find it, I will be one of the first.

Outside the Golden Sands I flag down a taxi and meet Rashid, a thirty-five-year-old Pakistani driver with a half-beard who has been circling the area for forty minutes looking for a customer. He's more dressed up than the other taxi drivers I've had. Wearing brown slacks, a long-sleeved cream-collared shirt, and a bright orange tie with matching orange epaulettes on his shoulders, Rashid sports a pseudomilitary look that inspires my confidence.

"Okay, Rashid, do you know where the golf course is that Tiger Woods is building?"

"Golf course, yes!" He peels out and we head south.

Within ten minutes, we've left the city and are driving through the desert. That's one of the many strange things about Dubai. It's massive and over the top, yet if you drive five miles inland from the Persian Gulf, there's nothing to see but sand. Especially today. "What's wrong with this weather?" "Yes, not good," Rashid says. It was cold and windy this morning, but I didn't think much of it. But now, as we drive deeper into the desert, visibility drops to a few hundred feet and the world around us turns brown. Rashid flips on his lights as blown sand starts to pile up on the highway. "What's going on?" I ask. *"Shmal,"* Rashid says. A *shmal* is the rarest of Dubai weather—a winter sandstorm. Twenty minutes outside town, Rashid makes a right at a sign for the Dubai Sports Complex. We follow the road until it comes to an end at an outdoor race track where, even in this weather, a fleet of Porsches is zipping around corners.

"Okay!" Rashid turns and says with a smile.

"Okay, what?"

"Race track!"

"No, *golf course*," I say. Like I did the night before with Mahmut, I show him my best golf swing.

"Oh, *golf*. . . ." He shakes his head, embarrassed.

I give him the rest of the information I have, which isn't much. "It's a golf course supposedly inside Dubailand." He lights up. "Dubailand!" He wheels the car around with the same speed as the Porsches next to us, and off we go again.

Dubailand is the Arab world's answer to Disneyland but, not surprisingly, a few hundred times bigger. Covering three billion square feet (another Dubai "fact"), the megacomplex will include theme parks, sports stadiums, apartments, hotels, and shopping. Between residents, tourists, and workers, Dubailand claims that it will boast a population of two and a half million people, an estimate that becomes even more absurd when I realize that's bigger than the entire current population of Dubai itself.

Rashid finds the main entrance. On the outside wall I see the black, round Arabic symbol I recognize as the logo for Tiger's golf course and housing development and underneath it, "The Tiger Woods." I love the "the." If you needed an original name but still wanted to capitalize on Tiger's involvement, I suppose that's the most obvious way to do it. We drive through a thirty-foot-high wooden gate, clearly mimicking the front gate of Jurassic Park, and continue on toward the Dubailand welcome center. Looping over and around the yellow building is a roller coaster with people in it. Not a real roller coaster, of course, and not real people. Dummies hang upside down in the cars with their hands up, having a fantastic time. Next to the roller coaster is a one-third scale model of the space shuttle, ready to blast off. And flying over the roof is a giant downhill skier. None of these is a working attraction, just things to whet your appetite until the actual Dubailand is built. Best I can tell, this welcome center *is* the only part of Dubailand that is built. And judging by the empty parking lot, the population hasn't quite hit two and a half million.

I hop out of the cab and experience the *shmal* for the first time. In the three seconds it takes to run to the double doors, sand is coating every exposed inch of me. When the automatic doors won't open, I force them apart with my hands and duck inside.

On the other side are three Pakistani workers, surprised to see anyone. Official current Dubailand population: five (I'm padding the numbers by counting Rashid, too).

No time for small talk.

"I'm looking for *The* Tiger Woods."

They stop and turn to each other, discussing the question in Urdu; then the head guy says in English, "Take him upstairs."

The lackey takes me to an elevator, and we climb to the second floor. Maybe those weren't dummies in that roller coaster. Maybe that's how Dubailand disposes of anyone who dares to look for The Tiger Woods before it's finished. The doors open, and I'm led down the hall to a giant map of Dubailand. Not what Dubailand looks like now, of course, but what it will look like two hundred years from now when it's completed. He points out the golf course and housing community on the map.

"There. The Tiger Woods," he says.

"How do I get there?"

"Al-Ain Road, then . . . right on *this*." He points to another street.

"And what's the name of that street?" I ask, hopeful.

"Hmm . . . I don't know."

Back in the cab, my fare has topped 90 dirhams (about thirty bucks), and I'm carrying only 120. "It's off Al-Ain Road, Rashid. Let's try again tomorrow." I slump back into my seat. "Al-Ain Road, tomorrow!" Rashid exclaims and begins the trip back toward the city. In the world of taxi drivers, there is no sweeter ride than a foreigner trying to find an oasis in the desert.

SECOND ROUND

12:25 PM • As Tiger sets to begin his round, I already know the mistake I've made. Five days ago in San Diego, I was stuck in the sun wearing rain gear. Today I'm stuck in the cold wearing shorts and no jacket. Tiger, of course, is thoroughly prepared for the conditions. Beneath his white Nike shirt he is wearing a black skintight undershirt made of space-age material and looks thoroughly comfortable. The high winds are whipping sand onto the golf course and have forced Tiger to wear sunglasses, a rare sight. He sports the black shades only between shots, but the additional piece of equipment is a real distraction since he never really knows where to put them. Throughout the first hole, the glasses travel from his face to the top of his hat to resting on the golf bag to the pocket on Stevie's bib. Along the way Tiger misses the fairway, misses the green, hits a poor chip, and makes a poor putt to start with a bogey.

12:50 PM • The 2nd hole at the Emirates Golf Club is a short, 351-yard par 4 with a lake along the right side. The water is usually only a semi-concern, but today's wind is blowing hard left to right, meaning a well-struck shot down the middle might still end up wet. I move ahead of the crowds and down the left side, figuring that's where Tiger will go to avoid the big mistake. He does, and his drive flies over our heads and through the rough before trickling into the desert. A British marshal scampers over and drops his hat on top of the ball to mark it.

As Tiger arrives, the marshal picks it up like a waiter revealing a gourmet meal. Instead, Tiger's treated to a fried egg, his ball sitting smack in the middle of a footprint. Tiger studies the shot, worried about whether he can even get a club on it from that lie. As he mulls it over, I feel something foreign on my shoulder. I slowly turn to find that a wee tourist has decided that the best way to see is to go on his tiptoes and rest his chin on me. Now, how can I not respect someone willing to do that? Besides, as the temperature continues to drop, I actually appreciate all the body heat I can get, even if some of it's not mine. Tiger indeed has trouble getting much club on it and advances it only thirty yards toward the hole. He scrambles for par, fortunate not to start with back-to-back bogeys.

1:13 PM ● Despite the weather, the crowd has doubled from only a few hundred yesterday to a thousand today. The rush to get to number 3 leads to anarchy as fans duck under ropes and run toward the tee box to beat Tiger there. Watching people from every race and religion running, I realize this is like the Olympics for out-of-shape people. The 3rd, a straight, slightly uphill par 5, is playing dead downwind, and Tiger takes advantage of it, launching a drive high into the air, carrying sixty yards past Monty's drive. He makes a 4 to get back to 7 under for the week.

1:57 PM ● As Tiger surveys a thirty-foot putt for birdie on the 7th, I am easily the most uncomfortable that I've ever been on a golf course. It's a little hard for me to explain. I mean, it's cold, maybe in the mid-50s, but every winter in college I was one of the last people on campus still wearing shorts to class. These chills may be more than just because of the storm. Last night I ate at Kentucky Fried Chicken's Dubai location, maybe not the smartest decision. I try to take notes but find my hands won't stop shaking, so I stuff them inside my short-sleeved shirt. When Tiger makes his long birdie putt, I'm compelled to pull them back out and clap.

3:53 PM ● On the range yesterday morning, Tiger finished his warm-up by hitting a handful of massive forty-yard hooks. I figured he was either having a stroke or there was a hole out here where that was the ideal shot to play. There are actually two. The first is here at the 13th, a 550-yard, dogleg left par 5. Like the 3rd hole earlier in the day, this too is playing downwind, and Tiger smokes it. Over the fairway, over the rough, past a set of palm trees, over all of us, finally touching down between two bushes in the desert. Three more feet in any direction, and he has no shot at all. When he and Stevie finally arrive after the long journey from the tee, Tiger shakes his head and says, "Best swing I made all day." Blocked by the bushes, Tiger hits a wedge into the fairway and, for the second straight day, leaves the birdie hole with just a par.

4:05 PM • Even though he didn't make a bogey and remains near the top of the leaderboard at 7 under, Tiger feels the need to regroup. He walks to the side of the tee and drops his head to think, then takes a few practice swings in slow motion, as if he's retraining his arms to do what has always been second nature. Dubai loves exaggeration, but the extra focus it takes to play quality golf in bad weather can't be overstated. Wind has a way of turning good shots into bad ones a lot more than it seems to make bad ones good. And for a self-described "control freak" like Tiger, I imagine nothing is more unnerving than believing he has factored in everything on a shot, only to have the wind switch directions or gust or stop altogether. Tiger breaks from his one-man huddle and drills a 3-wood stinger into the teeth of the wind, over the bunker, and onto the fairway.

The pep talk that I thought was unnecessary ends up helping him to play the last five holes 1 under par after playing the first thirteen at just even. His *shmal*-filled round of 71 is just enough to hold the lead by a shot heading into the weekend.

Back at the hotel, the first thing I do is take the hottest shower possible. After twenty minutes, the chills I've picked up during the day are still there. I bundle up in all the layers I should have been wearing at the course and order a pizza from room service. It is a creepy-looking pizza. It is round and there is cheese on top, but that is where the similarities to an actual pizza end. The dough is spiked with some curry-like spice, and the inclusion of butter and ketchup packets don't exactly bespeak the kitchen's confidence that they know what they're doing. But having not eaten anything since breakfast, I force down three pieces and fall asleep around nine.

Two hours later, I wake up and know at least one of my streaks is coming to an end. The last time I threw up was February 2000. There was nothing noteworthy about it. But after a few years had passed, I started to think, "Huh, I haven't been sick in a while." Eventually, it became something I boasted about at dinner parties. But now, in Dubai of all places, the streak comes to an end. Afterward, I am expecting that immediate relief, for my body to say that the worst has passed. It doesn't happen. And so I just lie there in the middle of the bathroom, picturing what a Dubai hospital is like. I haven't seen one, but it is safe to assume it is the biggest in the world. Or maybe it is built in the shape of a giant thermometer. Either way, I had a good run with Tiger. A hundred and eight holes. Six rounds. To borrow the line Gary Koch used when calling Tiger's snaking birdie putt at the 17th hole of the 2001 Players Championship, I am "better than most."

I never do call a doctor, figuring whatever they charge for house calls in Dubai is an expense no father of two with bad health insurance can afford. And in the morning I feel better. Not much, like 2 percent, but it is enough to give me hope that maybe I can survive six more miles around the course. Tiger isn't off till one, so I stay in bed till ten, then find Rashid's card and give him a ring. "Al-Ain Road!" he says when I tell him who it is. He'll be downstairs in ten minutes.

THE TIGER WOODS, TAKE 2 • Rashid is already outside, using the extra time to wipe the last of the sand off his Corolla. There are no signs of yesterday's storm, despite the fact the English-language paper outside my door led with the headline "Winds Shred Life in UAE." As we head back to the desert, I ask Rashid about his family. Turns out he has a wife and one child, neither of whom he's seen in two years. His story is pretty much the standard one in Dubai. He'll stay away from home for another five to seven years, then return with enough money to buy a house and support his family. He's not sad about it. If anything, he's proud. "In Pakistan, no money for taxi driver." His time in Dubai will be long but not without end, and when he returns home, he'll be a hero.

When we reach Al-Ain Road, our task becomes a question of which empty desert cross street to turn down. There are no street signs, no 7-Elevens, nothing. We take our first right and hope. After a few miles, a structure comes into view. We drive a little bit closer, and I see some sort of tower. Off on the right side of the cab, we pass a sign in the desert that read, "Military compound. No cameras allowed."

"I don't think this is it, Rashid."

"It's okay."

"Turn around, Rashid."

He doesn't listen and keeps heading toward the yellow security gate, walled in on every side. I stuff my camera under my jacket as we pull up to the guard window. There's no one there. In fact the whole place appears abandoned. On the other side of the gate, the empty desert road continues in a straight line. More of Dubai's smoke and mirrors.

"This isn't it."

"Yes." Rashid finally agrees.

We pass through the gates and make a U-turn as another car comes our way. Rashid waits and flags him down. As the burly man walks over us, Rashid rolls down my window. Thanks, Rashid.

"Do you know *The* Tiger Woods?" I ask.

He thinks for a moment then nods. "Al-Hibab Road."

Rashid repeats it, "Al-Hibab Road?!"

"Yes."

"Al-Hibab Road! *Salam Maleka!*"

This is as excited as I've seen Rashid in two days.

"You know where Al-Hibab Road is?" I ask.

"No."

Even if he did know where it was, we couldn't leave anyway. A pack of camels has appeared out of the desert and crosses through the unguarded gate and into the base. It's such a perfect Arabian moment that despite the signs, I pull out my camera and take some pictures. "They're going to Jumeirah Beach!" Rashid says, making a pretty good joke for someone with limited English.

We try every road within ten miles. Eventually, Rashid turns off the meter. "Too much money," he says. We stop at a junkyard and ask some workers. Nothing. We find an isolated model home development and ask the guard. "I don't know," he says. And so, after another hour and with Tiger's tee time approaching, I quit. "It doesn't exist, Rashid." If nothing else, that would certainly explain why Tiger hadn't been out to see it yet. There isn't anything to see. The Tiger Woods is buried underneath the sand like all the other things on my Dubai map, existing on paper but not in reality. In silence, Rashid drives me back toward the Emirates Golf Club, still sick and now also defeated.

THIRD ROUND

As he did last Saturday, Tiger starts the weekend in the lead and paired with a relative unknown chasing him. Last week, Kevin Streelman, this week a roly-poly former club professional from Ireland named Damien McGrane. But McGrane's reaction to playing with Tiger doesn't exactly have him bouncing off the walls when he met with reporters yesterday.

"Has it been a big ambition to play with him?"

"No, I wouldn't say it's my lifelong dream."

"Do you think you'll be nervous?"

"I hope not."

The sense is that McGrane is just one of the sixty-eight remaining European Tour regulars who doesn't particularly want to let Tiger show up at one of his own events, scoop up a giant appearance fee, and take home the trophy as well.

1:40 PM ● Tiger is even par through his first three holes when I run into Asif. He is the tenth person who has stopped me and asked to test-drive my periscope. Dubai claims to have everything a person could want, but no one has one of these. Asif is an East Indian Kenyan who was born in Canada but now lives in Dubai. For Asif, as for most of the people I've met here, Dubai is just a lily pad on which he'll float until life takes him somewhere else.

Still waiting for Tiger to turn on his magic, I ask Asif for any places in Dubai I have to see before I leave. "Forget about the tourist spots. You need to see the *real* Dubai." He tells me about the northern part of the city, where vendors sell gold and jewelry, and beat-up water taxis float along Dubai Creek. It sounds refreshingly different from the controlled glitz Dubai pushes on tourists. "And watch out for the whores," he adds. Maybe not so refreshing.

2:30 PM ● By the time Tiger sprays his drive into the desert on the 8th, he has lost his lead. At 1 over par for the day, he is now two shots behind Sweden's Henrik Stenson. And the hard-to-scare McGrane is still where he was, just one shot back. Most of Tiger's game is solid, but his driver is a disaster. The crowds have shrunk, too, with just a few hundred people outside the ropes. As big a draw as he is, European fans seem more willing to ditch even the world's best to track a player who is actually posting a good number.

The exodus puts me in the front row as Tiger looks at the trouble shot he has left himself. The ball is well below his feet, a downhill side-hill lie off the sand to an elevated green. Further complicating things is a row of palm trees right in front of him. Tiger stands behind the ball and runs the odds of pulling off different shots through his swoosh-covered supercomputer. I finally grasp just how hard it really is for even Tiger to win a golf tournament. Every part of his game is firing except one, and he's suddenly playing catch-up. Last week's blowout at the Buick Invitational isn't really the norm, it's an anomaly. In 2007, Tiger won seven times, but in six of those events his margin of victory was only two shots.

All of which makes a shot from the desert on Saturday's front nine just as critical as a shot on the back nine Sunday. He grabs a 5-iron and takes a few practice swings, exaggerating the motion of rolling his wrists over at impact. He's going low with a draw. Right between the trees. As he steadies himself over the ball, a marshal reminds us to "Stand, please!" in case we've somehow forgotten by the five hundredth time. A fan slowly lifts her camera phone and takes a silent picture. Tiger's shot splits the ten-yard gap in the palms and turns up the hill. It hits in the fairway and rolls, climbing the slope as best it can. When it stops, it's only seven or eight yards short of the green. A chip and a putt later, Tiger saves his par.

3:52 PM • But on a perfect day in Dubai, pars aren't good enough. Everyone is surging up the leaderboard, and Tiger is being left behind. Ernie Els is now 10 under after starting his back nine eagle-birdie-par-birdie. Tiger is still stuck at 8 under with two surging Swedes, Peter Hedblom and Henrik Stenson. I wish Nelson from Torrey Pines were here to look through his periscope and diagnose exactly what's wrong.

Tiger has appeared patient all day, but when he airmails the 13th fairway for the second day in a row, he's fried. He has to take a one-stroke penalty out of the bush and is not in that happy swami place he found on the 15th at Torrey Pines North last week. He stands behind his ball, notices the shadow of a fan's head near it, then lifts his foot and stomps on it, ordering it to move. He's acting as if the fan was making shadow puppets or something. He can take out his anger on his golf bag, but to do it on one of us seems like a dangerous precedent. It doesn't take him long to realize this, and when the head ducks away, Tiger immediately says, "Thank you." Then for good measure, "Thank you. I appreciate it." To succeed in golf, players are often encouraged by their sports psychologists to be themselves. The problem for Tiger is that he's an intense guy in love with a gentleman's game.

4:41 PM • Tiger lumbers through the back nine still at 8 under. When he arrives at the last hole, Ernie has finished with a 7-under 65 and a score of 11 under. Last year's champ, Stenson, is in the clubhouse at 10 under. Lee Westwood and Graeme McDowell have caught up and are both in at 8 under as well. Tiger is just 1 under since his brilliant opening round on Thursday. But he still has the 18th.

The 18th at the Emirates is the other hole where Tiger wants to hit his big sweeping hook. A 564-yard par 5, it looks a little as if someone took the 18th at Torrey Pines and bent it ninety degrees left, right down to the lake that fronts the entire green. Average-length hitters can't reach, but Tiger's drive is bombed and settles slightly into the rough, 230 yards from the hole.

Tiger knows he's behind. Some players get nervous by looking at leaderboards, believing that ignorance is bliss. I've noticed that Tiger can't stop looking. The more knowledge he has, the better. With Ernie at 11 under, he is going for the green. From up near the green, I look back and see Tiger take out his 3-wood. It seems like a lot of club from 230 yards until I see it start off high, a soft cut shot that he wants to land gently on the green. It moves a little right, then a little more. Even from two hundred yards back I hear Tiger start yelling at it, "Go . . . Go!" Halfway over the lake, the ball stops dead, like a harpoon without enough rope. It falls to the water and disappears with a splash.

The gallery is confused. I'm not confused, I'm miffed. *I sacrificed my eight-year throw-up streak just so I could witness a Saturday afternoon tank job?* There is no club tossing from Tiger, no bag kicking, no shadow stomping, either, just resignation that he's made his task tomorrow that much harder. He putts out for a bogey to some polite applause. He'll start the final round four shots behind Els.

THE REAL DUBAI • Feeling unimpressed by Tiger's play and still nauseous, I leave my hotel looking for the "real Dubai," as Asif called it. The worker at the front desk says I can walk to the Creek more easily than taking a cab. He obviously doesn't realize what I've been doing the last two weeks. But at this point, what's another couple of miles? Being a pedestrian here is tricky, though. There is so much construction going on that as I make the hike I'm constantly butting up against closed-off sidewalks or open trenches that force me into traffic, where I face a whole other set of dangers.

Within a few blocks of the hotel, everything changes. No cranes or malls or McDonald's; they have been replaced by hole-in-the-wall restaurants, Indian barbers cutting hair, and eight-story apartment buildings that go on as far as I can see. As I walk, I look in the windows and see some people watching TV; others are outside retrieving clothes from the balcony. It's funny, but the real Dubai isn't particularly Arab at all. It's Pakistani and Indian and Asian. And almost completely devoid of women. It makes sense considering that Rashid and so many others left their wives at home when they came here, but it is bizarre to spend even a little bit of time in a place where the men seem to outnumber the women a hundred to one. Which explains Asif's warnings about the prostitutes. I arrive at the "Creek," a dredged inlet from the gulf spreading 350 yards from one side to the other. Lighting both sides of the waterway are orange lamps to help guide boats across. One of them pulls up and offers to take me to the other side, but I wave him off and head for bed.

FINAL ROUND

After Rashid's and my failure in the desert, I call him one last time to show me two things I felt confident we could find: the Persian Gulf and the Burj Al Arab hotel. As far as the gulf goes, my ignorant American mind was picturing waves of oil lapping the shore. It's actually beautiful and blue, but don't call it the Persian Gulf. It's the Arabian Gulf, a reminder of the U.A.E.'s long-standing cultural tension between itself and its neighbor a hundred miles to the north in Iran. From there it's off to the tallest hotel in the world, where Tiger has spent his week. Only hotel guests are permitted inside the gates of the Burj Al Arab, which sits three hundred feet offshore, so Rashid and I make do with the view from afar. I feel as if I've become a skeptic on this trip, but it just doesn't look that big. This seems like a fact they couldn't get away with inventing, so I ask someone else on the outside looking in if it's true. She clarifies it for me—the Burj Al Arab is the tallest *single-purpose* hotel in the world. You've got to love Dubai. I take out my Burj Al Arab postcard and draw a little asterisk on its giant heliport.

12:10 PM • Tiger arrives at the 1st tee, going with the red mock T over the collared shirt this week, a look I'm confident in saying no other golfer in the world can pull off. Really, he could show up to play in a red tank top with a black bicycle helmet on his head and I'm convinced someone would nod and say, "Now, that is cool."

Tiger can pull it off because he plays like this: his drive on the first hole is straight down the middle, forty yards ahead of the Irishman McGrane, who is still playing with Tiger after hanging tough with a 72 yesterday. From there Tiger stuffs his second shot to three feet. He doesn't waste a second on the birdie, tapping it in and getting himself back to 8 under.

1:21 PM • Tiger is waiting at the 7th tee, in the midst of making a run at the leaders who are just teeing off. He's played the first six holes 2 under par and has pulled back to within a few shots of Ernie Els. But it's all on hold for a moment, as the group on the green is taking forever to putt. Tiger leans against a cooler and says to no one in particular, "How slow are these guys playing?" For a control freak, he does a good job disconnecting. He just swings his legs and checks out the scenery, noticing everything except the hundreds of people staring at him.

While he waits, England's Lee Westwood crosses by. Westwood is two years older than Tiger but until recently has been wrapped in an ever-present layer of baby fat. Working with trainers, he has lost six inches on his waist, picked up fifteen yards off the tee, and rediscovered the winning ways he had early in his career.

As he passes by, he sees Tiger's dropping score and smirks at him, a look I take as Westwood saying, "You're going to win every damn tournament this year, aren't you?" As if reading his mind, Tiger shrugs his shoulders and smiles back.

1:45 PM • The smiles come to an abrupt stop at the 9th green when, after two solid shots, Tiger three-putts. He birdied three out of his first four holes on the front but plays his last five in 2 over. The walk between nines takes me past a leaderboard, and I take a look to see where Tiger stands.

Tiger often speaks of a score he secretly has in his head during the final round that he believes he needs to shoot in order to win the tournament. Last night while walking back from the Creek, I did the same and came up with a round of 65. Fourteen under par. But with nine holes left, the leaderboard reads like this:

Els	−12
Stenson	−11
Oosthuizen	−10
Kaymer	−10
McDowell	−9

And tacked on at the very bottom, almost just to be nice:

Woods	−8

Tiger is just as far behind as he was when he started his round. I don't know what Tiger's number is, but he can't get to mine.

2:31 PM • Tiger makes a routine birdie on the par-5 10th and is facing a difficult pitch shot behind the green on the long par-4 12th. The lie is downhill and half buried, but the grass still looks wispy, a combination that makes how hard to hit it a total guess. It's the kind of lie that Judge Smails from *Caddyshack* might kick and say, "Don't count that, I was interfered with," but Tiger doesn't have that luxury.

From that weird downhill lie, with no more than twenty-five feet to the hole, Tiger takes a half swing with the face of his wedge wide open. It pops right out, lands softly on the green, and he watches as it rolls into the right side of the cup for a birdie. The fans let out their loudest cheer of the week, while a Brit next to me waves his cap and says, "Good show!" I didn't know people actually did that. The renewed smiles on everyone's faces tell me they think he can still pull this off.

2:46 PM • He'll have to keep it going on the par-5 13th. The hole has bullied him this week—in the water Thursday, the desert Friday, and yesterday, a bush. Today he avoids all the trouble and casually knocks in a three-footer for his third birdie in four holes. *Eleven under.*

3:01 PM • An hour ago, Tiger was completely out of this tournament. Now, as I make for the 14th green, I start to do the math in my head. If he birdies the short par-4 17th and the par-5 18th, he can get to 13 under. But something else would have to fall.

From 170 yards, Tiger drops his second shot to ten feet, just short of the hole. He tears off his glove aggressively as he strides to the green, wanting to get in as many holes as possible before the magic runs out. Watching him circle his putt, I sense that I am actually anxious. I'm legitimately worried that he will miss this and squander a chance to pull even closer. Maybe my nerves can be explained away as a spike in nationalism because we are both so far from home, but I think some part of me is beginning to care about whether or not Tiger Woods wins. His birdie putt starts just left of the hole, bends back toward the cup, and drops in the front. *Twelve under!* I join the crowd and cheer, outclapping most of those around me. He's birdied four of his five holes on the back nine. Tiger does a very subtle fist pump, like you might do to get Heinz ketchup out of a bottle. He grabs the ball out of the cup, hops over the hole, and keeps on going, off the green and up to the 15th tee.

As I head up the hill, I look to my right and see that Tiger and I are within a foot of each other. For the first time, I feel a need to say something to him. His resolve over these five holes has been too amazing to ignore. Without giving it any thought, I blurt out "Good putt, Tiger!" He doesn't stop. He doesn't look. He ignores me.

3:12 PM • Ernie Els may be four groups behind Tiger, but when Tiger steps to the 15th tee, Ernie is putting on the 11th green, no more than fifty feet away. During yesterday's press conference, Els said he likes to see what other players are doing. "And especially Tiger . . . he could get red hot at any time and you'd like to see what's going on." He might want to rethink that strategy. After hearing the cheer at fourteen and now seeing him in the flesh, the man nicknamed "The Big Easy" promptly yanks his four-foot par putt. It never even touches the cup, and he slips back to only 12 under. I don't believe what I'm seeing. In a mere five holes, Tiger has gone from having no chance of winning to being tied for the lead.

When Tiger is playing well, he's in everybody's head. But no big-name player has lost to Tiger as often as Ernie. At the 1998 Johnnie Walker Classic in Thailand, Els was up eight shots heading into the final round and lost to a surging Tiger on the second hole of sudden death. Two years later, at the Mercedes Championship, they dueled again into extra holes before Tiger drained a forty-foot putt to beat him again. And then there was two years ago, right here at the Desert Classic. Tiger and Ernie were tied after 72 holes when Ernie's 4-iron into the 18th green came up short in the lake, handing Tiger yet another victory. A win here would begin to heal a few of the South African's wounds.

ELDRICK OF ARABIA • 63

3:39 PM • With pars on 15 and 16, Tiger has to finish with back-to-back birdies to have a chance. The scorecard for the 17th hole at the Emirates says it's 359 yards long. But if Tiger can convince himself that the entire right side of the hole isn't a golf ball graveyard filled with stumpy palm trees, bushes, sand, and rocks, it's merely a 320-yard blind shot to the green. Needing birdie, there's no doubt he will be cutting the corner.

I run for the green, anxious to see where his drive comes down. It's harder to find a good spot ever since Els and Tiger crossed paths. In a moment that couldn't have done much for Ernie's fragile confidence, many of his fans peeled off and have decided to follow Tiger instead. From the green we can't see Tiger and he can't see us; our only clue is watching those fans positioned halfway to the tee.

We see their heads turn in unison, and our murmurs build as everyone braces for the thud. It lands on the front left part of the green, safe, and we cheer Tiger's gutsy play. He has a perfect angle to the back-right pin. This back nine has showcased almost every facet of Tiger's game. Chipping—12. Irons—14. And now, on 17, his incredible length and accuracy off the tee when he must have it. Tiger's bump and run for eagle looks good, but Tiger is begging it to turn a little more right. It skims the left edge and doesn't stop rolling until it is a missable eight feet away. As he walks to mark it, he turns and reads the leaderboard.

Els	−12	through 13
Oosthuizen	−12	F
Woods	−12	through 16

I narrow my focus onto the small circle of white-painted dirt around the inside of the cup. That's all that matters now. The putt slips over the front edge. Tiger steps toward the hole and punches the air. The crowd cheers again, silently chastising itself for ever wasting its time watching Ernie Els. Tiger is at 13 under and has the lead all to himself.

3:49 PM • But he still hasn't reached my number. Fourteen under. The high hook off the 18th tee is step one. He clobbers it, wrapping it around the desert forest and stopping it just before it hits the rough on the far side of the fairway. How important is that hook he was working on Thursday morning? By pulling it off, he is fifty yards closer to the hole than McGrane, who, despite playing well yesterday, has become only a footnote at this point. He and Tiger were tied when they started the round. Tiger now leads him by ten.

Tiger is almost close enough to power a 3-iron all the way to the front pin, but the last thing he wants to do is flirt with the water and give the tournament away. At least I'm hoping that's what he's thinking. Just to make sure, I find myself starting to give Tiger advice under my breath:

Don't be stupid, don't be stupid . . .

He grabs his 5-wood, then Stevie's towel, and rubs down the grip, needing every bit of tackiness for a shot with this much at stake.

The moment he hits it, there's no chance it's wet. Any of the wind that knocked down his 3-wood yesterday can't touch his 5-wood today as the ball flies the green, bounces, and then gets hung up in the deep rough in front of the back bunker. Tiger drops his club in frustration. To the chagrin of the European tourists next to me who are just down for a relaxing holiday, I restart my one-way dialogue:

Up and down, up and down, up and down! . . .

4:00 PM • At most PGA events, ringing the 18th green is a series of grandstands. Here there is only one large bleacher to the left of the green while behind it are three separate, glassed-in "corporate chalets" used by the sponsors and the sheiks themselves, many of whom are practically pressing their noses against the glass and staring down at Tiger playing his shot from the rough beneath them.

Because the ball is in the grass but his feet are in the bunker, he tries all sorts of stance/swing combinations before he finds one he likes. Besides that, he also has to factor in the thing he thought he was done worrying about—the lake. The green slopes severely back to front, and he just watched Damien McGrane hit not one but two balls into the water. If his pitch jumps out of the grass, it won't stop. He finds the spot on the green where he wants it to land, and returns to the ball, where he takes, I count, *seven* more practice swings. I've never seen anything done with such decisiveness.

For all of Tiger's hard work, he finally hits it, only to have it pop straight up and dribble onto the green, twenty feet short of the hole. Tiger fumes, tossing his wedge toward his bag in disgust. It clangs against his clubs and falls to the ground as Stevie hands him his putter.

And so it ends. After all his effort to pull close, he's just going to fizzle out with a par. He doesn't need to spend much time on the putt. It's going to do what he was hoping his chip would do, downhill and a couple of feet left to right. In the chalet behind the green, the sheiks are still watching, but not as intently. For eight holes at least, there was nothing boring about golf.

4:01 PM ● I never considered that he might actually make it. The first ten feet of the putt, I'm thinking about how I will kill time between the end of the tournament and my flight. But then I notice Tiger is beginning to backpedal as it gets close. Wait, I've seen this kind of thing on television. But it can't actually happen now. While I'm standing here. Suddenly, the putt disappears from view and Tiger turns and fires a huge right hook as the sheiks behind the glass rejoice. I throw my hands in the air and start to laugh. Fourteen under! The number. *My* number!

I pull out my notebook and start scribbling down his score and his stats. He has just delivered a 6-under-par 31 on the back nine on a Sunday. After three-putting the 9th, he only needed ten putts total to play the next nine holes. The crowd cheers, but either they're Els fans or they don't truly appreciate what just happened. Only a few dozen people in the grandstands are actually on their feet. Perhaps the rest are thinking the way I did until nine holes ago: that Tiger's style is, frankly, unbecoming. Or it might just be Dubai. If there's a place in the world that can numb your senses and distort your definition of the word *unbelievable*, this is it.

The only matter left to be decided is whether Tiger can be caught. Everyone else has already folded, but Els remains at 13 under and still has the 18th to play. His drive is solid, to the first cut of rough on the right side, close to where Tiger was. Chances are he will be on or near the green, looking at an eagle to win or a birdie to tie. Instead, his ball is swatted down by the same mysterious wind that grabbed Tiger's the day before, and it lands in the water at least twenty yards short of the green. Ernie passes by me, head down, once again on the losing end of a Tiger miracle. His body language matches that of the man next to me, who is muttering to himself, "Astounding . . . astounding . . . They handed it to him, didn't they? *Didn't they?*" No, Tiger handed it to *them* on Saturday. And on the back nine Sunday, he took it back.

I wheel my suitcase down the steps of the press tent and out to the long taxi line. Two Arab men, both in headdresses, one with a baseball cap perched on top, are directing the cabs and the people, matching up fans who are going to the same parts of town to speed up the queue. The two African men ahead of me are headed to Deira, and I join them, knowing from there it is only a short ride to the airport. One of them can't stop smiling and saying "That was amazing." The other won't stop shaking his head. Most of the fans this week had seemed to watch the action in a daze, almost impossible to impress. Njaaga and Jonathan are a couple of fantastic exceptions.

Njaaga is small, wiry, full of energy, while Jonathan is bigger and calmer, saving his thoughts for the brief moments when Njaaga isn't talking. Forty-something friends from Kenya, the two of them made the four-and-a-half-hour flight solely to see Tiger Woods. It wasn't just because they wanted to do it; Njaaga felt he had to. "In the Muslim religion, I read how in life you have to go to Mecca before you die. That is how this was." The closest he came to Tiger before this was in Milwaukee, of all places. When business took him there a few years back, he went out of his way to visit Brown Deer Golf Club, the place where Tiger made his professional debut back in 1996. "I just wanted to connect with him," he says. When the head pro realized how far Njaaga had come, he went into the back of his shop and dug up an old Greater Milwaukee Open hat for him. He points to it on his head, "And now I wore it to Dubai and he *won!*" I look at Jonathan. He's still shaking his head.

As we drive north on Sheik Zayed Road, we go back through Tiger's round, shot by shot, none of us having seen anything the other didn't but still needing to describe what happened just to make sure it really did. In a week where at times I wondered why I had come at all, in the end my only regret is that I didn't run into these guys until the taxi home.

At this point I realize Tiger can do things no one else ever can or will. That was my justification to Hillary at the beginning of the year, but now I actually believe it. That said, I still have my hang-ups. As our cab crosses the Creek into Deira, I know Njaaga is just the Tiger fan to ask about one of them. "Doesn't it bother you that he ignores us? That he's just this cold, calculated killer?" I am still wincing from my "Good putt, Tiger" that went unappreciated back on 14. Njaaga doesn't answer right away. He thinks about it and nods, affirming my point of view as a legitimate gripe. Finally, he speaks. "The way I look at it . . ." he pauses, picking his words carefully, "that's his work." He thinks for another moment, and then repeats it, "That's his *work.*" I'm starting to realize that Tiger Woods works best with his head down.

FIST PUMPS OF FURY

The WGC-Accenture Match Play Championship

The Gallery Golf Club at Dove Mountain
Marana, Arizona
February 20–24, 2008

There is a good chance my car might not make it across the Arizona desert once, let alone twice. A two-door Ford Explorer, it is the first new car that I bought and paid for all by myself. For years, I have protected and cared for it, never trusting anyone but myself to wash it. Two recent events told me things had changed. When I was home from Dubai, I put my son, Danny, in the back to go on an errand and, while I was strapping him into his car seat, he pointed at something on the floor.

"Dada, what is that?"

"That is called an air freshener. It makes Daddy's car smell good."

He looked at me for a second and then said, "But your car doesn't smell good."

The other incident was back in January, when I drove it into the side of our house. I was backing out of our narrow driveway, lost track of where I was, and heard a loud scraping noise. I got out and saw that the stucco wall was basically sanding down the back right quarter panel of my car. Theoretically, this should have been devastating. But I just shrugged, straightened it out, and drove away. My car has been exacting its revenge ever since by having random accessories break without warning. First was the handle that hung down from the inside of the passenger door to help passengers climb out. I was driving down the freeway when it just dropped off like a bat dying in its sleep. Next was the dashboard light that tells me how much gas I have in my tank. Was that important? The latest thing to go was the power on my driver's-side window. The car probably had another five thousand miles in it, but the eight-hour drive to the Accenture Match Play would be our last road trip together. And if Tiger were to lose in the first round on Wednesday, I'd be back home in thirty-six hours.

L.A. TO TUCSON • I have never gone on a trip in my life without knowing where I'd be staying. When my family took a month-long cross-country vacation together in the late 1980s, my parents had every hotel reserved before we left. I grew up convinced that if we hadn't booked that Flagstaff Days Inn two months ahead of time, we would have been forced to sleep in our car. Still smarting from my Dubai tab, I cautiously dove into the underground economy of Craigslist to see what my other options were. On the cheap end was a thirty-five-dollar-a-night room in an apartment downtown, but the three people renting it seemed a little too interested in finding out my sexuality first. On the expensive end was a Bates Motel–looking one-bedroom, one-bath overlooking the Saguaro National Park for seventy-five dollars a night, the perfect place to stay if you want to be killed in your sleep and have your body easily disposed of before sunrise. The best option was a guest house in North Tucson for sixty dollars a night. I had left a message with Cheryl, the owner, but by the time I left home, I'd yet to hear back.

Since the most distracting things along the five-hundred-mile route are prisons, there is plenty of time to think about life. And for me that means Tiger. Two tournaments, two wins. I shake my head. He just *had* to be thoroughly impressive from the very beginning. His Sunday comeback had sucked me into his vortex, and I am excited to see how in the world it can be topped.

In between prisons, I hear from Cheryl. The guest house is all mine.

I arrive over an hour late, mostly due to the fact that I don't realize there is an hour time difference between the two cities, but also because of the layout of Tucson itself. Ninety percent of the city sits east of Interstate 10, its only freeway. When I exit Prince Road, I naively start to organize my things at stoplights, thinking I'm almost there. Fifteen minutes later, I'm still driving, passing through mile upon mile of liquor stores, check-cashing places, and a dumpy-looking bar called the Elbow Room. They hold a top-tier golf tournament in this town? It seems like a chamber of commerce's worst nightmare. Eventually the seedy Tucson gives way to middle-class Tucson and I'm driving through the tract homes of Cheryl's neighborhood.

Cheryl has an Earth Woman sort of feel to her, her hair curly and graying with a peaceful face frozen in a consistent half-smile. The winter is her busy season as far as guests go, the big rush being the first two weeks of February, when Tucson holds its annual gem show. I'm sure Tiger came into town early to hit that. With her sons grown up and moved on, she figured if she could pick up some extra cash throughout the year, why not? The guest house is a few hundred square feet, and she diligently explains all the nuances of it, right down to making sure I know how to use a TV remote and work a plug-in fan. She even shows me how to stop the shower drain in case I feel like taking a bath.

Next, I have to sign Cheryl's meticulous checklist of every item that is currently in the guest house to prevent getting away with theft. Apparently that gem show crowd is filled with a lot of kleptomaniacs. The only glitch in the whole system is Cheryl's minimum four-night policy, meaning if Tiger can't hang on until the quarterfinals, I'll ultimately spend more money here than if I had spent three nights in an actual hotel where everything anyone would want to steal is already bolted to the floor.

I pay her the money and a deposit and say good night, but she insists that before going to bed I take any and all valuables out of my car, then whispers, "This *is* Tucson." I don't know what the town's official motto is, but I'm hoping that Cheryl's sticks.

FIRST ROUND: J. B. HOLMES

I have seen only one kung fu movie in my life, and staring at the sixty-four-man bracket for the Accenture Match Play, it is the best parallel I can draw to what Tiger Woods will face this week. In *Fist of Fury*, Bruce Lee plays Chen Zhen, a Chinese martial artist who goes to a Japanese school to avenge the murder of his teacher. When he enters, one of the students walks toward him and stretches out his arms to give Zhen a hug. Zhen promptly elbows him in the face, then tosses him against the wall. Another student with an exceptionally bad wig steps forward and starts to swing. Zhen blocks his punch, spins around, and then flips the guy like a baton, at which point the remaining forty students have seen enough and circle around him, ready to pounce. One by one, they rush at Zhen and then watch in horror as he chops, kicks, and generally humiliates each of them in unique and creative ways before he gives one final sneer and walks away victorious.

That would be Tiger's best-case scenario. He hadn't won the Tour's only regular season match play event in four years and had won it twice in only eight tries. For most of that eight-year stretch, he used the fairly legitimate excuse that the greens at the La Costa Resort where it was played were so bumpy and slow that plenty of perfectly stroked putts could never find the bottom of the cup. But last year, no doubt in response to his and others' complaints, the event was moved to Arizona's Gallery Golf Club at Dove Mountain, a private 36-hole club twenty miles north of Tucson. Out here the only bumps on the green are man-made. And in a moment that, at the time, was thoroughly enjoyable for me, it was just such a man-made bump, a ball mark that Tiger never saw, that kicked his par putt offline on the 19th hole and cost him last year's third-round match against Australia's Nick O'Hern.

Over the course of 72 holes, Tiger could make mistakes and still win. Dubai had proven that. But in match play, a stretch of only a few bad holes could end his week and his win streak. "It's a sprint," Tiger had told reporters yesterday. And if your opponent makes more birdies than you do, it's over.

Tiger's first experience with match play came at the age of thirteen. He made it to the quarterfinals of the Southern California Junior Match Play, shot 69, and lost. He came home and told his dad, "I shot a better score than he did, but he won the match. That doesn't seem right." Nearly twenty years after the loss, when a reporter asked if he remembered who beat him that day, he fired back, "James Mohan."

I am a little worried that this year's James Mohan might be J. B. Holmes, a stocky, goateed twenty-six-year-old from Kentucky who doesn't seem to scare easily. Similar to the NCAA tournament, the four brackets for the Match Play are decided by ranking, so whoever ends up facing Tiger Woods in the first round is near the bottom of that list. But J.B. is coming to the Match Play having just won the FBR Open up the freeway in Phoenix three days ago—by way of a one-hole playoff against Phil Mickelson. Under the pressure of sudden death, J.B. hit his opening drive 359 yards. If he is intimidated by top players, that is a weird way of showing it.

11:46 AM • From the top row of the Dove Mountain driving range, it's hard not to be distracted by the view. The lush green course lined with dormant brown rough sits in the shadow of Arizona's Catalina Mountains, the tallest of which is snowcapped. Looking west isn't so bad either: a thirty-mile vista where the desert is broken up by endless cacti, jagged brown peaks, and, far off to the north, an airline graveyard for planes that haven't been used since 9/11.

The bleachers are standing-room-only for one reason: Tiger is on the range. The first sound when Tiger hits a golf shot on the driving range is the thwack of steel colliding with the cover of a golf ball. The second is a few hundred people saying, "Umm!" as they watch it fly out of sight.

12:02 PM • I wedge myself into the right side of the tee on the 1st, a downhill 588-yard par 5. "Stroke Play Tiger" was pretty impressive the last two tournaments, and I am anxious to see how he compares to "Match Play Tiger." J.B.'s problem is that either way he will still be playing some version of Tiger. After the compulsory introductions and the subtle doff of his white TW-logoed hat, Match Play Tiger Woods hits his opening tee shot off the world right. It's not easy to silence the bleachers on the first tee of a golf tournament. These are fans who have sacrificed a few hours of watching more exciting shots in exchange for being able to tell their friends they saw Tiger Woods hit his first shot of the day. Yet the swing and resulting ball flight bring such an uncomfortable reaction you'd think Tiger had kicked a puppy.

I slink away to find out what exactly happened and find Tiger's ball resting in the side yard of the adobe house between the 1st and the 18th holes. Out of bounds. No one up at the tee knows this, so Tiger makes it halfway down the fairway when a rules official meets him and breaks the news. He's steamed and never does retrieve the ball. He just grabs his driver, hops into the cart, and makes the drive of shame back to the tee.

After his second drive (and third stroke), Tiger still hasn't caught up to J.B.'s first, a dead-straight high bomb that showed no sign of nerves. This first-hole disaster reminds me of a high school golf match where my team played Hueneme High, the worst team in our league. Theirs was a squad filled with players who had started playing the sport the day after they signed up to be on the team. The kid with whom I was playing hacked his way down the first hole, and by the time he arrived at the first green, he was exhausted, covered in sweat, his shirt already untucked, and laying ten. He stood on the fringe huffing, then tried to summon the strength to somehow take off his golf bag. He couldn't do it, spinning around two times before ultimately collapsing next to the green, refusing to get up.

This is going to be a long day, I remember thinking. The good news for Tiger is that he's only 1 down.

12:39 PM • After matching pars on the 2nd, J.B. has a downhill birdie putt on the 3rd hole that no one expects him to make. From my position below the hole, I can't even see the cup. So when he putts it and I hear the gallery higher up on the green gasp, I assume J.B. missed it— until he reaches into the cup and pulls it out. The crowd has shown its cards early in this match, and none of us wants to believe that the world's hottest golfer is 2 down through three holes.

1:07 PM • It's not getting any better. On the 635-yard par-5 5th, Tiger is busy fumbling around, his third shot having been mercifully saved from sliding into a grassy collection area when it drops inside a sprinkler hole. Before he takes his free drop, he reminds Stevie not to touch his ball until it has rolled at least two club lengths, a breach in the rules that would cost him the hole. When J.B. knocks his third shot to eight feet and makes the putt for birdie, it doesn't matter. Just like that, Tiger is 3 down through five.

1:15 PM • The only thing more out of whack than Tiger's game is the XM radio strapped to my arm. Some XM employees were lending them to fans for the day so we could hear the play-by-play of all the other action around the course. It was a great idea, but somehow I have lost XM's PGA Tour station, and the radio is permanently locked on the painful 1980s Gary Numan song, "Cars." I don't know how it happened. After the fourth time through, I take off my headphones and slip them around my neck.

Tiger lightens the mood at the 450-yard 6th when he drops his second shot hole high as J.B. misses left. J.B. makes a solid up and down for par, but Tiger has a real shot at three. A freshly-permed woman near me watches and says, "I'd like to see him do a pump!" Tiger makes the birdie, but no pump. Not when he's still 2 down.

1:29 PM • The 7th at Dove Mountain is normally the kind of hole Tiger can't lose. At 314 yards with no bunkers protecting the front of the green, Tiger can take a driver and knock it on. But J. B. Holmes can do the same thing with a 3-wood. It's a very rare thing to see Tiger outdistanced with every club in his bag. Perhaps feeling the pressure, he takes a big swing off the tee and is late getting his hands through the ball, missing right as he did on the 1st. I tune back in to XM to try to forget about the match and find Gary Numan on his last verse again, one line now sounding far too ominous:

> *I know I've started to think about leaving*
> *tonight . . .*

I can't take it anymore and remove the battery. Mercifully, J.B. only makes par to halve the hole. Tiger must be concerned, but one would never know it by looking at him. When he first came on Tour, he was twenty years old. Back then, his facial expressions during a round would run the gamut from goofy to fiery. At thirty-two, he seems to have settled in at sober. Even when he's being threatened by the lowest guy in the bracket, what used to be his poker face now *is* his face.

1:33 PM • Traditionally, "the turn" refers to the midway point where the golf course turns back to the clubhouse for the inward nine holes. Out here the turn comes between the 7th and 8th holes, where after miles and miles of heading directly downhill and away from the Catalina Mountains, we flip around and begin the long climb back toward the clubhouse. Calling this place "The Gallery" is very ironic. I can't imagine a worse golf course at which to be a spectator. The course and the view are beautiful, but never have 18 holes been spread farther apart from one another. Combine that with the number of snowbirds out here for the winter, and the abnormal number of first aid stations along our route makes sense. There is simply no way all of these fans are going to make it back to 18 on their own steam. And if Tiger doesn't start playing better, he might not make it there either.

2:23 PM • The par-5 10th is the first hole all day that both Tiger and J.B. play well, with each of them looking at eagle putts. After J.B. misses, Tiger concedes the birdie and focuses on his chance to claw back to 1 down. He runs it five feet by. It's an impossible stat to know, but I've got to believe Tiger's opponents concede a higher percentage of putts to him than they do to other players out of sheer respect for how clutch he is. Tiger slowly walks to the ball, talking to himself but still keeping an ear open in case J.B. says the three best words in match play: "Pick it up." J.B. seems torn about it but makes him putt it. It catches the edge and drops in. There's no cheer for this birdie, only a collective "Whew . . ."

2:55 PM • The two arrive at the 13th with Tiger still 2 down and only six holes left. After putting my battery back in, my XM radio is finally working and I catch the on-course announcer suggesting that J.B. is "starting to realize what is happening here." I think he's a long way past realization. If he were a pitcher throwing a no-hitter, this is like the sixth inning. Not close enough to start counting outs but not so far away that he hasn't briefly considered what it will feel like to be lifted on his team's shoulders.

The elevated back tee on 13 is the highest spot on the course. From on top, the tee shot sends players barreling downhill to the green 479 yards away. J.B. still has the honors and coolly hits his drive into play and out of reach for Tiger. J.B.'s length probably wouldn't bother Tiger so much if he weren't also hitting it so dang straight. Tiger again misses right. I'm surrounded by a dense pack of Tucson retirees, and we watch together in disbelief as the ball disappears into the desert. Tiger is down 3 with just five to play.

This is a true disaster. If Tiger had tossed down some birdies on the front as he did in Dubai, I'd feel more hopeful, but he has been flat from the beginning. Almost mortal.

Before I left home yesterday, I called my friend Ralph to see if he wanted to come with me. Ralph is the most passionate Tiger Woods fan I know, and for years we spent entire rounds of golf debating his true greatness. He had almost agreed to join me for this leg of the journey, until he remembered he had a cat. All I can think about now is how angry he would be if he were standing here, five hundred miles from home, his cat meowing helplessly in some kennel.

3:07 PM • Three down with five to play. After Tiger's 1994 victory in the finals of the U.S. Amateur, *Sports Illustrated*'s Rick Reilly called it "the greatest comeback in the tournament's 99-year history." On that day Tiger was 3 down with 9 to play. If Tiger wins this, I might just use that bathtub Cheryl taught me how to work.

Tiger and J.B. cut in front of me and across the cart path that connects 13 with 14. I grip the thin rope in my hands as they pass. Tiger's poker face is even more furrowed. No one feels like cheering. The only sounds are Tiger's metal spikes clicking along the cement ground.

The 14th is a 192-yard par 3 without many tricks to it. As J.B. studies the yardage book, an older man leans across the ropes and says in complete calm, "Tiger. Let the legend grow." It was the same thing Earl had told him in the middle of that historic '94 U.S. Amateur when he found himself way down. I don't think Tiger hears him, but he immediately lowers his head. I had stood four feet from him when he did this on the 15th hole at Torrey Pines North. Tiger is willing himself to slip into The Zone.

He refuses to watch J.B.'s shot. Once it's airborne, Tiger steps forward and tees up his ball. What J.B. does has no effect on his strategy: hit the green, make a birdie, keep going. Tiger looks calmer than he has the rest of the round. His shot lands in the flattest spot, the dead middle of the green, no more than fifteen feet away from the left-center pin. He has a chance. Before it stops rolling, I start running, across forty yards of groomed desert sand that looks like a Zen garden and past the corporate boxes, to a small gap between the grandstands and the TV tower where I can watch the most important putt of the match.

It couldn't break much, maybe dying a little to the right. Three feet from the cup, Tiger takes a step toward the hole with his left leg, and as the putt falls into the cup, he whips his putter back toward him with two hands as if he's snagged a fish on the end of it. He has to go a long way back, but he is in a position with which he's familiar. Two down with four to go. It's the same deficit he had at the 1996 U.S. Amateur. When he came back and won that one, *Sports Illustrated* merely dubbed it the most "dramatic" Amateur ever.

3:18 PM • With the scent of a Tiger comeback in the air, the number of photographers following Match 29 starts to swell. After Tiger puts his second shot to seventeen feet, they walk single file line up the 15th hole, weighed down by equipment and probably cursing this course even more than I am.

Next to the green I see J. B. Holmes's wife. Golfers' wives have become easy for me to spot on the course. With no exception, they're attractive, have enormous diamond rings on their left hands, and are unnaturally interested in golf. I first noticed her on one of the early holes, where, to her credit, she was weaving her way through the crowds without missing a shot. Even though J.B. hasn't displayed any emotion today, she has become a good barometer for me of what is probably going on inside her husband's head. Early on, she was full of smiles and cheers. When J.B. went 3 up on 13, she was standing on a chair with a perfect view of Tiger's bogey, and all was right in the world. But as I see her now, she's nervous, looking as if she just ate something she's violently allergic to and is waiting for the symptoms to kick in.

J.B. sends his birdie putt down the hill. It rolls so far past that when it stops, he is still away. His par putt coming back doesn't fall either. It's his only mistake of the day and couldn't have come at a better time for Tiger. A two-putt par will draw within one. From our angle, no one can see the cup. Tiger putts it but then quickly straightens and walks toward the hole as if he has just stroked the worst putt of his professional career. We all groan, thinking he might not win the hole after all, only to have the ball disappear for a birdie. Tiger doesn't react. Why should he? The message he sends by holing a putt he doesn't need to make is enough of an exclamation point.

3:33 PM • The 178-yard 16th is the last par 3 on the course, and the pin is in a nasty spot, back of center and pushed to the very left edge. Anyone who misses the green on that side will likely be playing his second shot from the desert scrub. After putting his last two approaches to about fifteen feet, he leaves this one to a safer twenty, right of the pin and below the hole. Tiger could take these last three holes and use them to teach an investment seminar on calculated risk.

Every fan in attendance seems to have abandoned the other matches in favor of this one. The only way I can see anything is by squatting down and peering through a small gap underneath the electronic scoreboard. It's the only thing making any noise, humming like an industrial fridge as Tiger tries for back-to-back-to-*back* birdies. As J.B. watches, doing his best to convince himself that this is exactly how he envisioned the match proceeding, Tiger's putt rolls uphill, slides left, and slams into the cup. He pedals toward the desert and fires a right-handed haymaker toward Phoenix. When J.B. misses, the match is all square with two to play.

3:42 PM • To all of Tiger's real fans, his victory is no longer in doubt at this point. They're running and laughing and slapping one another's backs as they head up the 17th hole. If the 17th had been a par 3 or par 4, I could understand their optimism. But it's an uphill, 601-yard par 5 that gives J.B. just enough of an advantage off the tee to plant some doubt. After Tiger finds the right rough with his drive, J.B. flies his thirty yards past Tiger's and straight down the middle. It is terrifying to look down a hole that is a third of a mile long and realize that both of these golfers are fully planning on reaching it in just two shots.

From the rough, Tiger still has 270 yards left. Uphill. I couldn't cover that distance with a teed-up driver and a rubber bouncy ball. Tiger thinks he can do it with a 5-wood. He unleashes it dead on line. It carries the last fairway bunker and keeps rolling, finally reappearing when it climbs onto the green, forty feet from the right-hand flag. J.B. reaches with an iron that ends up outside Tiger's ball.

From that far away in an all-square match, Tiger isn't trying to make an eagle. Then again, he wasn't trying to make his birdie on 15 either. On the hillside behind the 17th green, five hundred fans are on their feet before the putt is ever hit. With J.B. still a knee-knocker away for birdie, Tiger strikes the ball with authority, keeping his head down long after the putt is gone. We track it for him and watch as it waves to J.B.'s mark on the way by and falls in. An eagle 3! Tiger lifts his putter straight up with his left hand, then clenches his right fist and roars after it drops. The scream from the crowd overwhelms Tiger's as fans throw their own fist pumps into the air. He has just won his fourth straight hole to go 1 up, playing them in an unthinkable 5 under par. J.B. can only chuckle. Before turning and running up 18, I spot his wife. She has her hands over her face. I think she's crying.

4:15 PM • J.B. has a good look at birdie on the last hole but doesn't make it. It's over. J.B. shakes Tiger's hand and walks off, no doubt in search of a suitable cactus on which to impale himself. Tiger crosses through the line of fans and spots Lee Westwood up ahead on the putting green. Just like two Sundays ago in Dubai, Westwood doesn't speak to Tiger, only smiles. Tiger shrugs back, perhaps thinking *maybe I am going to win every damn tournament this year.*

The ESPN columnist Bill Simmons has said that he doesn't know how anyone can come up with more things to say about Tiger Woods at this point. To some degree he's right. How many times can I say "unbelievable" before it stops *being* unbelievable? Maybe I should swear off the word for the rest of the year. What feels more natural is to replace it with a different word. Until further notice, Tiger Woods is ridiculous.

Back at Cheryl's, I knock on her door to tell her the news. When she opens it, I see a set of bongo drums on the ground.

"How was your game?" she asks.

"Tiger won!"

"Yeeeeaaay!" she says, clapping her hands and joining in the celebration.

SECOND ROUND: ARRON OBERHOLSER

In high school, my best friends and I developed an unhealthy obsession with Pink Floyd. We started by buying their most famous albums, first *The Wall* and then *Dark Side of the Moon*, but it soon grew to the point that having every song they recorded wasn't enough. I started tracking down solo albums by the less successful members of the band. My friend James pounced on the movies they had made in their early years that included such must-have moments as the drummer Nick Mason standing in a buffet line ordering pie. "No crust!" he barked as the poor worker cut him a piece.

The peak of our obsession arrived on April 16, 1994, when Pink Floyd came to the Rose Bowl in Pasadena. The concert was the culminating event of years of undeterred adoration. We were only sixteen, but for each of us, that night was the greatest of our entire lives.

And the next day was the worst. We woke up in our separate houses and faced the reality that whatever happened that day or any day after could in no way be as significant as April 16.

That's how it feels as I sit in the bus driving up the long straight road from the parking lot to see Tiger play Arron Oberholser on day two of the Accenture Match Play. Arron's always seemed like a likable player, straightforward and well spoken. He had risen into the top fifty in the world after a strong 2006, but for months he's been trying to recover from bursitis in his shoulder, and with the inflammation finally subsiding, he's making the Match Play his first start of the year. It's hard to imagine much of a fight from someone who has played even fewer events than Tiger.

As Tiger did the day before, Arron hits it into the desert on the first hole to fall 1 down. Tiger never relinquishes the lead, making five routine birdies and zero bogeys to win 3 up on the 16th hole.

Given no choice but to accept how unbelievable, excuse me, ridiculous, Tiger is, I feel a burden to share it with people who might have never seen it for themselves. Plus, I can't stand the thought of trudging all alone to number 7 and back for three more days. So before Tiger's third-round match against Aaron Baddeley, I think of the perfect solution. I place my first ad on Craigslist.

THURSDAY NIGHT • "FREE TICKET for Friday," the posting begins. That should get their attention, I think. But it is only fair to tell people what I am expecting: "You've got to walk with me and you've got to be able to keep up—we're watching Tiger and Tiger only once he tees off." I wonder if I am being too harsh. What am I talking about? This is a *free* ticket. In fact, I'm not being specific enough, so I keep going. "No bathroom breaks, no long beer lines, no 'my feet hurt.' Tiger doesn't complain, you can't either."

The only reason I have any extra tickets at all is due to my college roommate, Rob. His dad is an Oklahoma State grad who had made a few runs at the Senior Tour before settling into retirement. He remains close to a number of pros, especially the ones who went to OSU. One of them is Scott Verplank, who is in the field this week. Even though I've never met Verplank, he agreed to set aside some tickets. Early on Wednesday I went to the will-call window to pick them up and saw he had set aside not just one set but two.

My Craigslist post went up around six o'clock. The first response came within a half hour, but none is funnier than one from a guy named David, who replies, "I'll take it." Before I can answer, he has sent me a second e-mail, "I will take it," as if the drill sergeant tone of my post made him fear I would punish him for using a contraction. But I had said, "First come, first serve," and that means Mike, a sixth-grade teacher who is off for rodeo break, is the person pretending to be my friend tomorrow. A few hours later I hear from George, Mike's brother, who gives me the bad news that Mike's wife isn't letting him go. Not even during rodeo break? But George has never seen Tiger either and is wondering if I might take him instead. I'm not sure what to do until George says he drives a Town Car for a living and that he would be glad to pick me up and drive me to the course. Just like that, I've gone from going alone to going in style.

THIRD ROUND: AARON BADDELEY

"So what is rodeo week anyway?"

"Stupid-ass Tucson s***," George explains as we head up Oracle Road, a shortcut to Dove Mountain. At least I hope it is a shortcut. George is thirty-three, stocky, and has a gun in his glove compartment. He's already shown it to me. Even though his car is technically a Town Car, its best years are behind it, and most of his rides involve taking kids under Child Protection Services to see their deadbeat parents in the middle of the desert. For him, this is just the latest in a series of tough Arizona jobs.

George used to steam clean jet engines for Honeywell. However, when the summer heat would hit 120 degrees on the tarmac, he would pass out. He'd wake up to find his grittier coworkers staring down at him, angry that he was once again slowing them down. Another time he worked for a telemarketing company, selling people computers over the phone. After being there a few weeks, he looked around and realized, "Hey, where are the computers anyway?" A few days after he quit, the place was raided by the feds.

All this to say, he wasn't so intimidated by a long walk on a cool, cloudy day.

12:17 PM • Tiger makes his strongest start of the week, with birdies on 1 and 2 to immediately go 2 up. The only person looking stronger is George. So far he has been a model student. He used the port-o-potty in the parking lot, he kept up with me on the walk to the driving range, and even though he bought a bottle of water, he did it before Tiger teed off. On the course, he's even outpacing me a little bit. When he realizes that we are stuck in the mob trying to walk from the 1st to the 2nd, he does what until this point I was afraid to do: he ventures off the cart path and starts bounding through the flora and fauna, long-jumping cacti two at a time.

12:34 PM • The par-4 4th hole at the Gallery is a total beast, 495 yards and the only hole where water comes into play. A long, dark lake protects the entire right side, even for the big hitters. Down the left side are more cacti, the cart path, George, and I. It's a drive that must scare Tiger. If he misses right, the hole's over. If he misses left, it's probably over, too. But at least left he might get lucky and bank it off my head and back into the fairway. "Incoming!" a marshal yells before running for cover. Tiger misses both George and me, but his ball comes to rest at the base of a prickly pear cactus.

Mark Rolfing, NBC's on-course commentator, comes over to inspect the lie. "What do you think, Mark?" someone asks. "Could hurt," he says. I'm about to be closer to Tiger than I've been all week. George is blending in nicely, wearing his XM radio and looking starry-eyed as Tiger approaches. But Tiger has a problem. He has no shot. The line to the green is blocked by the cactus, and he can't just punch it out without goring himself. He stares at it for a minute before grabbing an iron and then flipping it over. He's going to play the shot left-handed.

I'm actually left-handed, though I play golf right-handed. At one point I lost so much confidence in my putting that I thought perhaps I would do better from the other side of the ball and demo'd a left-handed putter from a pro shop. As it turns out, I'm equally bad.

Tiger's left-handed swing is depressingly good. But it's not perfect, lacking that confident release of the club through impact, as if his brain is resisting doing something imperfectly. After a few awkward practice swings, his real shot misses the middle of the club face, and the ball squirts off to the left. It looks as if it might reach the fairway until it hits one of the metal poles holding up the gallery rope and stops dead.

It took two and a half tournaments, but I have finally witnessed Tiger Woods make a mental mistake. He should have moved it. He purses his lips and closes his eyes, but he's not thinking those mysterious peaceful thoughts that led him to go 5 under on J.B. two days ago. This is unadulterated self-loathing at its finest. He flips the club back around to his good side and draws it back to take a giant whack at the cactus. I scan the gallery and see that no one looks worried about this. They are all like George, still beaming, unaware that if Tiger follows through on this, we will all be covered in needles. And, after the ensuing lawsuit, rich. But Tiger stops short, believing he has left the cactus sufficiently scared, and walks away.

1:00 PM ● Both players are putting for birdie on the 6th. Tiger is thirty feet, Baddeley fifteen. Tiger misses and "Badds," as Tiger and other players call him, makes it. The one thing Tiger hasn't faced this year is a hot putter, and Badds is always one of the best, ranking 4th last year in putts per round. His game has been a little off this morning; he has just dirtied his perfect white pants trying to escape the desert on the 5th. But Badds does have a history of being a giant killer.

Eight and a half years ago, when he was still an eighteen-year-old amateur, Badds pulled off one of the most forgotten upsets in golf when he toppled then number three in the world Colin Montgomerie to win the Australian Open. Gary Player called him "a better player at eighteen than Jack Nicklaus was at the same age." No pressure, though. Badds would turn pro, win the event again the next year, and then completely lose his swing.

He nearly quit the game but kept working and eventually met Mike Bennett and Andy Plummer, golf coaches who were trying to sell touring pros on a radically different swing style that they dubbed the "Stack & Tilt," the basic tenet of which is to do the exact opposite of everything you've ever been taught about the golf swing. This was intriguing to me since I already do just that. Basically, instead of swinging his weight to his right side on the backswing, Badds bends his left knee toward the ball, keeping his head directly over it. Coming down, he snaps the leg back and stands up, a simpler move that theoretically enables the club to make more consistent contact.

I tried it a few times and nearly broke my wrist from hitting the ball so fat. "Less tilt!" I remember yelling. But with Badds, it may be one of golf's prettiest swings, devoid of many moving parts. Within a year of overhauling his swing, Badds won his first Tour event at the Verizon Heritage in 2006.

1:16 PM ● Tiger arrives at the par-4 7th tee, sits down on a cooler, and takes off his shoe. He shakes it, and a rock falls out. I begin to realize my increasing level of obsession when I point it out to George as if it's a noteworthy event. The rock must have been the problem, I think to myself, because he flies his 3-wood all the way to the green and has just twenty-five feet for eagle.

As George leads the way, I notice Luau Larry again, the Hawaiian-shirted sportswriter. He hadn't traveled with me to Dubai, but he's back on the Tiger beat this week. Right now he's lying on the ground holding one of his tan legs. Without having to negotiate hundreds of fans outside the ropes, he has somehow managed to walk into a cactus. I look at it as a cautionary tale, and I focus back on the desert in front of me.

1:46 PM • Two days ago Tiger brought us the comeback. Yesterday was the stress-free win. After a slow start for Badds, today is shaping up to be the duel. They both make 3's on 7. On 8, Badds rolls in a long putt for another birdie, and then on 9, he nearly chips it in. Tiger responds with a birdie of his own. He points coolly at the ball as it drops in. I count up the circles on my scorecard and see there have been eight birdies between them.

2:17 PM • Eight birdies was nothing, I'm realizing. Tiger and Aaron both birdie the par-5 10th, both birdie the par-4 11th, and both birdie the par-4 12th! Fourteen birdies in twelve holes? George points out that this is suddenly feeling like video-game golf.

2:25 PM • And what good video game these days doesn't have violence? After not missing a shot all day, Tiger's drive on the 13th hits an old marshal right on top of the head. The ball bounces twenty feet back into the air and disappears into the desert. The marshal bends over in pain, and blood starts to run off his white hair. There are worse ways to die than from being hit by Tiger Woods. Like being hit by Retief Goosen, for example. Medics rush to make sure he's okay, but when Tiger walks up, the marshal is all smiles. Tiger gives him an autographed glove and a handshake. As the man is happily carted off the battlefield, Tiger goes to look for his ball. He finds it but loses the hole, and is back to all square.

2:40 PM • The birdie barrage was fun when Tiger was hanging tough at 1 up, but all square is a different matter. Badds stuffs it in close on 14 and again makes birdie. If I give Badds credit for a birdie on the conceded 13th, which wasn't that unrealistic, he has now birdied 6, 7, 8, 10, 11, 12, 13 and 14! That's eight of the last nine holes!

Tiger has had enough and sticks an 8-iron on the 16th to just four feet from the hole. Badds three-putts and concedes. Back to all square. At this point there's no walking. We are all running through the desert, with George leading the charge, cigarette in hand. The carnage inside the ropes has spread to the gallery outside. On the way to 17, we pass a beefy guy with blood dribbling down his leg. It's like D-Day out here; some people are getting dragged down by cacti, others are just giving up, either too tired to go on or too afraid they'll spill their beers.

3:14 PM • Badds hits first into 17, the uphill 600-yarder, and puts it twelve feet right behind the front-center pin. Tiger answers with an iron, just outside Badds's shot and left of the hole. Coming off Badds's three-putt on the last, I'm nervous about a hot putter zeroing back in, but he can't get his to drop and neither can Tiger. All square with one to go.

3:30 PM • Racing up the 18th fairway, I appreciate just how unreal George has been. Here's a guy whose only exercise involves flipping his meter on and off for twelve hours a day and he's somehow surviving seven miles, most of it running, some of it while downing a half pack of cigarettes. But on the final climb, he starts to fade. I turn and see the crush of fans steaming behind us. We can't stop. "We're almost there," I say. He doesn't answer, just puts his head down and keeps going. I pull ahead and run the last stretch, up and around to the far right side of the green. I make it, but my legs are shaking. I put my hands on my knees, turn around, and see there's no sign of George. I don't even consider going back. George would want me to go on. A minute later he cruises up and hands me an ice-cold bottle of water.

"We might need this if it goes extra holes." The student has become the mentor.

3:30 PM • The green on 18 slopes severely back to front, and the pin is cut in the middle toward the left side. The only easy putt is from below the cup. We can't see the players, but we know from their drives that Badds is hitting first.

3:31 PM • Slam. Baddeley's ball drops six feet right of the flag.

3:32 PM • Slam. Tiger's drops nine feet past it.

3:34 PM • The players receive applause as they walk to the green. The fans in the bleachers know only that the match is tied; they can't possibly appreciate the level of play it took to keep it like that. But those of us who have been hoofing it from the beginning cheer most loudly.

Tiger stands over his putt and has to be playing for birdie with Badds so close. "Oh, God . . ." The lady in the front row looks away before Tiger putts. Here she maneuvered to claim the best spot against the ropes, and she can't bear to watch.

Tiger misses. It's the first must-make putt I've seen him miss this year. Proof that he was only thinking 3, the ball rolls five feet past the hole.

Now one of golf's best putters has a slick right-to-left breaker to end it all. The woman in front can't watch this one either. Tiger glares at the cup as if ordering it to make sure this putt doesn't go in. Badds gently plays it a good two feet out to the right. I can't believe it will break that much, but it breaks even more and misses low. Like Tiger's, it keeps rolling and ends up three feet past the hole. Here we thought birdie would win, and now neither of them even has par.

In my head I flash to the way Tiger lost to Nick O'Hern in the third round last year. All Tiger had to do that day was make a straight, four-foot putt to win on the first extra hole. He hit it straight, but the ball lurched when it rolled across an old mark, and it missed the cup on the right side. The hole was tied, and Tiger lost outright on the next one. Tiger said afterward that he had been "so enthralled with the line" that he never saw the tiny crater.

Tiger won't make the same mistake. He inspects every inch of this one before pulling the trigger. It's in for a 4. "Yesss!!" George and I scream in celebration/relief. Badds makes his, too. We're going extra holes.

Because I knew to run to the far side of the 18th green, we can now head straight down number 1, while the other fans are blocked at the crossing near the first tee. George is impressed by my navigating, a compliment that means a lot more coming from a professional driver.

3:43 PM • Not everyone is happy that this has gone extra holes. Down in the fairway a father is having an argument with his son, who must be seven or eight. I don't need to hear the beginning of the fight to pick right up in the middle:

Dad: "It might be an *eighteen*-hole playoff, so get used to it!"

The kid whines.

Dad: "People are running. What are you doing? You're moping!"

Kid: "I don't *want* a playoff . . ."

Dad: "Then go home. Walk!"

I tell George to slip the boy and the dad his card. In a few weeks, they might be new customers.

3:43 PM • Badds is in the fairway on the 1st, with an iron in to a back pin on the par 5. He's about to take the club back when another kid, one who actually wants to be here, sneezes. It forces Badds to back off and start again. Then, impressively, Badds hits it to ten feet. For eagle. As Tiger steps into his second shot, the kid's father leans over. *"Don't sneeze,"* he says.

3:54 PM • Tiger puts it on the green as well but can only two-putt. For the second straight hole, Badds has a putt to win. This one is much easier than on the 18th, slightly downhill and nearly straight. He draws his buttery stroke back and releases the putter toward the hole. Tiger watches it, prepared to accept defeat, but right at the end it slips off to the left and misses the cup. Badds falls to his knees. Tiger quickly turns with Stevie already clomping ahead of him. There's no ruminating Tiger's fortune; we instinctively bolt for number 2, the 20th hole of the match. George and I pass a group of middle-aged men who are laughing as they go, saying, "I'm running at a golf tournament!"

4:04 PM • Tiger's play reflects a man energized by not one but two brushes with death. He hits his approach on the par-4 2nd to fifteen feet and continues striding toward the green. Badds is on the right side of the fairway with a better angle to the pin but leaves it out to the right, thirty feet away. A lot of the crowd has decided not to venture this far away for a second time, so seeing the action is not a problem, but George insists on running anyway. "I thought you were beat?" I say in between my gasps for air. He confesses that he downed a Snickers bar behind 18.

Badds's birdie doesn't fall, and for once today it is Tiger who faces a putt to win. It's almost completely straight, a little uphill, and heads away from the gallery and out toward the desert. I look back at George and see that for some reason he has taken one of his shoes off. He turns it over and shakes it, even though there are no rocks in it. "This is for Tiger," he says.

Tiger hits it, watches it for a moment, and while the putt is still rolling, he turns to Badds and removes his cap to shake his hand. The ball isn't even in the hole yet! With Tiger not even watching, it drops in. "Ohhhhh!!!" the crowd roars. George and I join the chorus. Tiger doesn't just win, he wins with flair. Up at the green, Stevie takes the ball out of the cup and heaves it into the crowd. Rain starts to fall for the first time all day, as if God had been holding back the weather till Tiger's work on Earth was done. As we turn around and make the mile walk back up to the buses, Tiger hops into a Lexus and disappears into the desert.

Yesterday I couldn't understand the fans who seemed convinced that Tiger would beat J.B. when their match was all square. Too many weird things can happen in golf. But having seen him walk away a winner time after time, I get it. In fact, I feel that same comfort. Tiger Woods is more than good. He's dependable.

I'm not a fair-weather fan. When I was in sixth grade, my Los Angeles Dodgers won the World Series. In the twenty years since then, they have won one playoff game, but I keep rooting. Between 2004 and 2006, I attended eleven different games. They lost all eleven. I even began trying different cities, going to games in San Diego and San Francisco to break my streak. No luck. A friend who is a Padres fan started inviting me when his team was in town just to increase their chances of victory.

I won't abandon the Dodgers, but I'm ready to root for someone who knows how to get the job done. The tournament deftly routes the line for the buses through the inside of the official souvenir shop. When George and I get back into line, he's wearing a neon yellow windbreaker, and I've swapped out my beat-up old hat for a new one. It's dark red with the Match Play logo on the side and a "TW" logo on the front.

QUARTERFINALS: K. J. CHOI

Come Saturday morning, only eight players are still standing out of the original sixty-four. Except for Vijay Singh and Tiger, most of the big names are long gone. Phil Mickelson and Adam Scott were out after the second round. Ernie Els, still reeling from the loss in Dubai, decided only at the last minute to come play, then promptly lost on day one.

Match Play is the rare tournament where the longer one survives, the earlier the tee time becomes. In order to whittle down the eight in time for tomorrow's final, today includes both the quarter and semifinal matches. Tiger's match begins at 7:45 a.m. and means I am back on the bus up the hill at 6:30.

Tiger's quarterfinal match pairs him against "The Tank," South Korea's K. J. Choi. A short and stout former power lifter who sings hymns on the golf course to relax, he manages to be intimidating and disarming at the same time. His swing plane resembles the way he used to lift weights, straight up and straight down, making for a consistent and boring fade with every single swing.

The Choi match is compelling only in that for so long nothing happens. From numbers 3 through 9, K.J. and Tiger par every hole. With Badds and J.B., the tournament had that Sunday energy to it. With Choi, all of a sudden it feels as if we are back to Thursday morning. At one point I begin to wonder if they have forgotten that the whole premise of match play is for one player to beat the other. Tiger eventually ends the stalemate with a chip-in eagle at the par-5 10th. He tosses in three more birdies over the next six holes and wins 3 up on the 16th green.

The victory puts Tiger into the final four, meaning that even if he loses in the semifinals, he will still have a spot in Sunday's consolation match for third place, which, of course, he would hate with every fiber of his *first place or nothing* mind-set. Either way, I need to find a courtesy phone. I've made it through my four-night minimum and need Cheryl's guest house for one more day. "I'm holding the room contingent on positive outcomes," she says. Groovy.

SEMIFINALS: HENRIK STENSON

Of all Tiger's opponents this week, Sweden's Henrik Stenson is the one I most fear. Part of that is because he wears wraparound Oakley sunglasses. But the logical part is that Stenson is quietly becoming one of the game's best players. And he has done it by stealing a page from Tiger's playbook. When his game bottomed out in 2001, Stenson's mental coach decided to put him through a spin-off of the Earl Woods finishing school. Believing his student needed to toughen up, he made Stenson hit balls while wearing a blindfold. When the blindfold came off, he finally trusted his swing and has since won four times on the European Tour, not to mention last year's Accenture Match Play right here at Dove Mountain.

Tiger never admits to being intimidated by anyone. Or even any*thing*. Last year Jason Sobel from ESPN.com asked him to name his greatest fear.

"Greatest fear?" His brain couldn't even comprehend the idea. "I don't really have any."

Sobel pressed. "No fears at all?"

"No, not really. I can't think of any."

I half expected Sobel to dump a box of poisonous snakes at his feet, but it didn't happen. The response was another example of Tiger's macho determination never to expose weakness. Nothing positive could happen if he were honest with his answer. If, for example, he confessed to a fear of people with muttonchop sideburns, chances are good they would suddenly be all the rage on the PGA Tour. But if Tiger were to be intimidated by another player, it certainly wouldn't be Henrik Stenson. Not only is Stenson one of the players Tiger flew past on Sunday in Dubai, he is also the player who was paired with Tiger that day back in December at the Target World Challenge when Tiger shot 62. Stenson? 72.

1:13 PM • Neither Tiger nor Stenson plays well the first five holes. As a result, they're spending most of their time throwing clubs and kicking their bags. I barely notice these fits of rage anymore, but they're completely shocking to Bryan, the forty-six-year-old mechanic with slicked-back hair who claimed my extra ticket today. When Tiger uses an especially colorful turn of phrase after pulling his second shot on the par-5 5th, Bryan's eyes go wide, and he asks, "Boy, have you ever seen him mad like that?" Uh, yeah.

Even though Bryan says "boy" and "gosh" and "golly" a lot, he is probably one of the toughest men I've met. He receives a cortisone shot once a year because of shooting pain up and down his left arm, the result of three decades of working with wrenches. The shot doesn't always help, and sometimes it doesn't take at all. For years he taught auto repair for the state, teaching kids in the juvenile prison how to fix cars. And really, when you're working closely with prisoners, what safer place is there to be than surrounded by blunt metal objects?

After building up a pretty good pension, a Tucson vocational school offered Bryan the chance to run its auto repair department. He said yes, throwing away his state retirement for the chance to be in charge of something for the first time in his life. Six weeks after making the move, he was informed that the program wasn't actually accredited and the Department of Labor was going to shut it down. Rather than give up, the guy who had no experience dealing with bureaucracy found a way to bypass months of red tape and convince the local community college to come on board and make the program legit. So when I notice Bryan limping down number 7, I don't push him to keep going. I figure he will probably push himself.

2:15 PM • I have seen Tiger this mad; I just haven't seen him mad this often. On the 9th, he slams his club back into the bag as Stevie happily escapes to go rake the fairway bunker. At 10, he slashes his club through the rough after missing the green in two. He's struggling but still 1 up.

Meanwhile, Bryan has officially hurt himself. He's not sure what's wrong, it might just be a cramp, but the limp is getting worse and we have three miles of uphill walking to go. This is Bryan's first golf tournament. His real passion is NASCAR, where if a driver were to win five straight events like Tiger, he would be reviled, not beloved. Part of that is because of the flare with which Tiger wins, but it's also because of how he loses. He doesn't whine like Jeff Gordon, or punch people, like Tony Stewart (although the thought of Tiger using one of his spin-out fist pumps to drop Rory Sabbatini would only increase his fan base). Looking back on last year's British Open, an event where Tiger finished a disappointing 12th place, his post-round interview is heavy-laden with self-effacement. "I couldn't" . . . "I didn't" . . . "I wasn't." His failures are his fault. The flip side is that when he wins, he can take ownership for it all the more.

3:27 PM • Stenson hits the green on the par-3 16th and makes a fifteen-footer for 2. The putt makes Tiger pay for six straight pars, and the match is suddenly all square. It's Stenson who blinks on the next hole, only managing a par whereas Tiger makes a sandy birdie to take the 1-up lead into 18.

3:45 PM • Walking toward the final green, I tell Bryan that, as George and I did yesterday, we should keep going to the far side in case it goes extra holes. I feel bad because Bryan has already gone the 16 holes with me this morning for the K.J. match, and now this one is going at least 18. We've logged well over ten miles at this point, and Bryan has admitted that he thinks he has a groin pull. When I give him the news, he just throws up his hands. "Why stop now? Why does it matter now?"

The pin on 18 is cut in the front-left corner, and Tiger is already safely on the green. With Tiger looking at no worse than par, Stenson's only hope is to make a birdie and hope Tiger misses. His approach shot is a little greedy and comes up just short of the flag, a mistake that sends his ball zipping back another ten yards and off the green. Now he must chip it in to keep playing. Stenson's steely look remains as he stares down his third shot. He pitches it up, and, like his second shot, it hits on the upslope and starts rolling back toward him. He could force Tiger to two-putt, but while his ball is still moving, Stenson walks up to it and slaps it into the gallery with his wedge as he takes off his hat. The crowd had given Tiger a winner's cheer when he reached the green, but now it's official. He is into the finals. And now that I look at them, Stenson's sunglasses aren't that scary after all.

CHAMPIONSHIP MATCH: STEWART CINK

In 1884, Thomas Potter, the secretary of the Royal Liverpool Golf Club and founder of what became the British Amateur, decided a 36-hole match play final was the ultimate way to decide a champion. This was back when the options of what to do with your day was a choice between hanging out with the sheep and watching golf.

On the other side of the bracket from Tiger is Stewart Cink, a lanky thirty-four-year-old from Georgia with a long, gentle swing that makes me feel as though the best way to watch him hit balls is from the comfort of a rocking chair. He and Tiger have already played together this year, during the third and fourth rounds of the Buick Invitational, where he started the weekend eight strokes back. He had no chance. Today he will be starting all square . . . and still has no chance. It's not his fault; it's just that with every match over the course of the long week, Tiger has made fewer and fewer mistakes.

7:45 AM • Next to the first tee sits the powder blue Walter Hagen Cup, the official trophy of the Accenture Match Play. It's made from Wedgewood china, making it the most fragile trophy in golf. Before the final match begins, the two girls in charge of seeing it's not broken spin it around so Tiger and Cink can pose next to it on the first tee. It's considerate of the tournament directors to give Cink his chance to see it up close, just once.

Feeling too drained after yesterday to take on another new fan, I've given my Sunday ticket to George again and tell him to feel no obligation to keep up with me. But he's still with me on the 1st green, so I ask about his Saturday night. Apparently, he drove to Mexico to place a sports bet, then he and his buddies stayed up late drinking, two of them passed out on the ground after fighting about who would drive to the gun show, he fell asleep on the couch, and the last guy was playing online poker until 5 a.m. I waited for him to add, "Isn't that crazy?" He didn't. I had the impression that that wasn't much different from every other Saturday night.

8:08 AM • Tiger birdies the 2nd. One up.

8:50 AM • Tiger birdies the 5th. Two up.

9:14 AM • Tiger birdies the 7th. Three up.

9:22 AM • Cink three-putts the 8th. Four up.

9:55 AM • Tiger sticks it on the 11th. Five up.

9:56 AM • Keep in mind that NBC's coverage doesn't start for *two hours*. Somewhere in the media trailers behind number 12, a producer is frantically trying to figure out how he can fill the last three hours of the network's four-hour broadcast.

11:22 AM ● Tiger gives NBC a reprieve, arriving at Dove Mountain's 18th only 4 up. And for once today, he's struggling. He finds the fairway bunker, then the greenside bunker, then chunks his sand shot, and angrily walks away with a bogey.

All Cink has left is a five-foot putt for par. If he makes it, it will stall Tiger's momentum and give him the slimmest of hopes that he can make a run during the afternoon round. As Stewart wiggles his feet before drawing back his belly putter, I look and see that everyone is certainly interested, but not in Cink. In fact I'm the only person watching Stewart. I follow the crowd's eyes to the far fringe of the green, where Tiger Woods is doing the riveting activity of putting on his watch.

If only Cink knew that no one was watching him. He might not have missed it.

It's his last chance to derail Tiger. After a one-hour break for lunch, Tiger returns, removes his watch, and stretches his lead all the way to 8 up, closing the match with a soaring wedge over a dry desert wash to two feet. When they get to the green, Cink doesn't make Tiger putt it. They remove their hats and expose their distinctive horizontal tan lines across their foreheads, a product of 117 holes in the Arizona desert.

As officials gingerly place the trophy on its wooden pedestal and photographers swarm the green, off to the side a middle-aged sound technician named Bob is panicking. He's already been told that NBC is going live to Jimmy Roberts in two minutes to interview Tiger, and he can't get any power to the mike. He flips the switches on and off. Nothing. He pulls out the extension cord and tries again. Nothing. "Thirty seconds, Bob . . ." His entire day is built around this one event, and he is on the verge of total failure. The fans who have had 29 holes to get plastered start laying into him, too. "Come on, Bob!" Twenty seconds. Bob pulls the extension cord and runs it through another outlet in the corporate tent next door. Five seconds. The dials light up. "We're good."

As NBC goes to Jimmy and Tiger, Bob nearly collapses from the stress. The same drunk fans applaud his save. "We love you, Bob!"

The win is Tiger's third straight win in 2008 and sixth straight win going back to last season. Because Jimmy's mike is working, I hear him recite the stunning fact that Tiger is now only ten PGA Tour wins away from Jack Nicklaus, whose seventy-three victories is second on the all-time list. It reminds me of one of the popular complaints I've picked up from other Tiger skeptics over the year: the notion that Tiger appears to be a better golfer than he actually is; that if Tiger had to face the same Hall of Fame players as Nicklaus, fields that included Arnold Palmer and Gary Player and Lee Trevino and Tom Watson, he wouldn't be such a dominant force in golf.

After this week, I don't buy it. At the Match Play, I saw a golfer who seamlessly adapts to any level of competition. When Oberholser could manage only three birdies in round two, Tiger needed only five. When J. B. Holmes threw down six, Tiger responded with seven. And when Baddeley somehow made ten birdies over twenty holes, Tiger was able to make eleven. After witnessing every hole of Tiger's season, the more compelling question to consider is which professional golfers playing today will never see the Hall of Fame because they had the misfortune of being born within ten years of Tiger Woods.

MATCH PLAY FALLOUT • My car survives a windy trip across the desert and pulls up to our house just after 1 a.m. late Sunday night. Everyone is asleep. Our house has cheap, creaky wooden floors, and over the course of the five months we've been here, I have learned the circuitous route I need to take between any two points to keep from making noise. I don't even have to think about it anymore. Open the door, take one small step to the left, then a big one forward and onto the rug. From there it is two paces toward our stereo followed by a hard right turn and then two giant steps into the hallway. The rest is easy: hug the right side of the hallway without knocking the frames off the wall, find the door to our bedroom, and I'm in. But after making it there, I decide I should go see Danny. I rub his back, "Hey, buddy . . ." I can't see him, but I can hear him roll over and look up through the dark. "Dada, you came back!"

It's weird, but by physically disappearing for these short stretches of time, I see that I'm not as invisible as I thought I was on my roof a few months before. When I'm gone, I'm missed. After every round of the Match Play, I would call home and tell Hillary the good news. She was excited on Wednesday and Thursday, but by Saturday she was one of the only people actively following Tiger's season who was wishing his unbeaten streak would mercifully end.

In coming home, I am the prodigal dad. "Come, family, sit at my feet and I will tell you about my adventures in the desert . . ." The next night I take everyone out to dinner at our favorite hot dog stand. Danny and I go and order while Hillary takes Katie to find a table. As I walk to get into line, she asks me to order a side of chips. I remember, but only when they deliver the food. "Oops, I forgot the chips." Hillary looks at me, disappointed, and says, "It's fine," in that tone that obviously means it *isn't* fine. Trying to be a Tiger-like man of action, I flag down a server and ask what it would take to have a side of chips. "Fifty-five cents." Fifty-five cents to be a hero? I can do that. I give him a dollar, tell him to keep the change, and do everything but stand up and take a giant bow. Hillary sees the whole thing differently, saying "I just said *'It's fine,'* we don't need chips. You're not listening to me!" It's not exactly the fist pump moment I imagined. But in fairness, I have only been following Tiger since January; I can't expect to have all my problems solved already. For now I can only conclude that the answer is not as simple as going to golf tournaments a couple times a month.

HATS OFF FOR THE KING

The Arnold Palmer Invitational

Bay Hill Club
Orlando, Florida
March 13–16, 2008

When Tiger won the Buick Invitational in January, he was merely accomplishing the expected. The comeback at Dubai was spectacular, except that it happened while most people in the United States were asleep. But with the Match Play, Tiger could not be ignored, and the sports world is responding accordingly. On the Golf Channel, former player turned analyst Frank Nobilo feels no shame in declaring Tiger "the greatest player that will ever play the game." On ESPN, *Pardon the Interruption*'s Michael Wilbon goes further, saying the question is no longer whether Tiger is the most dominant golfer of all time but whether he is the most dominant *athlete* of all time.

In January, Tiger had caused a lot of eye-rolling when he said on his Web site that winning the professional Grand Slam (all four major championships in one calendar year) was "easily within reason." Attaching the word "easily" to something that had never been achieved seemed a little . . . bold. By the time the Arnold Palmer Invitational at Bay Hill is in sight, the question of whether Tiger could win the Grand Slam has been pushed aside by an even wilder idea—could he have golf's first undefeated season? Turns out that Tiger has already done that, too. When he was eleven, he won all thirty-six junior events he entered.

Since Tiger actually lives in Isleworth, a gated community only a mile west of Bay Hill, this will be my one chance to stay at his place, but even after adding 117 holes to the tally in Tucson, he still doesn't know I exist. At some point I figured that he would hit a wayward shot, we would make eye contact, and there would be a moment of recognition where his nose would scrunch up and he would say, "Don't I know you from somewhere?" I would then run through all the adventures he and I have shared, whereupon Stevie would reach into his bag and serve me with one of Tiger's standard-issue restraining orders. And as long as I only had to stay a hundred yards away, I could probably still see most of his shots.

Thankfully, I have a backup plan, but it's dependent on someone I haven't spoken to in more than a year. My first job after college was as a production assistant on the sitcom *Sabrina, the Teenage Witch*. I'm still not sure why they hired me. I sat down for the interview, my first one since graduation, and the production coordinator who was interviewing me said, "First off, what's with your name? 'Robert.' That's a little different." He was serious.

"Uh, it's . . . just a family name . . . pretty common actually."

"Huh. Just never heard it before, I guess."

He flipped through a giant stack of résumés and found mine, setting it on top. From across the desk I could see the confusion. At the top where it said my name, I had inadvertently added a small "b" in front of the capital "R" in Robert, making my name read "bRobert." Here I was, an English major out of Princeton, and I'd misspelled my own name. "You know what, actually that's a typo," I said. "It's supposed to just be Robert. Or Bob." Four minutes later, I was walking back to my car. The interview was over. I drove away, assuming they would go with someone who could spell, but waiting at home was a message asking if I could start Monday.

Kelly was the assistant to the head writer and one of the people who couldn't believe they had hired me. Her boss didn't give her much to do, so she filled her days with involving herself in everyone else's lives, and when I went out on a date with another assistant in the office, she went around my back to find out if the girl had fun and whether she would go out with me again if I asked her. I was livid. Kelly said my point was irrelevant since the girl said she had a great time and would love to go out again. Four years later, Hillary and I were married.

Kelly eventually moved home to Florida and started working for the Golf Channel. I decide to go ahead and send her an e-mail. A week before I head to Bay Hill, she calls to say I can stay with her and her husband and casually throws in, "Oh, by the way, you want to be interviewed by the Golf Channel?" I'm on my way.

KING OF THE HILL • The first time Arnold Palmer saw Bay Hill was in 1965, four years after the plot of land was developed by a group of investors from Tennessee. He was invited down along with Jack Nicklaus and two other players to play in an exhibition match and proceeded to beat Nicklaus by seven shots. He decided he liked the place and made it his winter home before buying it outright in 1970.

Behind Torrey Pines, no other Tour venue has such a long relationship with Tiger Woods. At fifteen, Tiger came to Bay Hill and won the 1991 U.S. Junior Amateur, going extra holes for the first of his six straight USGA titles. When he unlocked the secret to winning at Bay Hill as a pro, he was unstoppable, winning Arnie's tournament four years in a row between 2000 and 2003, the last victory more impressive than any other. The night before the final round in '03, his then girlfriend, Elin, made a pasta dinner, and within a half hour he was violently ill in every possible way. They considered checking him into a hospital, but Tiger was worried that doctors wouldn't let him check out. He warmed up with only a handful of balls and headed to the 1st tee. In between running to the bushes, he shot the day's low round and won by 11 shots.

But since 2003, mysteriously, he hasn't won again. He hasn't even come close, finishing no better than 20th. The best explanation involves Bay Hill's rough, which has been grown longer in recent years to defend the course from longer hitters who tend to miss fairways. During his Wednesday press conference, Tiger was more than happy to offer his own nuanced theory for the dry spell: "I just haven't played well." If there were going to be an obvious tournament to derail his perfect season, this was it.

FIRST ROUND

7:31 AM ● Eighteen days ago I pulled out of a dirt field in the middle of the desert and headed home. This morning I pass beneath the twisting water slides of Wet 'n Wild and into the mammoth cement parking lot at Universal Studios Orlando. The tourist attractions are the lifeblood of this city sitting in the center of Florida. With my silver Rav4 rental car locked, I ride up an escalator, step onto a moving walkway, then hop onto a waiting bus headed for Bay Hill. If only there were four Egyptian women willing to fan me with palm fronds, it would be the perfect morning commute.

7:42 AM ● Our bus winds two miles through the police-lined neighborhood surrounding Bay Hill, a collection of houses ranging from modest to monstrous, and drops us off at the entrance to the "Arnold Palmer Priceless Moments Pavilion Presented by MasterCard." The tent is huge, which may have been the only way to squeeze its name on a wall. Inside are displays covering Arnie's personal life and professional life. Heading through this first time, I'm shocked to read that all seven of the King's major championships came within only a seven-year period. A young Jack Nicklaus ended his reign earlier than anyone expected, and when Arnie won his last, the 1964 Masters, he was only thirty-four.

There's no guarantee on how long we'll be able to see Tiger Woods play golf at its highest level. After he won the Wachovia Championship last year, he talked about how fickle a sport it can be. "This game," he said, "you have it for a little bit and it goes away, then you've got to get it back again." Someday he won't get it back again. And when that happens, he's already said he's not going to stick around. As he told Ed Bradley on *60 Minutes*, "When my best isn't good enough to win anymore, I'm gone. I'm racking the cue and I'm going home." For as special as Tiger is, it may be naive to think that just because his dominance hasn't been challenged by age 32, it never will be.

8:13 AM • The crowds are impressive early on this cool and clear Thursday morning, a solid two deep around the driving range. They also seem to be the least diverse, a sea of sixty-something Caucasian men. I ask Ken, who just so happens to be a sixty-something Caucasian man, to explain. He says they're all retired, and when you wake up at 4 a.m., this isn't early.

Tiger is nearing the end of his range session, sporting a cool blue shirt with subtle white stripes. I'm pretty sure his hat and pants are black, but they might be navy blue. I lean over to Ken again: "Do his pants look black or navy blue to you?" He doesn't answer. Since buying that Tiger Woods hat, I've turned a dark corner from observation to obsession.

All week in Arizona, Tiger had warmed up by making an exaggerated head turn through the ball, similar to what Annika Sorenstam does during her actual swing. He never did it during the tournament, but the move seemed to be a clue that he was struggling with rotating through the ball, a mistake that can lead to some big blocks to the right. Today his head isn't chasing the ball at all. He's just piping 5-wood after 5-wood down the center of the range.

8:50 AM • Tiger starts on the 10th hole this morning. Directly behind the tee is a single grandstand with a few hundred people filling its eight rows. A few fans sneak photos, their contraband phones popping up like a whack-a-mole game as Tiger looks down the fairway. The 10th at Bay Hill is exactly 400 yards, a slightly uphill dogleg right where the ideal shot is a 3-wood that cuts the corner and scares the people in the beer garden along the right side before drawing back into the fairway. Tiger has no problem with the tee shot, or his second, putting it onto the back tier and just eight feet from the hole. He reads the putt from both sides, then fixes a mark between his ball and the cup. He makes it. Tiger is under par before Universal Studios has even opened.

10:12 AM • Tiger cruises along, missing a birdie opportunity at 13 and parring 14 before we cross over residential Bay Hill Boulevard to the 15th tee. The final four holes at Bay Hill are one of the year's great closing tests. It starts here, a tight, 425-yarder lined with out of bounds and a group of magnolia trees so dark that their leaves appear almost black from the tee box. If you can make it through, the fairway cuts hard to the right to a green with bunkers in front, to the right, and in back. It's a nice, short par 4 that eases you into the homestretch.

Tiger lands safely between the magnolias but misses the green to the right with a pitching wedge. With a wedge? It's a rare mistake, and it costs him his first bogey of the week when he can't knock it close from the deep rough. He's back to even par.

10:20 AM • There's nothing short about the 16th, sixty yards longer than 15 and even more penal. Until last year it had always played as a par 5, but to bring winning scores closer to par, Arnie agreed to move the tees up and make it a long par 4, a change that forces players to hit a long iron or hybrid club into the green rather than lay up. If they pull their approach left, they'll for sure be in one of Bay Hill's seven lakes. If they're short, they'll find the tributary that runs in front of the green and connects to another lake on 17.

Tiger avoids every body of water and makes a nice up and down for par.

10:47 AM • Bay Hill does not ease up for its last two holes. The 17th is a 219-yard par 3 over water. Tiger gives himself a good look at birdie, but it doesn't fall. He grimaces at the missed opportunity and walks the twenty yards to the 18th tee.

10:57 AM • My dad once went to Florida, and on his return he declared it "the flattest place on Earth." Which is why I stand at the 18th tee shocked to discover that Bay Hill's most famous hole is a blind tee shot. From the 441-yard back tee, Tiger can't see the flag or the green and definitely not the lake, the course's most famous water hazard. Pros dislike blind tee shots because they have no specific target toward which they can aim. I prefer blind tee shots, figuring the less I know the better.

Tiger finds the fairway, and we walk uphill where all the hole's awful mysteries are revealed. If global warming ever does make water levels rise significantly, the narrow banana-shaped 18th green at Bay Hill may be planet Earth's first casualty. Everything about the hole, from the grandstands to the jagged rocks to the raised traps, forces a player to doubt whether the putting surface is really there at all.

Should Tiger need any further reminders on how easily this hole can ruin his round, he receives one courtesy of his playing partner, Mark Wilson. Wilson's second shot to the left-center pin hits the rocks and careens back into the lake. He walks forward until he finds a distance that doesn't make him sweat, drops a ball, and puts it in the water again. The workers on the big manual scoreboard facing the green were just finishing posting Wilson's name and scores after a solid 2-under start, but his quadruple-bogey 8 drops him out of contention.

Wilson's demise has no effect on Tiger, who makes a routine 4 and heads to the 1st tee still hanging on at even par.

11:35 AM • On the bus ride I had met Dave, a sixty-something fitness buff who is visiting family in central Florida for the week. He had confessed to being a big Phil Mickelson fan but had never seen Tiger in person. I invited him along so he can see what all the fuss is about.

Outside of Tiger's opening birdie, Dave hasn't seen much, and I'm worried about losing a possible convert. Now, after his third tough pitch out of the deep rough today, Tiger still has twenty feet left for par on the 2nd. As Tiger looks over his putt, I explain to Dave how Tiger's focus seems to spike when facing long par saves. Birdie putts are opportunities to move ahead. But clutch par putts keep him from losing ground. Tiger waits until I'm done with my explanation, then drains the twenty-footer to stay at even par, and Dave looks at me as if I am Tiger Woods' svengali.

12:32 PM • If the 6th at Bay Hill weren't buried in the front nine, it might be the course's most famous hole: 558 yards, every bit of which is played around Bay Hill's largest lake, a near-perfect circle of water that appears large enough to sink the *Titanic* without anyone knowing.

The question for any golfer standing on the tee is "What's my line?" Tiger and Stevie spend a good minute checking the yardage book, making sure they're doing the math right. If Tiger isn't aggressive enough, he'll end up in one of the traps along the right. If he's too aggressive, well, the problem is obvious. In 1998, John Daly hit six balls into the water and left the hole having made an 18.

Tiger picks his target and hits it so completely straight, there's no need for him to watch it. He bends down and salvages his tee. Because the hole continues to curve around the lake, the second shot isn't as long, but is just as dangerous for players who want to reach it in two. Tiger calmly puts his ball on the green and lags his eagle putt to four feet for birdie—no need for Match Play–type miracles quite yet.

After the birdie at 6, Tiger pars out for an even round of 70. I can find no reason for the tepid play other than Tiger's explanation from yesterday—he just needs to play better. He missed a few drives into the trees on the right, on two occasions he missed the green with a wedge in his hands, and when he did find the greens, he couldn't make a putt. I was not surprised when Dave apologized and left me on number 7 to follow golf's human highlight reel, Fred Couples. At age forty-eight, the 1992 Bay Hill champion had rolled out six birdies and a much more exciting round of 65. Tiger will start tomorrow 5 shots behind him and will need to fix something at the Isleworth range tonight.

SECOND ROUND

As the season has worn on, I have become more and more savvy about how to smuggle my cell phone. The first morning at the Buick Invitational, I took it with me and had it in my pocket. I walked past a smiling security guard who said, "Is your cell phone turned off, sir?" I smiled back, "It sure is," and kept going, only for him to change tones and snap, "You *can't* have cell phones on the course. You'll need to hand it over." It was a trap and, frankly, a good one. For the rest of the week I simply denied I had it. At the Dubai Desert Classic, I could have duct-taped it to my ear and security wouldn't have said anything. The Match Play stepped it up with metal detectors and wands, but George said if I stuffed it inside my pants, they wouldn't find it.

Friday at the Arnold Palmer Invitational I not only bring my cell phone, but I also need to use it, which is a much riskier proposition. While Tiger is on the putting green, I see a text message saying the producer of Golf Channel's nightly news show would like to interview me tonight about my adventures but that he has a few questions in advance.

I slip behind a fence near what turns out to be the club's laundry facilities. Workers scurry in and out with sheets, towels, tablecloths, and napkins. Judging by that, these fans must be the messiest on Tour. As I wait to be connected, I feel a breeze that smells like cold cuts intermittently blowing on my neck. I turn and see a round security guard with a bushy orange mustache standing one foot from me, his hands on his hips. He's wearing a black guard outfit and a matching hat with the word SECURITY on it in yellow letters in case there is still any doubt.

I decide to turn away slowly, hoping he'll be called off to a real emergency or maybe just lunch. He doesn't budge, so once the producer comes on the line, I start inserting inane, showbiz-sounding questions into our conversation to make me sound important, like "What time we on camera tonight?" and at least three or four times wedge in the phrase "Tiger and I." When the phone call ends, he's still there. "Hi." I say, figuring my phone is goners, but hopefully not me with it. He pushes the button on his walkie-talkie. "Security to base." We stand in silence. There's no answer. "Got a few minutes?" he asks, facetiously, I presume. We walk to his nearby golf cart, and he tells me to have a seat. We take off around the ninth green as incoming fans stare at me as if I've done something wrong. Which, okay, I have. I try to act cool, put my feet up on the cart, and make small talk.

"What's your name, man?"

"Lynn."

"*Lynn?*" I'm so convinced I have heard wrong that I start to spell it. "L-Y—"

"N-N," he finishes, sternly. I change the subject.

"So have you seen Tiger this week?"

"Yesterday on eighteen," he tells me. "He's almost as big as I am." For clarity's sake, Tiger is roughly 190 pounds. Lynn is pushing 300 if not already there. Even if he is just comparing their heights, it's the best example yet of how much everyone wants to look at Tiger and find some way to believe "I *am* like him."

We arrive at Lynn's destination, the main security office, where Sandy sits behind a desk. I already met Sandy yesterday. She is the petite but gruff woman who responded to my question of whether I could bring my periscope this week by scoffing and saying no.

The moment of reckoning has come. Sandy looks to her burly

guard, wondering what awful thing I have done. I put my head down. He speaks. "This guy is writing a golf book, setting up interviews, that sort of thing. He *needs* to be able to use his cell phone on the course." Lynn's a softie! He asks Sandy if she has any more stickers for security-approved cell phones, the ones reserved for doctors with patients who might die if they aren't reachable. Sandy begins looking around her desk, a workspace covered in security hats, volunteer badges, and old newspapers. After a few seconds, she gives up and with that same curt manner as yesterday says, "Is your phone on vibrate?"

"Silent."

She shrugs. "So just don't make any phone calls. And if it goes off, you better believe Tiger Woods will toss your phone as far as he can throw it."

3:20 PM • Tiger's second round officially started two hours ago on the 1st hole, when his ball came to rest and the marshal looked down and joked, "Hey, how come Tiger's playing a Pinnacle?" From there he would finish his first eight in only 1 under par. It's not too thrilling, considering Vijay Singh is already in the clubhouse having shot 66-65 to post 9 under heading into Saturday. Tiger's in trouble. And as he stares down a twelve-foot birdie putt on the 9th green, I finally understand why. The green is patchy, dying, and, in some places, dead. I don't know how anyone can make any putts except by sheer luck.

Tiger's win streak has been the big news at Bay Hill this week, but close behind it is the tale of something even more unstoppable: nematodes—parasitic worms that have been feasting on the roots of Bay Hill's TifEagle greens since last summer. The greenskeepers knew something was wrong, but after being unable to cure it, they sent a sample to a professor of plant pathology at Clemson, where the Ph.D. discovered the worms. At that point, it was too late; the worms had caused too much damage. Because so many of Bay Hill's greens are elevated, I hadn't seen the destruction until now. Jim Furyk told reporters that the greens were "fine." Tiger called them "not very good." They were both being generous. This 9th green is so bad that large sections of it have clearly been painted with green fertilizer to cover the damage.

Supposedly these worms are barely a few millimeters in length, but I have found articles saying nematodes as long as twenty-seven feet have been discovered inside the carcasses of dead sperm whales, and some part of me is waiting for a big one to burst through the brown turf as in Frank Herbert's *Dune* and swallow a player, preferably Vijay.

I focus back in on Tiger, who, on second glance, has left himself a birdie putt that avoids any bad spots. He makes it, but it's now apparent that for Tiger to make a serious run, he must find a way to putt well on unpredictable greens.

3:56 PM • The par-4 11th at Bay Hill, like the 3rd and the 6th holes, wraps around the right side of a big round lake, 438 yards from tee to green. Tiger takes an aggressive line off the tee with a fairway wood, his ball stopping so close to the water that when he hits his second shot, his divot lands in it, leaving Stevie with a little less work to do. The line for his approach is even gutsier than his tee shot, landing ten feet left of the back left pin and only a few feet right of being wet. He misses the putt.

4:28 PM • On the 13th hole, Tiger again knocks it into birdie range. And again misses. I'm standing with Darnell, a Tiger fan who came all the way from Bermuda to watch him this week and is just shaking his head. "It's one thing to be respectful, but somebody has got to say the truth. These greens are *bad.*" It's true, but at the same time, other players are posting low scores on these same greens. They are making some adjustment that Tiger isn't.

5:03 PM • On the long par-4 16th, Tiger misses right off the tee and finds himself completely blocked by the bleachers facing the 17th green. Most marshals tend to overreact upon seeing Tiger's ball and force the gallery back three times farther than we need to go. The marshal at the 16th seems intimidated by the enormity of moving three hundred people and lets us stay where we are, within a yard of the ball. Stevie shows up, sees the lack of room he's been given, rolls his eyes, and asks the marshal to take charge.

We're moved just in time for the arrival of Tiger, who strolls up, takes one look at his ball, and immediately asks for a rules official. He waits. So we wait. It has been a frustrating two days, and he stands still with no emotion. But when the rules official arrives and tells Tiger that he has the option of playing the shot as it lies, Tiger smiles and laughs. "No, I do not want to play it *as is*." The only other time I have seen his genuinely friendly personality break through like this was late in the finals of the Match Play when he bounced a drive off a woman's leg. He walked up with a toothy smile and said, "I'm sorry. I am *so* sorry. I wasn't trying to hit it over here. I was trying to hit it over *there*." Both examples make it obvious that the space between his game face and his smile is a lot thinner than he would like his opponents to believe.

5:10 PM • Tiger ultimately takes a free drop off the cart path, then an additional drop away from the bleachers. His second shot shoots through the trees and winds up in that terrible fifteen- to twenty-foot range. No surprise, he misses. The longest putt he has made all week remains his Thursday par putt on number 2.

5:32 PM • On the 18th Tiger hits it *again* to fifteen feet. He has hit nearly every green on the back nine and has eight straight pars to show for it. Vijay remains the leader at 9 under, while Tiger sits stalled at 2 under. He needs this. He is above the middle-front hole position, a putt that should have some good speed to it. He leaves it dead on line but a few inches short. That makes him 0 for 6 on the back nine with makeable birdie putts. He makes his par, reaches into the cup, and, revealing his true sentiments, flips the ball behind his back and into the lake.

A 70-68 start for Tiger. He makes the cut by only four shots and will begin the weekend farther out of the lead than when he teed off this morning.

THE GOLF CHANNEL • This isn't my first time in front of the camera. Between my junior and senior years of college, I worked as an extra for the summer. For three months I bounced from show to show, literally being used to fill empty space. I had a recurring role on the teen show *Boy Meets World*, where I routinely played the mute, out-of-focus high school student. In the short-lived drama *Vengeance Unlimited*, I played a pivotal role as the out-of-focus guy who walks past the same window four or five times.

Thanks to that summer, I'm not particularly nervous about being interviewed by the Golf Channel's Todd Lewis, the cheery former sports anchor at the CBS affiliate in Orlando who joined the network at the beginning of the year. Besides, I have plenty to talk about—my adventures with Rashid, running six miles with George, and, of course, Tiger. If I do completely blank once the red light goes on, Todd assures me I can go back and do another take. While the makeup artist goes to work on me, the different on-air personalities stick their heads in to say hello. They don't need to introduce themselves but they do anyway— "Hi, I'm Brandel," "Hi, Rich Lerner . . ." "Hey there, Kraig Kann . . ." It's not false modesty. They come off like a group of guys that doesn't tolerate ego. It's refreshing, and it makes sense.

After all, the Golf Channel is a long way from Hollywood, just a one-story building wedged in the middle of a nondescript Orlando business park. The channel may be available in 75 million households worldwide, but if it were ever to grab even 1 percent of that number, everyone at the network would party long into the night at the local Bennigan's.

The stage is completely dark but for the lights on the set. With the exception of Todd, the cameraman, and me, everyone else hangs back in the control room, watching the feed from the stage floor. Todd preps me with a few of the questions he will ask, I nod, and off we go. We finish the first take, and I'm excited to go again to see if I can make myself sound interesting this time. Todd listens as I explain how I'm going to improve on my second take. He puts his finger to his earpiece, smiles, and says, "They're telling me we're done." Driving to dinner, I console myself with the thought that, if nothing else, I was finally in focus.

THIRD ROUND

There is irony in the fact that my first experience following Tiger was in the Sherwood Country Club parking lot last December. It's the exact same place I had stood as a thirteen-year-old when my dad took me to my very first golf tournament, Greg Norman's Shark Shootout. He and I walked up from the dirt lot and caught sight of the clubhouse, an all-brick mansion that was the most beautiful building we'd ever seen in our lives. We just stood there in silence, gawking. Someone walked behind us and said, "That's the *tennis* clubhouse." We kept going up the road and came to the main clubhouse, something so massive and over the top it was hard to believe that no war-ending treaties had ever been signed behind its white pillars. We wandered past the front and down through the empty parking lot when a car pulled up. Out stepped Arnold Palmer.

My dad had grown up in Pittsburgh and cemented his love for Palmer from the gallery at the 1962 U.S. Open at Oakmont. The tournament built to a Monday playoff between western Pennsylvania's favorite son and a young, pudgy kid named Jack Nicklaus. The whole way around, my dad remembers the hometown crowd not just rooting against Nicklaus but actually booing him. It was bad enough that he was from Ohio, but to be from Ohio *and* beating Arnie was sacrilege. In the end, Nicklaus held off Palmer—and the crowds—and won by three shots. It was the first major of his career.

Seeing Arnie in person at age thirteen was immobilizing. I didn't know how a human being was supposed to handle a moment of such significance. My dad told me to run and find a golf pencil. I did and was back in time to catch the King walking by. I remember my dad said, "Morning, Arnie," as if he were part of his regular foursome. Arnie smiled and said, "Hello." I said nothing, just held out the pencil, and my ticket. He signed it, then headed into the clubhouse, a cashmere sweater stuffed under his arm. I remember thinking how normal he was. That he *could* be one of the guys in my dad's foursome. That he would rib him after a bad shot and applaud the good ones and wouldn't think about heading home after the round without having a drink and a sandwich in the bar. Even back then, I knew that was what made Arnold Palmer special. He was one of us.

11:27 AM • When the seventy-eight-year-old Arnie appears on the range at Bay Hill, he receives the welcome he deserves, a standing ovation from the bleachers. He's wearing a soft orange shirt, gray slacks, and half-hidden beneath his slight paunch, a green belt from Augusta National, one of the *ninety* clubs to which he belongs. He stops to talk to Fred Couples, and picks up Fred's 3-wood to waggle it, still appreciating the feel of a shaft he is too old to hit. He moves from Couples to Tiger, who pats him on the back. When the season started, Tiger was one PGA win behind Arnie. Less than two months later, he has already passed him.

11:51 AM • I move down the number 1 fairway a few minutes ahead of Tiger and read in the daily pairing sheet about Vijay's second-round 65. At first he seems to be playing at a level he can't sustain, having chipped in not once but twice yesterday. Then I read that Vijay is still recovering from a bout of food poisoning he picked up in India last month, as a result of which he claims to have lost eighteen pounds. Tiger was onto something back in 2003—apparently the secret to winning here is to become violently ill.

11:57 AM • Tiger starts his round by missing right and leaving himself a downhill lie from the deep rough to the green. Tiger peers down at his lie, almost afraid to look, then shakes his head. He goes with a short iron, opens the face and his stance, and takes a giant rip at the ball, the club almost flying out of his hands from the speed of the swing. The crowd loves it. It ends up twelve feet away. After yesterday, I know he can two-putt from there, but he actually makes it. Three under. Exactly the start he needs. From this far behind, he needs to post a low number on the front nine and scare as many of the two dozen players teeing off after him as possible.

12:22 PM • The afternoon wind is picking up as Tiger reaches number 3, a mini version of number 11, just under 400 yards around the lake. It's downwind, and Tiger plays aggressively along the left side of the fairway near the water. He leaves his second shot ten feet away, downhill. *Again* he makes it! Four under. He said to reporters yesterday that more than the line, the bad greens are messing with his speed; that he just needs to adjust to hitting them harder than he is used to doing here. Consider the adjustment made.

Another adjustment he has made today is to manually fix as many defects in his line as he can. Before his birdie putt on the long par-4 4th, I decide to count. One . . . two . . . three . . . four . . . five . . . six. Most of us don't fix that many marks in a month. But it pays off as he drops it in for his third birdie in his opening four holes. "That's the Tiger we know and love," a fan says. At 5 under, he's pulled within four of Vijay, who hasn't even teed off yet.

1:05 PM • Back on the 6th, the massive par 5 around the lake, Tiger's drive leaks right and jumps just a yard into the rough. The first one on the scene is Luau Larry. It's the first I've seen him this week. His leg reveals no sign of the Tucson cactus incident, and he walks up to Tiger's ball to take a look at the lie. A fellow sportswriter jokingly asks, "What do you see, Feherty?" Larry always appears humorless, but I'm hoping he'll see the rare opportunity to try out his best Irish lilt. To my disappointment, all Larry says is a flat and accent-free "It's okay."

1:43 PM • An okay lie isn't good enough for a birdie, and Tiger plays the rest of the front nine 1 over to make the turn at 4 under par for the week. Vijay remains at 9 under. No one else is lower than 6 under, meaning that Tiger's 33 on the front nine has put him within striking distance.

2:15 PM • On the 11th, the wheels have come off for Ben Crane, Tiger's fair-skinned playing partner, whose face has been recently coated with a thick layer of white sunblock. Tiger made the hole look easy with a two-putt par, but Crane pulled his second into the lake, dropped, played his fourth onto the green, then rolled his bogey putt well past the hole.

Anyone plays slowly en route to a triple-bogey seven, but even when he's playing well, Crane remains one of the Tour's slowest members. As Crane looks over his double-bogey putt, Tiger walks to the back of the green and stands next to Dottie Pepper, NBC's on-course commentator fitted with headset, mike, and a battery-packed belt. They start whispering and laughing about something as Tiger crosses his arms, then puts them on his hips, then crosses them again in an exaggerated fashion. I'm not sure what's going on until I look back down the 11th fairway and see Pat Perez, the Tour's most impatient player, going nuts waiting for Crane. On cue, Pat crosses his arms, then puts them on his hips. Tiger and Dottie laugh at Tiger's dead-on impression. Once again, Tiger is using other players' weaknesses to his own advantage, never once letting Crane or Perez do anything but make him smile.

3:09 PM • By the time Tiger arrives at the fairway on the 15th, Vijay has dropped a shot and Tiger's down only four. The wind has been growing stronger all afternoon, and on the tree-lined 425-yard hole, it begins to gust straight into the players' faces. Tiger faces a tough second shot from the right side of the fairway, an approach that he will have to somehow get around the hole's trademark magnolia trees.

Golf purists criticize the modern player for his inability to shape shots, and as usual, Tiger is the exception to the rule. Where other players hunger for control, Tiger's Nike balls are custom-designed with an extra-soft cover so he can turn the ball even more. He aims his stance to the left and the face of his forged Nike blade to the right, and slashes across the ball from out to in, sending it left of the magnolias and then cutting back hard to the right and straight at the pin. It's not amazing, it's not unbelievable. I don't even think it's ridiculous. It's beautiful. It drops out of the wind and stops three feet from the hole. No nematodes can stop this putt from going in the cup. Tiger is within three.

3:26 PM • Tiger pipes it down the middle on the 16th, the scariest par 4 at Bay Hill. The pin is cut only four or five paces off the front edge near the water, and the wind continues to gust in his face. Showing his range of shots, he chokes down this time and hits one low, with less fade than before. While the ball is in midair, the fan in front of me, Kevin, declares that it will be close. I trust him. He's a key performance analyst at Boeing and has an Indiana Jones–style hat with the chin strap pulled tight, a pair of binoculars, and a range finder to determine exactly how far away each player is. The ball skids to a stop no more than four feet away. "A lot of these guys on Tour are golfers," Kevin says. "Tiger's an athlete." Tiger makes another three. Six under.

3:44 PM • As long as none of the leaders pulls much farther away from him than 10 under, he will have a chance tomorrow. After a par on 17, I make my way down the left side of 18 and see that the leaders have gotten closer to Tiger, not further. The wide-eyed Nick Watney had it to 9 under, but bogeyed the 13th to fall to 8. The Swedish-born/Southern-raised Carl Pettersson fell back to 8 after a bogey on the 9th. And Vijay has just played the 5th through 8th holes 5 *over* par and slipped two shots *behind* Tiger. The traditional Sunday-afternoon crumble at the feet of Tiger is happening, but it's happening on a Saturday.

3:55 PM • Tiger pars the 18th, signs his scorecard for a 66, and moves to the outdoor media area, where he is quickly surrounded by reporters and cameramen. A crowd of a few hundred of us gathers on the other side of the metal barricade to eavesdrop, but we can't hear a thing. Still, none of us leaves. An old man next to me brings out the digital camera he has hidden in his pants and is trying to take a picture, but he's too short. I take it from him, hold it up high over the mob, and snag a good one. I try to zoom in and make it even better when I look up in the grandstands and see a group of marshals pointing me out to, of course, Lynn the security guard. As he lumbers down the stairs to nab me, I slip between the crowds and escape for the bus.

THE BAD DOG • When Tiger leaves Bay Hill, he drives home to Isleworth to work out and watch the leaders finish. As Kevin, the Bay Hill superfan, had said, Tiger is an athlete, and after years of keeping his workout regiment under wraps, he finally revealed it to *Men's Fitness* last year. He typically goes to the gym six days a week, sometimes up to three hours at a time. I don't know why this should surprise me. When Tiger was a kid, he overcame a debilitating stutter by talking to his dog. Sometimes, he would talk so long that his dog fell asleep.

The first thirty minutes of Tiger's workout is purely stretching, from the obvious body parts like his back, all the way to his toes. Weightwise, Tiger generally does high-rep sets versus power lifting and bench pressing. At 190 pounds, he already has plenty of bulk. The big concern for his trainer is keeping Tiger's body symmetrical, not wanting any part of him to be out of balance with the rest, a flaw that could upend everything else. The rest of his routine is rounded out with cardio and core training, which leads to the most disturbing quote of the article: "I like doing sit-ups, thoroughly enjoy them. I think they're fun." If a man can convince his mind that sit-ups are fun, there is no limit to what he can achieve.

I also decide to strengthen my core and go to Steak n Shake. It's my fifth time to this hamburger joint in three days. Even though the service and food are growing progressively worse, I can't resist going back again and again. The combination of meat, fries, and shake gives me all the things my body needs after five hours on the course.

If I had known what was taking place back at Bay Hill, I never would have left. The leaders who had shown some cracks as Tiger made his late charge completely collapsed once his 6-under total was officially posted. Bart Bryant was a few shots ahead and found the water on 16 to fall back into a tie with Tiger. Nick Watney, who had already slipped to 8 under when I left, pulled his drive on 16 out of bounds, then hit his fourth shot into the water left of the green. He'd make a quadruple-bogey and finish at 4 under. Carl Pettersson double-bogeyed the 10th and bogeyed the 15th, falling past Watney to only 3 under. And while Vijay recovered from a front-nine 40, he couldn't pull ahead of Tiger, joining the party at 6 under. By the time I return to Kelly's house and check the scores, Tiger is tied for the lead with four other players and has landed in the final group.

After thoroughly enjoying the highlights of the field's collective demise, I need to hit some balls. Considering I have dragged my clubs with me across the country, I might as well use them. The only lit driving range nearby is the Bad Dog Driving Range. There are four sizes of buckets from which to choose: "Runt," "Lap Dog," "Pick of the Litter," and . . ."The Bad Dog," 180 balls guaranteed to make all ten fingers bleed. I go with Lap Dog. Rather than hit balls without a purpose, as I usually do, I try to maximize the pressure and pretend I'm actually playing alongside Tiger. After a few dozen swings, he stops me. "Wait," imaginary Tiger says. "One shot. Closest to the hole. You get inside my ball, you can write about our round. If not . . . we never met."

I take a breath, focus on the red flag 105 yards away, factor in the left-to-right breeze, and swing. It bounces once, kicks right, and, best I can tell, settles up next to the eight-inch-wide red-painted flagpole. I win, Tiger. I imagine his reaction, silent and cold, then saying "Two out of three?" I refuse the temptation to end on anything but a good one and leave the rest of the balls behind.

FINAL ROUND

Last night Tiger went from in the mix to in the lead, and as a result, Tiger mania is sweeping central Florida. A few thousand fans are already with me lining the 1st fairway, anxious to be part of his win streak. The spectrum of the fans officially falls between two extremes. Next to me is a guy in his early twenties, dressed like Tiger Woods. Red Tiger Woods Nike shirt, black pants, black hat. He's completely humorless. There's no smiling, his arms are crossed. For him, this is war. He needs to concentrate on Tiger and will not be distracted by any of my dumb questions. When I ask him if he's a big Vijay fan, he turns, gives me an eerie Tiger-like scowl, eyes barely visible beneath his hat, then turns back to face the fairway.

The other extreme is partying behind me. Even though Tiger hasn't teed off, Daryl and his rowdy friends have just arrived from their preround victory celebration at the beer garden. Daryl flew in from Seattle, but the rest of the group is local. He introduces me to the rest of his buddies. There's Jessie, then Joe. "Yo, Francis!" I meet Francis. I think that's it until Daryl asks, "Anybody seen Cedric?" I count five. Daryl says there's eleven of them total, and if I want to have fun, I need to stick with them.

"If you can keep up with me, I'll walk with you guys for a few holes," I say. Daryl's insulted.

"If *you* can keep up with *us*." Oh, it is on.

"All I know is I'm one beer more sober than you are."

Joe pipes in. "One? Try two or three."

These guys are sort of interested in golf and very interested in women. When Suzann Pettersen, an athletic blonde who happens to be the number three female golfer in the world, walks by, Daryl turns around and takes notice. "I have *got* to go visit Sweden!" he says, loud enough for her to hear. Neither of us tells him she's from Norway.

It's not the first time Pettersen has been here this week. She came to watch Tiger yesterday, too. After Tiger smashed his drive on the 12th hole, she turned to her parents and started laughing. Walking down the fairway, I asked her what the biggest difference is between his game and hers. "He just hits it so much harder than I do," she said. When top-tier athletes from the same sport start showing up at events, something special is happening.

2:06 PM • I troop along with Daryl and company as Tiger makes a solid par on the first. On the 218-yard par-3 2nd, Tiger knocks his shot about eighteen feet short of the cup, a definite birdie chance. Before Tiger has even gotten to the green, Daryl and the group start walking to number 3.

"Where are you guys going?" Daryl turns around and keeps walking backward while talking to me.

"Oh, we don't stay for putts."

"What are you talking about?"

"If we stay for putts, we'll fall behind. Francis knows *all* the tricks." My time with them lasts only one and a half holes. But I get over it quickly when Tiger makes the birdie they missed and takes the outright lead at 7 under.

3:51 PM • Throughout the rest of Tiger's front nine, Daryl and I are repeatedly leapfrogging each other. After raising his putter to celebrate a ten-foot par save on the 4th, the rest of Tiger's front nine is precision. He hits every green and defies the nematodes again on the pockmarked 9th for a twenty-foot birdie putt from off the fringe that puts him at two shots clear of the pack at the turn. The only thing he can't do is make a stupid mistake.

4:00 PM • And then he makes a stupid mistake. After laying back off the 10th tee with just an iron, he plants his second shot no more than seven feet from the hole, then three-putts. The birdie try never touches the hole. The par putt lips out. One minute earlier, I was wondering whether the Tour's trophy engraver has ever tried carving Tiger's name with his eyes closed. Now I'm realizing what one small bogey has done. It has given the other players the worst possible thing in the world—hope.

When Tiger's mom, Tida, was interviewed in 2006 for the *60 Minutes* piece on Tiger, she explained the mind-set she had passed on to her son about competition. "You have to, no matter how close friends you are . . . you must kill that person." The bogey at 10 is the equivalent of Tiger lifting his foot off the field's collective throat and asking "Everyone all right down there?" He is suddenly tied at 8 under with Bart Bryant, who had birdied the 10th when he passed through five minutes earlier. Other players are suddenly energized to make moves, too. Cliff Kresge climbs the leaderboard to –7. So does Hunter Mahan. The relaxing back nine I had envisioned is over before it starts.

4:35 PM • Tiger scraps around for pars on the next two holes and comes to the 364-yard 13th, a short par 4 with water in front. It's short enough that Tiger can hit a long iron off the tee and still only have a sand wedge into the green. He has to reapply the pressure, and stuffs a sand wedge just over the pond and within twelve feet of the tucked front pin. I scan his line for dead spots, but it's only Tiger's fault if he misses this one. He raps it hard uphill and into the grain, and it falls in on the front side.

Any birdie is a big birdie right now, but his timing forces his chasers to take some risks on those tough final four holes.

4:45 PM • With Tiger still putting for a par on 14, I steal Daryl's "trick" and jump ahead. The crowds have swelled this afternoon to five deep, the thickest Sunday crowds of the year. Down at 15, I catch up with Bart Bryant in the group ahead in time to see him make a four-footer for a birdie of his own and back into a tie for the lead.

Watching Bart Bryant, I can't help but think of Ed Fiori, the forty-three-year-old journeyman who knocked off Tiger at the Quad Cities Open in 1996 to deny the rookie his first Tour victory. As Fiori was then, Bryant is in his mid-forties and is built more like a high school gym coach than a finely tuned athlete. There is something unnerving about that age, a window of time when a golfer's body will sometimes let him play well, but the world won't think any less of him if he doesn't. If a twenty-eight-year-old loses down the stretch to Tiger, it's a choke. If a forty-five-year-old loses, it's a valiant effort. It isn't that Bryant doesn't have anything to lose. A win would earn him an invitation to the Masters next month and the CA Championship next week. But for now he must be relishing a position where the expectations couldn't be lower.

4:51 PM • At 9 under, Tiger and Bryant are two shots clear of anyone else. They aren't in the same twosome, but they're close enough to keep tabs on each other, giving the tournament a match play feel. Tiger plays conservatively off the tee on the par-4 15th, hitting only a 5-wood to make sure he stays between the magnolias. Of course, it helps that his 5-wood still goes 250 yards. He two-putts for par to keep pace.

5:09 PM • Tiger lays back off the 16th as well, taking a 3-wood on a par 4 that is 485 yards long. For a player who early in his career had the reputation of swinging out of his spikes and then dealing with the consequences, he has displayed a tremendous amount of patience throughout this win streak. He has never once looked harried. When he was down four strokes at the turn in Dubai, he told Stevie he needed to shoot 30 to win, then meticulously picked off birdies one by one, playing for the safe side of each green rather than firing at every pin. The mature Tiger Woods may not always be as flashy from tee to green, but his restraint only makes him even more dangerous.

The result of Tiger's safe drive is a 200-yard approach. He still manages to leave it hole high in the middle of the green. As his birdie putt falls off to the left, Tiger bends over his putter as if he's falling on his sword.

5:28 PM • Just as Bryant did a few minutes earlier, Tiger has a birdie look at the par-3 17th, but can't make it. He angrily pounds down a bump he has deemed the cause of the miss. Even though he came alive on Saturday to slide into first place, the longest putt I have seen him make all week remains his par save on number 2 way back on Thursday.

After three days, I've learned that to get from the right side of 17 to the left side of 18, I will have to sprint past the tee box and make it to the crosswalk before the marshals close the ropes. When Tiger's birdie effort doesn't drop, I take off full speed, which is a few steps faster than it was back at the Buick, and arrive at the crosswalk right as the marshal places the white rope back on the pole. He flashes me a fake smile and turns around. I can either wait until Tiger has teed off and then try to find a spot down the bleacher-lined left-hand side or keep going down the right, where I will only get as close as the front edge of the lake before reaching a dead end. The crowds down the entire left side are at least ten deep, and no one is leaving.

I run down the right side. On my way, Tiger's tee ball passes me, a low 3-wood placed perfectly to the left side of the fairway. It's my first view of Bay Hill's 18th green with its traditional Sunday pin placement, three quarters of the way to the green's right edge and only a few yards from the water. The trouble short is obvious. The trouble long is hard to miss as well, three bright white bunkers curving like a boomerang around the green's back side.

5:35 PM • Up ahead, Bryant rolls his thirty-five-foot birdie putt toward the hole. From two hundred yards away, a fan near me says "Miss," under his breath. "Miss. Miss it." He's like D'Annunzio in *Caddyshack* trying to spook Danny Noonan. Bryant indeed misses and taps in nonchalantly for an impressive 67, safely in the clubhouse at 9 under. We cheer, having to give the guy credit for not buckling under the pressure. Tiger needs a par to tie or a birdie to win. As always, he has done it before. In 2001, he faced a fifteen-footer to beat Phil Mickelson and made it. First he must hit the green.

As Tiger and Stevie start to discuss the shot, the wind begins to gust differently than it has all day. It switches direction 180 degrees and begins to blow in our faces, as if a special-effects team just flipped a switch to make Tiger's second shot to the 18th that much harder to judge.

He has 170 yards. With the wind, it's at least another ten, maybe more. He chooses a club and backs away as the wind gusts again. A siren blares in the distance, then fades. Tiger steadies himself one more time and hits a hard cut toward the middle of the green. It clears the water and lands safely on the other side, twenty-five feet above the hole to the left. He hands Stevie his club with his right hand as Stevie gives him an open-palm low-five with the other.

The low-five is a much safer option than the forever awkward celebration they shared after Tiger chipped in for birdie on the 16th at the 2005 Masters. Stevie followed one of the greatest shots in golf history by trying to christen the moment with a high-five. He managed to make contact with no more than one of Tiger's five fingers, then stood there waffling between a fist pump and a forearm bash to make up for it. It exemplified why Tiger Woods was never meant to play a team sport. Someone else was always bound to make him look worse than he was.

His Ryder Cup stats prove it. In his singles matches, he hasn't lost since 1997. But in team play, the greatest player in the world has a losing record—seven wins, twelve losses.

5:45 PM • From my spot on the corner of the lake, I'm looking straight across the water as Tiger walks the length of the putt, down to the hole and then back again. There are so many things to distract a lesser life form. An NBC crew guy shuffles down the grassy bank behind him, gripping his boom mike. From under the bleachers, Arnie emerges and stands watch in his navy blue Bay Hill blazer.

Tiger's head is on a pivot, but it's only in order to keep the line of the putt always centered between his eyes. He walks slowly; nothing is rushed. He actually appears to relish the pressure of the moment. I met a clinical psychologist one day at the Match Play and asked him for a professional opinion on Tiger's ability to perform under duress. He chalked it up to Tiger having an overdeveloped cognitive and neuro-motor reserve, and when the other parts of his brain are stimulated by stress, he can access a "storeroom" of calm. Everyone always wonders how he or she can perform under pressure like Tiger. The Ph.D. I met said it's irrelevant—what Tiger does is something most people couldn't physically do even if they knew how.

5:47 PM • He takes two last strokes before stepping into the ball. As he draws the silver putter back, I notice a bird on the lake dive beneath the water. Dogs can sense earthquakes. Maybe loons can, too. The moment he hits it, the crowd starts to cheer, sounding like a distant wave that won't stop breaking. With the ball having traveled only two feet from Tiger's putter, someone in the back row of the bleachers stands and put his hands up as if he already knows it's in. That is trust. The rest of the grandstands are on their feet when it's halfway to the hole and still on line. As the putt banks to the right, the cheers from those with better views continue to swell and we take our cues from them, screaming the ball down toward the cup. I stop tracking the actual putt when I see Tiger take a few steps backward. *He's done it again.* When it drops, Tiger turns and, in one glorious motion, slams his black TW hat to the ground. Taking my cue from him, I toss my own hat into the air and roar in delight. If there were only a way to harness the energy released around that green, it would power the city of Orlando for a week.

Without waiting for permission, the still-screaming fans around me duck under the ropes and begin racing toward the green. I grab my hat off the ground and do the same. To spend exactly 333 holes roped in and then be running free is thrilling. I know we're heading toward Tiger, but I don't think anyone has thought through what we'll do if we reach him.

Twenty yards from the green, a handful of old marshals bolts across with some rope and stretches it from the lake to the grandstands, bracing itself for the stampede that might very well roll on past them without giving it another thought. I hit the rope. It stretches tight around my waist under the crush of the thousand fans behind me, but the line holds. On the other side of the rope is Larry Johnson, a wiry marshal who finds himself with the most memorable job of the day. "Did they prepare you for this?" I ask. "Not enough!" he says, both laughing and terrified at the same time.

Four tournaments. *Four wins.* Each one more thrilling than the one before. His 64th PGA Tour win ties him with Ben Hogan on the all-time victory list and puts him two ahead of Palmer. As workers scurry to the green to set up microphones and place all the blue-blazered tournament officials in a straight line, I remember an interview David Feherty did on CBS with Tiger during the Buick. He asked Tiger whether twelve wins in a row was possible—twelve being the number it would take to beat Byron Nelson's record of eleven straight victories in 1945. Tiger paused but never took his eyes off Feherty as he casually said, "Uh-huh." When I heard it, I blew it off as another example of Tiger's out-of-control ego. How could he consider breaking a record that ranks as golf's most untouchable achievement. But going back to last year, his win streak stands at seven. If Phil Mickelson hadn't held him off at the Deutsche Bank Championship last September, this would be win number ten.

Eight minutes later, Tiger is back on the green, now wearing a blue blazer of his own and standing in front of Arnie. As Tiger accepts the silver trophy, the man whose statue rests on top of it elbows him in the side and sarcastically calls him a "jerk." Tiger steps to the microphone and tries to sound modest about his finish. "I just happened to get lucky and make a putt." Someone behind me yells back, "It's not luck!" If it happens once, it's luck. If you do it in Dubai and at the Match Play and again at Bay Hill, it's otherworldly. Supernatural. After that putt, there's no way I can wait two or three weeks to see him play again. And for the first time this season, I won't have to.

DRIVE FOR SHOW, PUTT FOR . . . D'OH!

The WGC-CA Championship

The Blue Monster—Doral Golf Resort & Spa
Miami, Florida
March 20–24, 2008

There are three online reviews on TripAdvisor for the Econo Lodge in North Fort Myers, Florida. They are titled "Very Disappointed," "Don't stay here!!," and "Never stay here, no matter what." Unfortunately, I don't read them until after I am very disappointed and staying there. I had driven down the west coast of Florida from Orlando Tuesday night until I couldn't stay awake any longer when the Econo Lodge appeared majestically in front of me.

The problem is that I am sharing a wall with Moe, a belligerent alcoholic I have heard but not seen who, between his drinking and related carousing, has broken everything in his room by sunrise. At 7 a.m., I abandon the notion of sleep, check out, and head for the Rav4. Outside, Moe is standing in front of his room, dressed but unshaven, tattooed, brown curly hair in knots, preparing the manager for what he's about to see. The manager courageously steps inside as Moe shakes his head, as if even he can't believe what he's done. Driving away, I see a gangly woman slip out Moe's door, followed by a poor maid walking to the Dumpster with a handful of used limes.

My accommodations for the CA Championship in Miami can't possibly be this bad. I'll be staying with Craig—a writer himself who has read about my adventures on ESPN.com and received permission from his fiancée to let me crash on their couch for the week. "We're not creepy," he promises, something that's hard to disprove just by saying it.

To get from Fort Myers to Craig's home in Fort Lauderdale, I drive in a straight line for a hundred miles, across the width of South Florida, on a stretch of highway called Alligator Alley. There are no cities along it, and Kelly had promised that I would see actual gators while I was driving. It seems hard to believe, equivalent to tourists who eat on Rodeo Drive thinking they'll be sharing a bread stick with Angelina Jolie. But sure enough, after only a few miles there is a clearing, and a healthy seven-footer is sitting on the side of the swamp, waiting for a tourist's Rav4 to run out of gas. I check my gauge and keep driving.

In 1959, the New York real estate magnate Alfred Kaskel bought 2,400 acres west of Miami. But saying "acres" makes it sound too civilized. It was swampland, and people thought he had lost his mind. Three years later, the first PGA Tour event was held at Doral—a name Kaskel created by smushing his wife's first name, Doris, together with his own. During the third round that year, Doral's water-flanked 18th hole averaged more than a stroke over par and the head pro dubbed it "a monster . . . a blue monster." The name stuck for both the hole and the course.

For a venue to stay on the Tour schedule for nearly fifty years, it's either hallowed ground (Augusta National, Colonial Country Club) or a little lucky. Doral survived a scare in the mid-'80s when Eastern Airlines, its sponsor of seventeen years, went bankrupt. It was given new life again last year when the PGA Tour took the Ford Championship at Doral and rebranded it the CA Championship. Ironically, "CA" is the rebranded name of Computer Associates, the IT management firm that has taken on sponsorship in the hope that people will forget their chairman is currently serving a twelve-year prison sentence for securities fraud.

But Doral's safe spot on the schedule isn't because of CA, it's because it's also the second of the year's four World Golf Championships (the first being last month's Accenture Match Play). The major pro circuits concocted the WGCs in the late 1990s as a way to bring together the best players on Earth more often than just for the year's four majors . . . and make some healthy TV revenue in the process. In addition to the top fifty players in the world, this week's exclusive seventy-nine-man field includes the top three from the Japan Golf Tour, the Australasian Golf Tour, the Asian Tour, and the South African Sunshine Tour. They're lured by a big purse and the fact that there's not a two-day cut. As long as they finish all 72 holes, they're guaranteed at least a last-place $35,000 paycheck. Who knew that dominating the Sunshine Tour could bring such perks?

All any of this meant for Tiger Woods was that he would be receiving a $360,000 raise. After winning the Ford Championship in 2005 and 2006, he went right ahead and won the CA Championship in 2007 and the bloated first-place check of $1.35 million. It was more prize money than he took home for winning the PGA Championship that same year.

Unlike Bay Hill, the conventional wisdom heading into Doral is that Tiger can't lose. The rough is shorter than last week, its greens are worm-free, and even though he won't be staying at home, Tiger will probably be able to make do with the sleeping quarters on board his 155-foot yacht, brought down from central Florida for the week.

FIRST ROUND

11:15 AM • Just four hours from Orlando, and the weather is completely different. The air is heavy, and elephant gray clouds drag themselves west to east across the South Florida sky. Tiger is on Doral's putting green, surrounded by more than twenty international flags and lagging putts from fifty feet away. The first putt is terrible, stopping twelve feet short. The next two are within four feet. The last ball is tracking toward the cup when K. J. Choi walks up and stops it with the end of his putter. Tiger is shaken out of his focus, sees the offender, and smiles. Direct interference may be the only way for the field to stop him at this point.

12:26 PM • There's nothing monstrous about the first hole at Doral. It's a 529-yard par 5 with only a few scattered palm trees to the right and left. Tiger booms his drive down the middle, so far in fact that he only has a mid-iron left. He lands it on the green and two-putts. One hole, one birdie. It's hard to know what a winning score is going to be this week. Last year, Tiger finished at 10 under and won by two shots. In 2006, he doubled that number, shot 20 under, but won by only one shot. I suggest that he just birdie the remaining 71 holes to take the guesswork out of things.

1:00 PM • The 2nd hole is even easier than the first—a 376-yard par 4 where Tiger's meticulously planned strategy is apparently to swing out of his shoes. I know it's early in the round, but so far I don't get this course. It's flat, boring, and easy. If that were the criteria to host a World Golf Championship, I should invite someone from the Tour to play Woodley Lakes Golf Course near a muni near my house that is often coated in a thin layer of goose excrement.

1:07 PM • The Blue Monster shows itself on number 3. It's the first water hole on the course and a mirror image of the 3rd at Bay Hill, a long par 4 turning around the left side of a lake. Last year this hole had the fourth-highest stroke average of any hole played on Tour. Today's wind must not be blowing the typical direction, because all Tiger needs is a fairway wood and a wedge to have ten feet for birdie. After missing the birdie on 2, he makes one here. Two under.

2:07 PM • Tiger pars his way to the 7th, a par 4 that reminds me of all the least interesting holes at Torrey Pines and Bay Hill. Long. Straight. Bunkers on both sides of the fairway. There are no choices, no risk/reward. Just hit it between the sand traps and onto the green. It's almost as though when a golf course architect doesn't know what else to do, he hits the "F7" key on his keyboard and out pops a hole like this.

4:15 PM • After a bogey on the 7th, Tiger picks up two more birdies on the par-5 8th and the par-5 10th. But 3 under is only a so-so score today. As he waits his turn on the 14th green, he looks at the leaderboard and sees that Australia's Geoff Ogilvy is done with a 7-under 65 and Phil Mickelson is in with a 5-under 67.

Mickelson long ago decided that his best tack as world number two is to gush about how much more talented Tiger is, then rise to the occasion and beat him just often enough to keep some people wondering. Of the three times Tiger has lost a fifty-four-hole lead on the PGA Tour, one came at the feet of Phil, who stole the 2001 Tour Championship away from him. And last year they dueled in the final pairing at the Deutsche Bank Championship with Phil holding Tiger off to win by two. Their relationship can be summed up by the fact that the only off-course activity they ever share is Ping-Pong between Ryder Cup and Presidents Cup matches. It's civil, but unless there's a win or loss at stake, the sport's two most talented players have nothing in common.

Seeing Phil ahead of him may be the motivation Tiger needs. He rolls in his birdie at 14 and gets to 4 under. With the players having crossed to the next tee, the marshal lowers the ropes and we funnel down 15. But the marshal doesn't see that Craig Connelly, Paul Casey's caddy, is still running the gauntlet. After zigzagging through the crowds, Connelly arrives on the tee and tells the marshal, "You forgot a guy!" The marshal looks toward 14 to see whom. He clarifies: *"Me!"* Connelly has an excuse for being on edge. In the first thirteen holes, Casey has six birdies, four bogeys, and only three pars.

Meanwhile, Tiger seems to have found a groove. His shot on the 175-yard 15th is within ten feet. He makes it to get to 5 under and is tied with Phil.

5:00 PM • If Tiger ever hits a longer tee shot this year than the one he hits on the 17th, I'll be shocked. After yells of "fore right!" from the tee, his drive smacks the cart path along the right side and bounds forward toward the hole. I pace it off and then triple-check the yardage—385 yards. And his angle to the hole could not be better, allowing him to play straight up the skinny neck of the green. He pitches it toward the hole; it jumps onto the green, curves toward the stick, and almost falls in for eagle. His third birdie in four holes puts him at 6 under, ahead of Mickelson and within one of Ogilvy.

5:12 PM • The Blue Monster has a few too many "F7s" for my taste, but Dick Wilson, the post–World War II architect who designed both this course and Bay Hill, certainly knows how to design a hard finishing hole. Unlike the par 4 he shaped at Bay Hill, there are no secrets here. 467 yards. Slightly elevated green. *Don't go left.* The lake that runs down that entire side of the hole is so terrifying to players that I've seen twice as many play from the trees on the right than ever actually hit the water. It's not all nightmares, however. The greatest finish at Doral came back in 2004 in a playoff between the penguin-shaped Craig Parry and my own ticket benefactor, Scott Verplank. Parry found the skinny strip of fairway, which was impressive in itself, then took a 6-iron and knocked it into the hole for an eagle and the win. It was such an impossible feat that the typically intense Verplank never went through the five stages of grief. He went straight to acceptance and started laughing. Last year Tiger came to the 18th with a three-shot lead and took the opposite approach. Rather than test the water, he laid up with his second shot, then two-putted for bogey and the win.

With the afternoon wind replaced by black clouds, Tiger blasts his drive and misses right, into one of the traps and 140 yards from the flag. He takes his pitching wedge from Stevie and burrows his feet into the sand. *Just make a par and get out of here.* His shot lands on, but the green is no less subtle than the water next to it. Tiger has left himself a good seventy feet up and over a ridge to the hole.

As Tiger walks to his ball on the front of the green, the threatening clouds have started to sprinkle, the third time this year that rain has held off until Tiger's nearly done with his round. He keeps his head down, nearly making the birdie but running it up the ridge and five feet by. In the time it takes him to walk to his ball, the sky unloads. It's just what the 18th at Doral needs, more water. Tiger acts as if he doesn't even feel it, which is possible considering his focus. With the rain cascading off the brim of his hat, he looks down at the ball, and then misses the par putt wide. It's the first time he has bogeyed an 18th hole since Dubai and only the 2nd time all year. It drops him back to 5 under and into a tie with Mickelson. If he wasn't planning on coming out firing on Friday, he is now.

FLORIDA CRAIG • My home for the week is only a few blocks from the beach in Fort Lauderdale, a yellow two-bedroom bungalow surrounded by heavy tropical trees and plants. Craig sits at the kitchen table reading *The Wall Street Journal* and wrapped in a blue bathrobe and a three-day old salt-and-pepper beard. On Friday morning, I haven't been awake for thirty seconds when he asks his first question of the day.

"What do you think Tiger is going to shoot today?"

I have no idea. "Sixty-nine."

"What makes you think that?"

Craig's life is an obsession with finding answers. Three and a half years ago he was an NYU law student working as an intern in the office of then attorney general Eliot Spitzer. His responsibilities were simple. Every day he would walk into an office lined from floor to ceiling with boxes of subpoenaed files and pick one, often at random. For the next eight hours, he would pull out every single page, examine it, then slip it back into place. The goal was to find evidence that Marsh & McLennan, one of the nation's largest insurance brokers, was at the center of a multicompany price-fixing scheme. Not even Spitzer knew exactly what that evidence would look like. And somehow Craig found it. On a single 8½-by-11-inch piece of paper. Within a few months, the CEO had resigned and Marsh & McLennan agreed to return $850 million to its policyholders.

A few years removed from sniffing out the smoking gun, Craig is trying to finish a book about corporate fraud in the Eliot Spitzer era, a topic that became a little more complicated when his former boss resigned as governor of New York seven days ago. At this point, Craig is slowly being driven mad by the frenzy of it, alternating between chewing tobacco to stay awake and Tylenol PM to sleep. After downing his morning coffee, he decides to push away from the keyboard and see Tiger Woods in person for the first time in his life.

SECOND ROUND

10:31 AM • Craig and I find a spot in the bleachers as Tiger begins his morning warm-up. Seeing his favorite athlete in the flesh has left Craig silent for a few minutes, but the questions are now flowing again.

"Who was the best man at Tiger's wedding?"

"Some childhood friend, I think."

"So it wasn't Stevie?"

"No, uh-uh."

"What do you think that says about their relationship that he was Stevie's best man but Tiger didn't ask Stevie to be his?"

"Huh. Never really thought about it." It isn't that Craig's questions aren't good. They are fantastic, actually. But my mind is somewhere else. I am stuck on the woman behind us who is embarrassing herself by asking her husband whether Zach Johnson will receive an invitation to the Masters this year since he won it last year.

Tiger's relationship with Steve Williams, like all of Tiger's relationships, remains hard to pin down. But unlike his marriage, this one exists almost exclusively in the public eye. It began here at Doral back in 1999. Stevie was on the bag of four-time major winner Ray Floyd when he received a call from Tiger, who floated the idea of Stevie coming on board. In a telling moment, Stevie hung up on him, believing it was a prank. Stevie doesn't put up with a lot of, well, crap. At the 2002 Skins Game, three years into their partnership, a fan snapped Tiger's picture while he was hitting out of a bunker on the 18th hole. Stevie took the camera and dropped it into a lake. In the second round of the 2004 U.S. Open, he kicked the lens of a New York *Daily News* cameraman, then snatched another camera away from a fan two days later. Stevie is aggressively loyal.

There is no quality Tiger demands more from his entourage than that, but then to ask Stevie to stand in his shadow during a day off at his wedding may have just seemed too cruel. As for why Stevie asked Tiger to be his best man, that one's easy: if you have one chance to make the biggest control freak in sports history play second fiddle to you, you do it.

11:12 AM • Tiger tees off on the 10th hole in three minutes, and we're not there. Craig and I are at the putting green waiting for his dad, Ray, who was supposed to join us but hasn't shown up yet. While Ray isn't Craig's birth father, he raised him from age five. Craig has called him

"Dad" for as long as he can remember, and when he turned twenty, he officially took Ray's last name. It's a strong bond, but when it looks as if Ray might make us miss Tiger's tee time, Craig says, "Screw him," and we run to the tee.

11:29 AM • The 10th hole at Doral is a 551-yard par 5 that takes a seventy-degree turn left halfway down the fairway. The entire left side is protected by water, with no traps to save you. All three players in Tiger's group wisely miss right with their second shots into the greenside bunkers.

Tiger tries to spin his third out of the trap, but it hits short and keeps rolling, almost off the back and into the water. With Tiger preparing for his fourth, I ask Craig if his dad has any distinctive features that might make him easy for me to spot. "He has a Van Dyke mustache." That shouldn't be hard. Within twenty seconds I see a skinny sixty-something guy in shorts walk by with a mop of brown hair and a matching Van Dyke mustache. "That him?" Craig turns around. "Dad!" Craig makes room for Ray, who arrives in time to see Tiger tap in for par.

12:06 PM • The par-5 12th hole at Doral doesn't seem hard, but the obscure stats say otherwise. Last year on Tour, it was the par 5 that had the fewest players attempting to reach it in two. It's long, for sure, 603 yards and uphill. But it should really receive some sort of Audubon Society award—to make it tighter off the tee, hundreds of new trees have been planted on the right side over the last few years. It also features a green completely surrounded by bunkers.

None of that scares Tiger from piping his drive and then going for it with his 3-wood anyway, from 265 yards. His second shot splashes down almost hole high in the left greenside trap. Craig, Ray, and I charge ahead and position ourselves behind the green for his third. The electronic scoreboard says he has thirty-eight feet to the pin. He smacks the sand and the ball pops up, bounces twice, and rolls toward the hole.

Tiger raises his wedge above his head, signaling anyone who was only half paying attention what is about to happen. It rolls into the hole for eagle. Craig lets out a therapeutic "Whoooooooa!" as Tiger casually kicks the sand off his spikes. As he retrieves the ball from the hole, they update the leaderboard. Tiger is on top.

12:57 PM • The cheers from his eagle echo across Doral, especially as the other scoreboards are updated, but it doesn't scare Ogilvy, who has again pulled ahead of Tiger as we reach the par-4 16th. The 16th is a 372-yard dogleg left par 4. That isn't how Tiger would describe it. In a straight line from tee to green, it is more like 325 yards. Craig, Ray, and I take a shortcut down the left side and pass another lake. There's so much water on this course that this one isn't even in play on any holes. Tiger's smashed drive comes down in the rough twenty yards short of the green. He pitches to ten feet, where his birdie putt thinks about lipping out before falling into the left side of the cup to tie Ogilvy again, this time at 8 under.

1:50 PM • Tiger returns to the 529-yard 1st. Holes like this must be what it was like for Tiger back in 2000 before his power caused every par 5 in the world to be lengthened seventy-five yards. Driver, 7-iron, six feet for eagle. He makes it for his second eagle of the day and is all the way to 10 under.

2:21 PM • Even though he had made birdie look easy on the tough 3rd hole yesterday, today he pulls it left and Craig and Ray have their first outside-the-ropes adventure with Tiger. With trees in front and water right, Tiger decides to just pitch back into the fairway. Once they're gone, Craig is still shocked that hundreds of people just ran full speed to crowd around a golf ball as if it were the last source of heat in a Siberian prison.

3:21 PM • A few holes later, Craig and his dad are on their own when I run into Chris, a tattooed fan who is wearing a red shirt covered in Tiger-related statistics:

> 1 Sam Alexis
> 86 worldwide wins
> 64 PGA Wins
> 13 Majors
> 9 Player of the Years
> 1 FedEx Cup

He says he ironed on every letter himself. I marvel at his work. "How did you get everything so straight?" I ask. "Used my eyes," he explains.

Up at the green on the par-5 8th, I reconnect with Craig and Ray in time to see Tiger make his best putt of the week, a fast, downhill ten-footer for birdie. Ray is a college professor at the University of Miami and limits his response to the putt with applause and a grin. Craig is a ball of energy. When Tiger crosses through to the 9th tee, Craig presses himself against the ropes and screams "TIGER!!!!" into the left ear of Louis Oosthuizen's wife, who has been putting up with the day's (typical) madness to support her Sunshine Tour–playing husband. She takes a deep breath, knowing there is just one hole left. The way Tiger is playing, I want to keep going.

3:46 PM • Tiger's last hole of the day, the par-3 9th, requires a 169-yard carry over water to a middle pin. The line is great, but the club is wrong, and it blows twenty feet past the hole.

It's not a realistic birdie putt by any means. It's speedy and has at least two different breaks in it. And yes, Craig has witnessed a pretty solid round—two eagles and two birdies—but I feel as if it hasn't quite been enough, so I call upon my Tigerpowers and contact the Man for the first time this week. "Come on, Tiger. How about a little more magic . . ." I whisper. Tiger starts his putt three feet right. It can't possibly break that much. But it hits the slope, just like the long bomb he made at the Buick in January, gains speed, cuts back to the left, and straightens out toward the cup. Tiger raises his putter straight above his head and walks the putt in the last foot. Most people give him a warm Friday cheer as he waves not once but twice as our roar gives way to sustained applause. Craig's reaction has more of a *Sunday-I've-lost-my-mind* feel to it. He screams as he jumps up and down, never once thinking about Eliot Spitzer.

The round of 66 puts Tiger one off the lead and into the final group on Saturday. We head for the car, rehashing the day as we walk. There are a few seconds of silence before Craig fills the void.

"So what do you think Tiger will shoot tomorrow?"

THE BIG WINNER • Once again, my spam folder has hit triple digits. It is one of the unforeseen consequences of filling out entry form for every single prize that is being given away on the PGA Tour this season. At the CA Championship alone, I have turned in close to thirty completed stubs to win a trip for two to the World Golf Hall of Fame. They are attached to the bottom of every ticket for the week, and when it poured on Thursday, the whole way back to the car was littered with opportunity. I'm sure it's exactly the vacation my wife has in mind for the end of the season.

She also won't be too excited about the his-and-her Jet-Skis that might be coming our way when my name is pulled from the raffle box at Bay Hill. But I had to. It was right next to the booth that was giving away tickets to see the Orlando Magic in a few weeks, and even though I won't be in Florida to use them, I am still keeping my fingers crossed.

Winning a prize would make up for the harassing e-mails I keep getting from the bamboo furniture factory in northern China that is anxiously wanting to do business with me. It will also help me forget the other e-mail that was apparently sent just to insult me. I never opened it, but the subject was "what a stupidface you have here bobsmiley."

Not all the e-mails in my spam folder are rude, however. The ones from my "Buick Concierge" are so personal I'm worried Hillary will read them and become concerned about the health of our marriage. "Hello Bob," she coyly begins. I know it is a she because next to the text is a photo of a woman standing in a gray pantsuit. After a slow intro, she turns up the heat. "Something piqued your interest. Perhaps it was a sleek, smooth exterior or the thought of spending time in a tranquil, peaceful cabin." *What is she talking about?* "Whether you desire the sheer beauty of Enclave, the sophisticated elegance of Lucerne, or the distinctive style of LaCrosse, you are interested in a wonderful vehicle." *Actually, I was interested in the free golf balls.* "I look forward to taking this journey with you. I'll e-mail again soon. Sincerely yours, The Buick Concierge." I've made Valentine's Day cards for my wife that are less suggestive than that. But all will be forgiven when we're sitting poolside at that new resort northeast of San Diego. We just have to sit through one little time-share presentation first.

THIRD ROUND

After Thursday, Tiger was at 5 under and the 2006 U.S. Open winner Geoff Ogilvy was at 6 under. After Friday, Tiger was at 11 under and Ogilvy was at 12 under. Ogilvy told reporters heading into the weekend that if he could just stay one shot ahead of Tiger every day, he'd be happy. For the thirty-year-old Ogilvy, the Open at Winged Foot was his last victory, and I understand why. In the twenty-one months since, he and his wife, Juli, have had two kids. While at Doral, Juli is sleeping in one room with two-month-old Jasper and Ogilvy is next door with year-and-a-half-year-old, Phoebe. He is having all-nighters, just not the ones that typically derail a young athlete's career.

9:35 AM • Joining Tiger and Ogilvy is another Australian, Adam Scott, who is three shots back of the lead at 9 under. I had figured the pairing of such big-name players would make today a zoo and have brought the periscope, but there's no one here. The locals must know something that I don't.

I head down the first fairway to meet Miller, my first acolyte. A six-foot-four University of Iowa freshman, he had read my original ESPN article about the Target World Challenge and decided to spend his spring break following Tiger for every hole of the CA Championship. It was quite a journey. First, his dad drove from their home in Kansas City to pick him up at school. Next, he flew to Texas to meet his sister and her boyfriend, Robert. From there the three of them drove twenty hours from Dallas to Miami. While his sister has stayed back at the pool, he and Robert have been here every day since Tuesday.

The big highlight? Tiger's bunker shot for eagle yesterday.

It wasn't the shot itself they cherish but the joy of the sand blowing into their eyes after he swung. It isn't the first time I've seen fans revel in bizarre moments. Last week at Bay Hill, Tiger hacked a shot out of the trees and sent grass flying. As Tiger walked away, a fan lit up and turned to his friend to say, "I tasted his divot!" Fans long to feel connected to Tiger, but since he provides such little personal interaction, we often find ourselves grasping for whatever scraps he leaves behind.

10:10 AM • The three players in the group could not have three more different starts. Tiger misses his opening drive well left, then finds a hole between trees and puts his second shot on the back of the green, leaving himself a long putt for eagle. Ogilvy misses right off the tee, hits a palm tree with his second, then drops his third into the greenside trap. Scott has no problems with anything and hits his second shot within ten feet for eagle.

Miller points out that even though they started at –12, –11, and –9, all three of them could be at −11 when the hole is finished. Can I call him my acolyte if he's more perceptive than I am? Ogilvy saves par from the trap to stay at 12 under, while Adam indeed makes eagle to get to −11. Tiger has a simple six-footer left for his birdie but, strangely, lips it out.

10:30 AM • Tiger is changing his strategy on number 2. After two days of hitting driver within forty yards and not making birdie, he lays back to a hundred. That doesn't work either. He rolls his birdie putt five feet by. Most of the season, I haven't been watching Tiger's short-par putts. He simply doesn't miss them. Yesterday he was ten for ten on all putts inside ten feet. But the missed birdie on the 1st has everyone sticking around, making sure that was just a temporary glitch in Tiger's flawless mechanics.

Unfortunately, it isn't. His par putt, like the last hole, lips out. After three-putting 18 on Thursday, he told reporters yesterday that he fumed about it all the way back to his boat. Now he has three-putted both of his first two holes.

10:36 AM • No one is more bothered by this two-hole start than Dave, a middle-aged Tiger fan in a Cuban guayabera shirt with a rich calypso accent. "Come on, Tiga . . . don't let dem do dat to you . . . ," he says as he heads toward number 3. Since I spotted him behind the first hole, he has been giving color commentary on the action, but not to get attention. He doesn't even seem aware that anyone hears him; he just can't contain it. After Tiger misses another makeable putt on the 3rd, Dave verbalizes what we're all fearing: "Oh, Jesus, 'av mercy. We are in deep sh**."

Calypso Dave has been here every day. Thursday wore him out, but he went home afterward, took a hot shower, rubbed lotion on his feet, and was back on Friday. "You're following *only* Tiga?" he asks. "Who else would I follow?" I say. He nods in approval, then starts to hum and keeps walking.

11:31 AM • On the 5th green, Scott makes another birdie putt to wrestle the lead away from Ogilvy. Tiger is in position to keep pace with a twelve-foot birdie of his own. "Tiga, I'm going home if you don't make dis," Dave says. A third lip out. Dave curses but doesn't follow through on his threat.

I'm glad I've found Dave because now that I've become a fan myself, I need someone who has my same level of expectations. I've been appalled over the last two weeks to realize how many people in Tiger's gallery have no interest in what he actually shoots. These aren't fans, per se, just people drawn here by the phenomenon; and if Tiger does something spectacular while they're watching, even better. They take many forms. There are the frat boys who bring their girlfriends in high heels. There are the soccer moms whose first reaction to Tiger is usually "Isn't he adorable?" The most irritating to me are the easily impressed spectators—the ones who are so ready to gush that they compliment Tiger on a "good shot!" that has already disappeared with a poof into a sand trap.

Calypso Dave would never do this, and in this moment he knows the only appropriate response to Tiger's putting is anxiety. As for Tiger, he just stretches his neck from side to side and walks to the next hole.

12:24 PM • Tiger makes his first birdie of the day on the 7th and is in position to erase more mistakes at the par-5 8th, where he has given himself another good chance. This time I notice his stroke. His typically smooth artist-like rhythm with the putter is gone. He merely swipes at the putt and misses. Something is wrong.

12:28 PM • On the 9th tee, Tiger separates himself from Scott and Ogilvy and walks to the side of the tee box to talk to himself as he had in San Diego, Dubai, and Tucson. This has become a predictable part of his routine when he is struggling and never fails to spark a return to form. I wait for him to lower his head, but his focus is broken as he looks across the lake and sees Mark Calcavecchia, the heavyset forty-seven-year-old, who is huffing and puffing in the humidity as he walks down the 10th fairway. Last year, Calcavecchia joked with reporters that after playing a lot of golf, he "couldn't run out of a burning house." Tiger never does refocus. He looks at the proudly out-of-shape Calc and laughs, then hits a mediocre shot to the green.

1:05 PM • At the beginning of the day, I didn't understand why there were so few people here. Now I know. After the cameraman on the 10th films Tiger making an ugly par, he pulls out his plastic rain cover and secures it around his equipment. I look up to the sky and see some dark clouds, but, even more alarming, I see the MetLife blimp heading north as fast as it's two eighty-horsepower engines can fly.

1:11 PM • The first drops of water start to fall as Tiger plays down the 11th. His thirty-foot birdie putt burns the edge as the drips turn to rain. I'm halfway to the 12th tee when a single blast of air horns rings out around the golf course, signaling the immediate suspension of play.

Within fifteen seconds, Tiger has his watch on, the physical manifestation of his return to reality. I turn around, and a fleet of Cadillac SUVs is suddenly idling behind the green. The caddies throw the bags in the back and hop in, with Ogilvy, the leader by three, brazenly taking shotgun over Tiger. The Escalades slip out an exit used by maintenance workers, and two minutes after the horns blow, every player on the entire course is gone.

We spectators, of course, are afforded no such luxuries. Having long ago lost track of Miller and Calypso Dave, I move under a tree to wait it out and notice that I am the only golf fan at Doral who isn't leaving. One man even pulls a giant palm frond off a tree and covers his head as he flees. The locals seem convinced that this will get worse before it gets better. I give in and head back.

4:40 PM • Three and a half hours later, it is still raining. If it weren't for my streak of never missing a hole, I would be long gone. But I can't risk the chance that the storm will pass, the course will dry out, and they'll try to play a few holes before dark.

Over that stretch of time, I have huddled under leaky grandstands, I have stood inside a concession stand, I have received a complimentary massage from some women who work at the Doral Spa, and I have collected another dozen entry forms for that dream trip to the Golf Hall of Fame. I have even been so bored that I stood and watched as Stevie sat by himself and ate a sandwich.

But finally, after doing all that and with the electronic scoreboard giving no more information than "Weather delay," I am out of things to do. I spot a man with a name tag and ask how I can find out if play has been canceled for the day. "Play *has* been canceled for the day," he says. That was easy.

The deluge could not have come at a better time for Tiger. He can return to his yacht, go back to bed, and pretend that today never happened.

ISLEWORTH RED • This has been my longest stretch away from home since either of my kids was born. Eleven nights and counting. Back in L.A., going that long without a father figure was having its effect on Danny. Apparently he had spent most of Saturday walking around the house carrying a bag and declaring "I have a purse just like Mama!" Hillary tried to counteract it by teaching him how to shoot baskets into a trash can. I have never seen her shoot a basket in my life and suspect that this might be just as damaging to his eventual manhood. I need to get home, but it turns out I will be staying in Florida even longer than I thought. And the reason has nothing to do with the weather.

During the first round back at Bay Hill, I was talking with a guy from Tampa who asked me if I were going to the Tavistock Cup. The Tavistock Cup is the annual two-day event between Tiger's Isleworth Golf Club and the rival golf club in Orlando, Lake Nona. It's not an official event on the Tour schedule, but every year it trades off locations and this year it just happens to be at Isleworth. I knew all about it. I just didn't know it started on Monday.

When I told Hillary I was adding a third tournament to my Florida trip, her reaction was the same as my mechanic friend Bryan's when I made him keep walking with me to the far side of the 18th at the Match Play with a pulled groin: "At this point, what does it matter?" Once I tracked down someone willing to part with one of the hard-to-get passes for the event, the only thing I needed was a collared red shirt. "*Isleworth* red," the member told me. Apparently, if anyone in the gallery shows up without wearing one of the two team colors, he will be denied entrance.

So after Saturday's shortened round at Doral, I go where surely no other person at the über-wealthy Tavistock Cup will be going to procure a red shirt: the Salvation Army. It has a great selection, actually. I almost get to the register with the first one I find, but notice it has the name "Glenda" stitched onto the front. Another one is the shirt from someone's old Target uniform. A third one has a big crawfish on the lapel. At last I find a plain, logo-free collared red shirt. It is only $2.99, which leaves me enough for a new (old) pair of khaki shorts. If I am really going to see Tiger's neighborhood after all, I need to look presentable.

THIRD ROUND, SUNDAY

8:45 AM • About forty serious Tiger fans have beaten me to the 12th tee, where round three will pick up again. I look toward the driving range and see Tiger slowly walking with Stevie down the 10th fairway. Even though it's round three, Tiger is already sporting his Sunday red shirt. Except it is really a Sunday pink, which isn't the powerful statement he really needs to be making at this point.

Keeping pace with him are a few dozen other fans. It's exactly like that *SportsCenter* commercial where Tiger is walking by himself through the quiet ESPN offices, only to reveal that he still has a gallery trailing behind him. Though the fans have to walk around the 11th green, Tiger and Stevie walk in a straight line, under the ropes, across 11, back under the ropes, and up onto 12.

Tiger is all smiles. When Adam Scott arrives, Tiger shakes his hand and says, "Good luck, man." When Geoff Ogilvy walks up, Tiger shakes his hand and says, "Good luck today, buddy." *Buddy?* This is the guy who is now leading by three! What happened to Mom's "You must kill that person"?

Ogilvy is already standing behind his ball when the horns blow. Without looking back at Tiger or Adam, he says, "Good luck, boys," and stripes his drive right down the fairway.

9:30 AM • Tiger misses a twelve-foot putt for birdie on the 12th, but the real sign that he still isn't comfortable with his putter comes on the 13th. While Ogilvy and Scott are busy chipping, Tiger stands off to the side and works on his stroke. Back and through. Over and over. This is something most golfers and many pros do all the time between shots, but never Tiger. He can no longer afford to hide the fact that something is faulty with his mechanics. Ogilvy and Scott have both played, and it's Tiger's turn to putt, whether he wants to or not. He misses again.

10:08 AM • After two more pars, Tiger hits a solid approach on the par-4 16th, past the far right pin within twelve feet. Ogilvy is a few feet outside Tiger and casually makes the quick downhiller. Tiger had to learn something about the speed by watching it, but that's not his problem. His putt wobbles off to the right. Another unhelpful par. As Ogilvy walks to the next tee, Tiger just stands in place and stares at his ball in frustration.

10:44 AM • One more incredible lip-out on 17 and a final missed birdie putt on the last, and Tiger is finished. At least with the third round. One bogey, one birdie, sixteen pars. Seventy-two. Still stuck at 11 under par, his awful putting has put him 5 back of Ogilvy. He's been passed by plenty of others, too, and they aren't a bunch of nobodies: Adam Scott, Vijay Singh, Jim Furyk, and Retief Goosen. He could expect one or two of them to slip, but all of them? Not likely.

Tiger said in his Wednesday press conference that one area where he has seen the most improvement is his ability to fix things in the middle of his round, saying it has allowed him to take a round that should be a 73 or 74 and turn it into a 64. So either he failed to fix his game today or he did fix it and his 72 was really an 82 in disguise. I fear he's stumped. After signing his scorecard, he walks past security, ignores the autograph seekers, and disappears into the resort. He has three hours to figure things out.

FINAL ROUND

Before I went to bed last night, Craig asked me what I thought the chances were that Tiger would still win this week. I said 60 percent. After the closing seven holes of round three, I'm down to 20 percent. As easy as Tiger has made clutch putts appear this year, the ability to stroke the putter on the correct line is so much more feel than any other aspect of the game of golf. When a player is putting well, there's nothing technical about it. And when a player is putting *really* well, it's almost mystical.

In the best round of golf I ever played, I was 3 over par on the front, which was good but not unbelievable. As I stood on the 10th hole, looking at my thirty-five-foot birdie putt, I suddenly felt I would make it.

And I did. And then I birdied the 12th. And the 14th. And the 16th. Short, long, uphill, downhill, it was irrelevant. The ball was going to go in. This wasn't happening on any course; this was my home course—the same place where as an eight-year-old I would purposefully hit it into the bunkers so I could play in the sand. Even more special, I was playing with my dad, who was so nervous for me that he hadn't spoken in two hours. I came to the 18th green facing a twisting downhill putt for a par and a back-nine 33. I didn't stand over the putt and say, "Okay, now make sure you open the blade exactly five degrees when you take it back . . ." I looked at where I wanted the ball to go and then hit it there. And I made it.

Right now Tiger is looking where he wants it to go and it simply isn't going there. The longest putt he has made in the last two days: six and a half feet. Even if he knows what he is technically doing wrong, I'm not convinced that even Tiger Woods can master the feel he needs to execute it in time.

2:01 PM • Of course, I never considered that his solution would be to just knock it inside six and a half feet. He makes a four-footer on the 1st hole for a quick birdie. Twelve under par. On the short 2nd, the easy hole he has managed to play 1 over for the week, he rolls in a birdie from fifteen feet. Twenty percent chance of winning? Shame on me.

2:19 PM • He finds himself with an eight-foot par putt on the 3rd to keep the momentum going. If it were to go in, I would consider him cured. But for the fifth time in two rounds, Tiger lips out a putt. Golf is not a game of inches. It's a game of millimeters, and that fractional loss of alignment with Tiger's stroke is enough to jeopardize a streak that goes back to last September.

As Tiger walks to the 4th tee with his head down, the air horns blow and Tiger is once again ushered toward a waiting Escalade. Even more frustrating, it's not even raining. There are some dark clouds to the south, but not here. No fans leave this time except for Miller from Iowa, who has a twenty-hour drive to Texas ahead of him tonight. I feel bad because he came all this way and caught Tiger's worst tournament of the year. He feels bad because he never once heard Tiger curse. If he keeps putting like this, it's only a matter of time.

3:25 PM ● After a baffling hour of suspended play that saw a total of seven or eight raindrops and zero lightning, many of the fans have decided that God is punishing us for missing church on Easter and have headed home. I take an empty spot in the front row next to the 4th tee. The 4th hole at Doral is the last place any player wants to restart his round. It's the most difficult par-3 on the course, 236 yards over water. Earlier in the week it was playing into the wind and Tiger had to hit a 5-wood. He was still short of the green.

Finally, I see the fleet of Escalades off in the distance. It starts in a single line and then begins splintering off in various directions around the course. Tiger's Cadillac doesn't pull any closer than the 14th tee, leaving him and Stevie to walk the rest of the way on foot. Tiger is not on the tee for more than thirty seconds when a Tour official with an earpiece walks up to the players with a smirk and whispers something. Stevie eavesdrops and immediately picks up Tiger's bag and starts walking away. Tiger follows him and does a half turn toward us and waves. "See ya, guys." And then he's gone.

Huh?

It's another delay.

In the seven hours since he teed off on the 12th hole, Tiger has played only ten holes. I've never been more exhausted and seen less golf in my life. And again, no rain. It's fishy. I'll blame the Australasians. Here's my thinking. Clearly they see that one of their own, Ogilvy, is in the lead and notice that Tiger is desperately trying to make a Sunday charge. It's golf's version of icing the kicker. Satisfied at my increasing ability to blame anyone but Tiger, I stretch out on the grass and wait for the imaginary storm to pass.

4:45 PM • I have never fallen asleep on a golf course before. It is incredible. A cool Miami breeze, the smell of fresh cut grass, no rain . . . Unfortunately, when I awaken, Tiger is still 5 shots back.

The caddies come into view first. Tiger is trailing behind. He has to be tired of this ritual. It's been two and a half hours since the original delay. At some point in the blur of this endless afternoon, I have run into Craig's dad, Ray with the Van Dyke mustache, who came back today with Craig's mom and some family from Minnesota. I tell Craig's teenage nephew Stephen that if he starts to applaud when Tiger arrives at the tee, I'll join in. Stephen leads the way, I follow, and the other thirty fans who have stuck around add to the warm welcome. On a day like this, even Tiger needs some extra motivation. He nods, appreciative. If he somehow pulls this off, I can definitely say I played a role in his comeback.

Despite our support, Tiger takes a long iron off the tee and hits it terribly. I put my hands on my head as I watch it start dead right. The ball should be wet, but the wind that has come up in the last two hours holds it back and it stays on the bank right of the green.

After so many rain delays, there are fewer fans here than in Dubai, no more than a hundred, so I have an unobstructed view of Tiger's five-foot putt to save par. He starts it two inches outside to the left, and it never moves. It's dead straight. He either misread it or made a poor stroke. Or both. Back-to-back bogeys on 3 and 4, and he is right back where he was four hours ago. Heck, he's right back where he was twenty-nine hours ago! The Australasians have gotten their wish. They have killed Tiger's momentum.

7:03 PM • The next six holes are an exercise in futility. Tiger makes an easy birdie on 6, then puts himself behind a palm tree and has to scramble for a par on 7. He plays like a tactician on the par-5 8th, hitting the fairway, then the green and two-putting for another birdie. But on the par-3 9th, just when he seemed to be finding a way to scrape out a good round, a photographer snaps a shot right in his backswing. "Not in my swing!" he yells the second the ball is airborne. The ball is yanked way left and nearly slips into the lake. He walks to the far side of the tee box as Stevie turns around and looks for the culprit.

Every player deals with photographers. But only Tiger has to do so on every single shot he plays. I want Stevie to go after the guy and swallow his memory card whole. I want him to take his telephoto lens, place it on a tee, and have Tiger Sasquatch it all the way back to the media tent. But he doesn't know who it was. Neither do I. The photographers, of course, all do the collective "Not me!" look and stare up and down their line as if whoever did do it is really going to raise his hand and own up.

Then, adding insult to injury, Tiger's par putt lips out.

And so does his birdie putt on 10. *Seven* lip-outs in twenty-eight holes. I have friends who would melt their putters in a furnace if that happened. The reality of Tiger's failure is finally setting in. When he walks off the green, most of the fans don't say anything. They just watch him go in confused silence. The only cheer anyone tries is one of consolation. "It's okay, Tiger . . ."

7:15 PM • Play is called for darkness as he makes another uninspired par on 11. His day will end in the exact same place it started—next to the tee at number 12—meaning it just took Tiger ten hours to play 18 holes of golf. As he walks to a waiting golf cart, one delusional fan still has life in him and yells out, "Plenty of golf left, Tiger!" Well, he's five shots out of the lead with seven holes to play, and almost every player in front of him has won at least one major. If he pulls a victory off, it will be the greatest comeback of his career.

Tiger's streak isn't the only one in jeopardy on Sunday night. When play is suspended for darkness, I figure that means the first round of Monday's Tavistock Cup will simply be pushed back until Tuesday. But a lot of the Tavistock players are committed to being at next week's regular PGA Tour event on Wednesday, so the best they can do is push the tee times back a few hours until Monday afternoon. So? Well, my guesstimate is that Tiger will finish his fourth round in Miami around 10:20 a.m. He is now scheduled to tee off at the Tavistock Cup in Orlando at 1:42 p.m. Taking a private jet, the three-hour-and-twenty-two minute window is no problem for him. But all I have is my Rav4 and a Google Maps printout that says the drive will take three hours and *forty-nine* minutes. I have quite a day ahead of me.

FINAL ROUND, MONDAY

Even a World Golf Championship becomes a ghost town on a Monday finish. Gone are the Cadillac salesmen and their brochures. Gone are the chipper volunteers handing out CA visors to every person walking through the gates. In fact, gone is anyone at the gate. I just waltz on in. In the big WGC merchandise tent, all that is left is fifteen brown CA Championship T-shirts. Yesterday they were marked down to $10. Today they're $5. The concession stand near the 18th green isn't even being manned by volunteers anymore. A Miami rehab center has agreed to work the registers and sell what's left of the food in exchange for 8 percent of the receipts.

But Tiger is still here. And he is still wearing the same worthless pink shirt from yesterday.

8:20 AM • If there were ever a day this year where Tiger might recognize my face, it is this morning. Back out at the 12th tee, there are no more than twenty of us lined up single file along the left side of the tee box. There isn't even any press, with Luau Larry nowhere to be seen. It's such a small group that it feels awkward when Tiger shows up and we stand in silence. It seems almost rude of us to not say something. So a brave man with his hands in his pockets does.

"Good luck today."

Tiger turns and faces him. "Thank you," he says. It's the first fan Tiger has looked in the eye this season whom he hasn't hit in the head with a ball first. Another fan sees the rareness of the opportunity.

"So can you do it today?"

Tiger thinks about it as he bounces the end of his driver lightly on the wet grass with his left hand.

"It'll be tough."

"Six birdies?" another man asks.

"I don't know. Might not be enough. Might need seven." The conversation comes to a casual and natural end. It is such a random, intimate moment in a year that has been everything but. He is a real person, briefly. And the fact that he has a number in his head gives me hope. Because it shows that even though so many things have gone wrong in the last two rounds, he hasn't given up. He has clearly spent at least a minute thinking about what specifically he will have to do to pull this off.

Seven birdies in seven holes. His best run in stroke play this year remains the back nine at Dubai, where he had six birdies in nine holes. But if his putter catches fire, anything is possible. My confidence renewed, I map out the game plan in my head:

Hole 12: par 5 = 3
Hole 13: par 3 = 3
Hole 14: par 4 = 3
Hole 15: par 3 = 2
Hole 16: par 4 = 2
Hole 17: par 4 = 3
Hole 18: par 4 = 4

As long as he eagles the par-5 12th and the drivable par-4 16th, he could get to 19 under and have to par only the tough 13th and nasty

18th. And if the wheels fall off Ogilvy as they did for Els back in February, well, who knows what might happen?

8:30 AM • As we wait for the horn to blow, Tiger's ball is already sitting on the tee. Which is good. I need everyone in this group to play as quickly as possible. I've got a 1:42 tee time back in Orlando.

The horns sound, and Tiger hits it down the left side, in line with the bunker. A fan calls out, "Come back!" There are so few of us that Tiger finishes his thought: "A little! A little!" The shot misses the bunker and stays in the left rough.

Playing with Tiger is Denmark's Anders Hansen and South Africa's Tim Clark, neither of whom can remember who has the honors from yesterday. They clearly don't know this is costing me precious seconds.

8:46 AM • Tiger has a twenty-foot putt for birdie on 12. He makes it! It's jolting to see a putt of any length drop after his clumsy putting over the last forty-eight hours. Thirteen under . . . you just never know . . .

9:06 AM • Tiger misses his birdie putt on the 13th, which is understandable on a 245-yard par 3, but when he misses only a *nine*-footer on 14, that hurts. We all groan in agony. These fans get it. You don't come out early on a Monday morning to watch Tiger play only seven holes when he's down by 5 unless you truly believe he is amazing enough to find a way to win.

9:17 AM • The whole year has seen far too many people scream "Get in the hole!" but when I see Tiger's shot into the 175-yard 15th, I reflexively yell it because, well, the ball looks as if it might go in. It is dead on line with the flag on the right side. The cup itself is blocked from view by the fronting bunker, but after it disappears behind the trap, I see the dozen fans up at the green start jumping up and down as they cheer. I run up to find Tiger's ball is literally two inches left of the cup. I didn't factor an ace into my preround equations. It's his best shot of the week, and if he loses, no one except the twenty of us will remember. The birdie drops him to 14 under. Ogilvy hasn't moved and is still at –17. Tiger is only three back with three to play.

9:26 AM • Tiger is back on the almost drivable 372-yard 16th. He grabs his driver, sees that the group ahead is still on the green, and tells Tim Clark, "I'll wait." I love it. When the green has cleared, Tiger tees up his ball and asks all of us on the left side of the tee to please move back. He sets up and gives one last look around the corner, and I smile. I know Tiger Woods is about to swing as hard as he physically can. When his club face explodes into the ball, I imagine that just over the fence to our right, inside the Miami police shooting range, fifty cops just hit the deck. It goes a long way, but is too high and balloons into the air. "Damn it!" he yells. I start running, somehow thinking that my personal speed has some correlation with how fast Tiger will play.

Tiger's ball comes to rest on the front edge of the bunker short of the green, but it's not totally in the sand. It's a bad break. From there he could be aggressive, but he might flop it into the sand if it comes out too soft. The best he can do is to pitch it twenty feet past the hole and hope to make the putt coming back. The putt is close, but he misses. Still three shots back.

9:55 AM • Tiger still isn't quitting. He sticks his second shot into the 17th only four feet from the hole. He makes it to get to 15 under. Ogilvy hasn't done a thing and remains stuck at 17 under. Neither has anyone else. If Tiger can summon whatever juju Craig Parry used to eagle the 18th four years ago, he can actually still win.

10:06 AM • His drive on the last hole is a bomb, over 320 yards, down the right side of the fairway and the absolute best possible angle for

Doral's traditional Sunday pin position—back left. He arrives at his ball dead serious. His heroics this morning have given him a chance, albeit small. Had he made that birdie on 14 and the ace on 15, a par here might have been enough for a playoff. The shot is a little downwind, and at the last second he swaps out his pitching wedge for a 9-iron.

Stevie backs away, and a thought crosses my mind. Am I about to witness the greatest shot in Tiger's career? After all, every tournament so far has yielded a mind-boggling shot that has made the previous tournament's mind-boggling shot less . . . boggling. Tiger gives a last look at his target (the bottom of the cup) and swings. It's right on line, but it looks a little short. "Go! Go!" I yell. It hits ten feet short on the upslope to the back tier. "Bounce!" I scream. It bounces once, then stops and spins back down the hill, twenty feet from the hole.

On Saturday, I couldn't have conceived of a way in which I would be applauding a Tiger loss, but as he shakes his head and walks to the green, we cheer. The last time Tiger lost, one of my children wasn't even born yet.

If there were ever a day for him to phone in the rest of his round, it would have been today. He never even gave it a thought. Before he hits his birdie putt, I bend down and retie my shoes. This is the *easy* part of my day. Tiger's putt glides up the hill, breaks left, and stops a foot away. His streak is dead, but mine is still alive. The moment the ball stops rolling, I take off like a madman past the clubhouse and make for the Rav4.

CHEZ TIGER

The Tavistock Cup

Isleworth Country Club
Windermere, Florida
March 24–25, 2008

I have three and a half hours to make what should be a four-hour trip. Once I leave the Blue Monster and turn left on Doral Boulevard, it's another half-mile sprint to my car. Well aware of the challenge I am facing today, I didn't risk general parking and the likely wait for the shuttle bus. I'm parked illegally at a bank, facing out, with the gas tank topped off. On the passenger seat, directions that say I'm 243 miles from Isleworth.

As I turn on the Palmetto Expressway, I get the sinking feeling that maybe Tiger's 15 under par finish could get him into a playoff and I'm a complete fool for leaving. I call Craig, who is at home watching the coverage. He gives me the play-by-play down the stretch. When Jim Furyk makes his six-footer to post 16 under, I lay into the accelerator and head north. Ten minutes later, Ogilvy wins with a 17-under finish. Tiger putted like Frankenstein and lost by only two.

I've calculated I need to average eighty miles an hour to pull this off, which means I also need to avoid slow toll lines, road construction, and, most costly, Florida state troopers. The one thing I forget to factor is my own stupidity, which comes into play when I miss the turnoff for the turnpike. The mistake costs me a precious five minutes.

California doesn't have turnpikes, and I'm not sure I understand the concept. Apparently I'm paying Florida for a highway that is just two lanes. It gives me no choice but to become the kind of driver I normally can't stand as I weave between traffic, tailgate the fast drivers, and flash my lights at the slow ones. At one point, the passenger in one of the cars I'm trying to pass leans out his window and says, "Take it easy! It's only Monday!"

By noon, I assume Tiger is leap-frogging me in his private jet, traveling 700 percent faster than I am with his seat fully reclined. He's too high to catch a whiff of the mile-long dump that parallels the turnpike just west of Palm Beach. I fumble to shut down my air-conditioning, but it's too late. The car reeks.

The road heads north past Jupiter Island, where Tiger owns close to twelve acres stretching from the Intracoastal Waterway to the Atlantic. He bought the first ten acres in late 2005 for $38 million, a local record. He demolished the preexisting property, but the last report is that Tiger's not sure when he'll finish the proposed 10,000-square-foot home and move the family from Isleworth. I wonder if his Realtor mentioned he's only seven minutes up the turnpike from that landfill.

I reach my halfway mark, 122 miles from the course. Tiger will be on the driving range in thirty minutes. For the first time since I was sixteen, my speedometer climbs to ninety. In doing so, I pass a guy in a black Mercedes convertible and do a double-take. As he drives along with the top down, he's steering with one hand and playing a miniature trumpet with the other. I can't decide which of us is more reckless.

Only an hour left, and I'm still 79 miles from Orlando. I don't even know if I'll cut it close at this point. I spot a trooper lurking behind an overpass and shift from drive down to third so he doesn't see any brake lights. The Rav responds, dropping to a respectful seventy-one miles per hour.

With six minutes to go, I'm off the highway and onto the main drag of Tiger's hometown of Windermere, a sleepy hamlet where I'm learning that drivers obey the twenty-five miles per hour speed limit. After going ninety, it feels like slow motion.

It's 1:42 p.m. Tiger is on the 1st tee, and I am still looking for a parking spot. My streak is dead, too. Four hundred and five consecutive holes until now. If I had just caught that first turnpike turnoff or picked some faster toll lanes, things might have been different. I want to be bitter and sulk, but I remember the lesson Tiger taught me this morning at the CA Championship: keep fighting, all the way, no matter what. So once inside the gates of Isleworth, I start to run.

Every year, a few days after the Los Angeles Marathon has ended, there is inevitably a local news story about someone who is still on the course, someone who has severely injured himself along the way but won't quit and is willing himself (now through rush-hour traffic) toward the finish line (which doesn't even exist anymore). I'm that guy. And after a good mile of running past mansions, each one more amazing than the one before, I have nothing left. My legs are heavy from the long drive, my feet are still wet from walking Doral, and all I've eaten today is a free granola bar I grabbed at Bay Hill. So when I hear a golf cart coming up behind me, I do something that probably doesn't happen much around here—I stick out my thumb. The middle-aged Isleworth member behind the wheel slows down, I hop on the back, and my new friend John takes me the last half mile.

On the tee at number 3, I once again find Tiger. It's been three hours and fifty-eight minutes since I left him at Doral. As I catch my breath and relish what may be the most beautiful place I've ever seen, a new streak begins.

THE BUZ AT ISLEWORTH • The best player at my home course growing up was a guy about my dad's age named Buz. Another member once bet Buz that he couldn't make a 4 on eighteen straight holes. He went out and made seventeen 4s in a row before coming to the last hole, a par 5, where he accidentally made an eagle 3 and lost the bet. Twenty years later,

Buz claims it never happened, but my friends and I remember the story clearly. I was in awe of Buz from that day forward, believing that making eagles when you are actively trying not to is playing the game of golf at a level bordering on the paranormal. I couldn't imagine how the kids at Isleworth handle the fact that their club's best player is Tiger Woods.

Tiger might not be here if it weren't for Tour veteran Mark O'Meara. Like Arnold Palmer, the first time O'Meara saw Tiger was at the 1991 U.S. Junior Amateur at Bay Hill. After watching the fifteen-year-old kill a drive on the 9th hole, O'Meara said, "Okay, I've seen enough." He knew then that Tiger was the next big thing. They developed a friendship, and when Tiger left Stanford in 1996, O'Meara opened his home to the Tour rookie, even trying to set him up on dates with his own kids' babysitters. In return, Tiger pushed O'Meara during early-morning practice rounds and encouraged the declining pro not to set-tle for less in his golf game. Two years later, at the age of forty-one, O'Meara won the Masters. Three months after that, he won the British Open. When Tiger's eight-figure endorsement check from Nike cleared, he could afford to live, well, anywhere. He bought a house in O'Meara's Isleworth neighborhood.

Isleworth isn't old by golf standards. Twenty-five years ago it was a sprawling piece of land southwest of Orlando covered in orchards and surrounded by lakes and cypress trees. A group of investors headed by Arnold Palmer bought the land, built the course, and developed the high-end community before selling it to the Tavistock Group in 1993. When Tiger Woods moved in a few years later, a number of young stars followed suit. The roster of Tour players at Isleworth quickly ri-valed that of Orlando's other Tavistock-owned club, Lake Nona, and the neighborhoods began debating the question of who might win in a match between their best players.

The Tavistock Cup is now in its fifth year, and while it isn't an of-ficial event, it has a $3.8 million purse and is broadcast to more than eighty countries. If nothing else, it's beautiful to see that in such a crazy, mixed-up world, rich people of different gated communities have found a way to peacefully coexist.

FIRST ROUND

The only thing that reveals how long a day this has been for Tiger is his pants, which after seven holes of golf and a plane ride, lack their usual crispness. Gone, finally, is that pink shirt, replaced by his personal Team Isleworth mock T. The shirt is red, the sleeves are black, and on his left arm is his name and the Nike swoosh, lest anyone forgot.

The Tavistock Cup is comprised of two eleven-man teams competing to earn points toward a team total. Today's matches consist of two-man better-ball medal match play, a format whose name alone ensures that no one can understand what is happening. Essentially, Tiger and his partner (a senior tour player and friend of Tiger, John Cook) will each play a ball and take the lower score between them to build an eighteen-hole total. Their two Lake Nona opponents (Henrik Stenson and Northern Ireland's Graeme McDowell) will do the same. The low score after the round earns two points and a tie wins one, a loss zero. Tomorrow's format is four-ball singles, with each player competing against both of the two opponents in their foursome in an eighteen-hole stroke play match. Making it stroke play rather than match play guarantees that every match, even the blowouts, go the full eighteen holes.

2:15 PM • The teams hit their drives, and I head down number 3 fairway. And I mean fairway. To my delight, the Tavistock Cup doesn't set up any ropes along the holes, thus allowing the privileged two hundred of us who are here to walk wherever we would like, including right behind and next to the players. Heading toward the green on the expansive par-5 3rd, I am literally walking in Tiger Woods' footsteps.

It's such a different perspective on a golf tournament. The entire hole is laid out in front of me, not to the side. Unlike trudging through the rough or the desert, the spongy fairway beneath my feet is comforting, safe. Tiger and I are nearly one.

"Please allow room for the players, sir."

"Sorry."

Okay, so there are limits to how close I can get.

2:24 PM • Well, I have tried for two holes to pretend that I actually care about who wins, but I don't. And as much as they build up this rivalry between the two clubs and claim to keep the trophy secured in a four-inch-thick vault, I don't think anyone else cares that much either.

When I was at Doral, someone referred to the Tavistock Cup as "the biggest cocktail party in golf." That seems to be about right. Residents in blue and red shirts stroll the fairways with their Top-Siders and their Bloody Marys, at times too burdened by their unwieldy celery sticks to applaud. So, for once, I begin tuning out exactly what is at stake and enjoy the scenery and the scene.

Standing out from the sweater-around-the-neck crowd is Stevie, who is wolfing down a Styrofoam container of French fries. I don't think the Tavistock Cup is his favorite assignment. Throughout the season I have noticed that he puts on his caddie bib at the last possible second and always takes it off before Tiger putts out on the 18th. Someone noticed he wasn't wearing it when Tiger made his birdie to win at Bay Hill. Stevie's explanation: "I wasn't thinking playoff." Today he's not wearing it at all. For someone doing an intrinsically subservient job, I see it as his subtle form of rebellion. As for the fancy Tavistock Cup golf bags the players have been given, he has no choice. He drags Tiger's about ten yards before begrudgingly picking it up and heading down the fairway with his fries.

2:38 PM • On the 4th hole at Isleworth, a 479-yard dogleg left, Tiger cuts too much off the corner and finds a fairway bunker. I walk right up to the edge and look down at him. He eyes the flag cut way right, then notices that a couple of photographers have positioned themselves exactly in his line at the front edge of the bunker. "Uh . . . yeah," he says, "that's not a good spot." They move, and he casually hits one of his most impressive shots of the year. From 161 yards (I'm standing on the marked sprinkler head), his iron from the sand starts out high and at the middle of the green. A safe shot. Then it suddenly bends hard to the right and lands within twenty feet of the hole. A brilliant shot.

3:35 PM • As we approach the clubhouse, the crowds have swelled from a few hundred to maybe a thousand, which is still not enough to prohibit me from walking in a straight line wherever I want to go.

"Sir, you need to give the players more space."

"Sorry."

4:15 PM • Between the 1st and 10th tees at Isleworth sits a replica of Arturo Di Modica's famous sculpture of the Wall Street bull. The head of the Tavistock Group is the British tycoon Joe Lewis, an investor who, a week and a half ago, lost more than a billion dollars when Bear Stearns was bought by JP Morgan. The bull is supposedly not for sale. Not yet.

Tiger cuts the corner off the tee on the 409-yard 10th, hitting it ninety yards past the other players in his group. His eighty-eight-yard pitch into the hole sucks off the front, and he has to chip his third. After a quick look at the line, he hits it and watches as it lips out, his eighth one in three days. He smiles and turns to Stevie. "Looks familiar, doesn't it?" It's slightly reassuring that he is still not on his game this afternoon. If he had shown up and made everything in sight, I might have ordered a stiff drink of my own.

5:17 PM • Isleworth is set in and around a series of enormous lakes, the largest more than a mile and a half wide. In the summer, the club sometimes brings in professional water-skiers to coach the neighborhood kids. It explains the over-the-top prizes on the par-3 11th, where five brand-new ski boats are floating in a pond to reward any player who makes a hole in one. Even wilder are the eleven brand-new black Cadillac Escalades lining both sides of the 223-yard 15th. To win one, a player doesn't need to ace the hole. He only needs to win the closest-to-the-pin contest. If he does make a hole in one, every member of the team wins an SUV. When a dealer is willing to line a hole with almost a million dollars worth of cars, it's safe to assume the tournament doesn't include a pro-am.

6:20 PM • Tiger and John Cook arrive at Isleworth's 18th green with their match all square. While I don't care who wins the cup, I don't particularly want to see Tiger lose twice in one day.

Tiger has already made par, but Lake Nona's McDowell and Isleworth's Cook still have birdie putts. In a showing of team solidarity, Tiger goes over and helps Cook with the line. And he doesn't do it halfheartedly. He walks halfway to the hole and does the same routine as if he were putting, feeling the line by swinging one-handed. He gives Cook his read. Cook likes it, but the putt doesn't fall. Now it's all in the hands of McDowell, whose putt is on line, but too hard. It hits the cup, lips out, and actually catches air before stopping a foot away. The match is halved and both clubs earn a point. It's nice to see a lip-out actually help Tiger Woods for a change.

IMG-FREE • I sit down for dinner at nearby Jersey Mike's sub shop and start to flip through the complimentary Tavistock program. The paper they used to print it is of such high quality, the binding so thick, that when I try to hold open the pages with my soda, the cover flies back at me in rebellion. Given the ads inside, it's apparent its producers are well aware of their readers' taste. One realty listing is for a $12 million "French farmhouse" that boasts of having its own massage room and "apothecary theatre lobby." I know what a theatre lobby is, and I know that an apothecary is a pharmacy. How in the world those combine into something enticing is beyond me, but then again, I'm not the Tavistock Cup's target audience.

Tiger sizes up what will be yet another birdie on the 4th hole at Torrey Pines South at the Buick Invitational on Saturday, January 26, 2008. *(Robert Beck/ Sports Illustrated/Getty Images)*

Tiger makes his way through a blur of fans. Flanking him is the terrifying Officer Brian Freymueller of the San Diego Police Department, a man so large that small planes have been known to make emergency landings on his shoulders. *(Donald Miralle/Getty Images)*

Tiger reacts to sinking his deconstructed birdie putt on the 12th hole during the final round of the Buick Invitational. *(Jeff Gross/Getty Images)*

Tiger and the gallery dress warmly during Dubai's freak winter sandstorm—except for me (wearing the striped white shirt in the front row four fans to the left of Tiger). Tiger shot 1-under while I picked up hypothermia in the Arabian desert. *(Ross Kinnaird/Getty Images)*

My quest to find The Tiger Woods is delayed by a pack of camels. Rashid: "They're going to Jumeirah Beach!" *(Courtesy of the author)*

After losing his lead, Tiger pulls his drive into the desert on the 8th hole on Saturday in Dubai. *(Karim Sahib/AFP/Getty Images)*

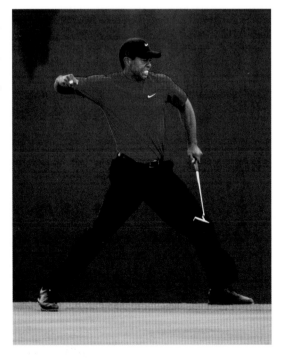

Fourteen-under! Tiger hits my number to complete his Sunday comeback at the Dubai Desert Classic. *(David Cannon/Getty Images)*

Tiger drains his eagle putt on the 17th hole to take a 1-up lead on J. B. Holmes during the first round of the Accenture Match Play, February 20, 2008. *(Scott Halleran/Getty Images)*

Despite Aaron Baddeley making 10 birdies, Tiger still manages to win his third-round match. The win erased any last doubts about Tiger's 2008 form. *(Scott Halleran/Getty Images)*

In the early morning north of Tucson, Tiger pitches from off the green against K. J. Choi in the quarterfinals of the Match Play. *(Robert Beck/Sports Illustrated/Getty Images)*

Tiger waits on the 1st green during the Sunday finals of the Accenture Match Play. Twenty-eight holes later, he would close out Stewart Cink 8 up. *(Scott Halleran/Getty Images)*

Tiger celebrates his winning putt at the Arnold Palmer Invitational on Sunday, March 16, 2008. He would later say he had no recollection of slamming his hat to the ground and only learned of it when he saw his caddy Stevie holding it. He asked, "Why do you have my hat?" *(Andy Lyons/Getty Images)*

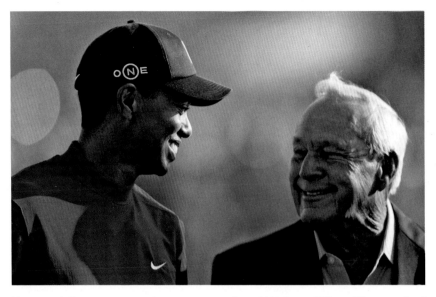

Tiger and the tournament's eponymous Arnold Palmer. When Tiger stroked the final putt, Arnie nodded and grinned, knowing Tiger would make it. With the victory at Bay Hill, Tiger moves two in front of The King on the all-time PGA Tour win list. *(Andy Lyons/Getty Images)*

Tiger tees off on the 18th hole during round one of the CA Championship at Doral on March 20, 2008. *Don't. Go. Left. (David Cannon/Getty Images)*

Above left: Tiger raises his sand wedge after making an eagle three from the greenside bunker on the par-5 12th on Friday at Doral. Through two rounds, the Blue Monster was no match for him. *(Warren Little/Getty Images)*

Above right: Putting woes and a pink shirt end Tiger's undefeated streak on the final day of the CA Championship. *(David Cannon/Getty Images)*

Right: But March 24 isn't all bad. After speeding from Miami back to Orlando, I arrive at Isleworth, Tiger's home course, where I enjoy the freedom of no ropes at the Tavistock Cup. *(David Cannon/Getty Images)*

Above: Practicing by himself, Tiger hits to a flagless 12th green prior to the Masters on Tuesday, April 8, 2008. *(Harry How/Getty Images)*

On the final day of the Masters, Tiger reacts in disbelief to yet another missed putt and the end of any hope for a Grand Slam season. Two months earlier, Vegas bookies set the odds of him pulling it off at an astounding 11-2. *(David Cannon/Getty Images)*

Tiger appears to be back in perfect shape as he works on the putting green with coach Hank Haney on Wednesday, June 11, 2008, the day before the U.S. Open. *(Courtesy of the author)*

On the second day of the Open, Tiger plays off the cart path on number 1 and tweaks his knee. He birdies the hole for the first of five straight "3's" and a front nine 30 to move into contention. *(Donald Miralle/Getty Images)*

Tiger makes a 60-foot putt for eagle on the par-5 13th on Saturday at the U.S. Open. The roar that follows will reach outlying planets in seventy to eighty years. *(Harry How/Getty Images)*

Four holes later, Tiger receives a hand from Stevie after he chips in for birdie on the 17th to pull within one of the clubhouse lead. *(Fred Vuich/Sports Illustrated/Getty Images)*

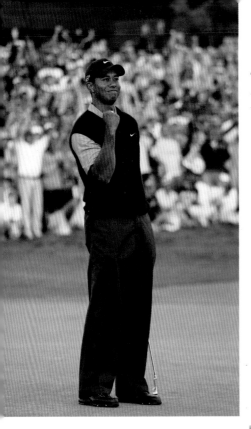

Tiger joins his fans in celebrating the 40-foot eagle putt on the 18th hole that gave him sole possession of the 54-hole lead heading into Sunday. *(Ross Kinnaird/Getty Images)*

Facing page: At 5:52 p.m. on June 15, 2008, Tiger makes a 12-foot birdie putt to force a Monday playoff against journeyman Rocco Mediate. What would have been his most devastating loss became the most clutch moment of his career and perhaps the most electrifying putt in golf history. *(Robert Beck/Sports Illustrated/Getty Images)*

Tiger grabs his knee after a painful drive on number 2 during the final round of the U.S. Open. Quitting was never an option. *(Ross Kinnaird/ Getty Images)*

Tiger plays out of a bunker on the 9th hole to the 15th green during Monday's playoff. He salvages a par but heads to the 16th hole one stroke behind Rocco Mediate. *(Robyn Beck/AFP/Getty Images)*

Tiger and Stevie celebrate after winning the U.S. Open in 91 holes. *(Travis Lindquist/Getty Images)*

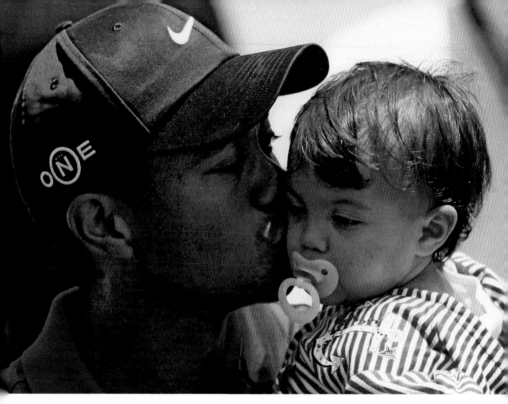

Tiger kisses daughter Sam after the landmark victory. Critics said fatherhood might drag down his performance; since her birth, he has won 10 out of 15 tournaments. *(Travis Lindquist/Getty Images)*

While waiting for the trophy ceremony on the 18th green, Tiger and Rocco share their first laugh since walking off number 1 tee earlier that day. In between, Rocco admitted to NBC's Mark Rolfing, "I think I had him a little scared." *(Doug Pensinger/Getty Images)*

Tiger Woods, winner of the 108th U.S. Open. He would later call it his greatest victory ever. *(Robyn Beck/AFP/ Getty Images)*

The closest I ever came to meeting the man: my Buick Clubhouse picture with virtual Tiger Woods. *(Courtesy of the author)*

What I am anxious to read are the profiles on the players. They are all asked a variety of banal questions, such as "Name something you do that's 'green.' " Who knew that England's Justin Rose and his wife make their own compost? I turn to Tiger's Q and A, expecting to read answers filtered through his management team at IMG. What I find are the same seemingly ridiculous questions but, in response, a collection of answers that read as more honest and devoid of calculation than anything he's said in years.

What does he hope someone invents before he dies? "Teleporting." This is a guy who hates to waste time. His favorite childhood cartoon character? Optimus Prime from *Transformers*—the leader of the Autobots who battled without end. If NASA ever okays a trip to outer space, will Tiger go? "Damn right!" The possibility of what is to be gained from a challenge excites him more than the risks. I keep reading. What reality show would he like to be on? "I hate reality shows and would never be on one." As a sitcom writer, no answer could endear him to me more. But my favorite answer is his last. "What disease do you want to see cured in your lifetime?" Most players give the obligatory sad response, naming some illness and then presumably hanging their heads and asking for a tissue. The disease Tiger would like to see cured? "The yips!" My soda almost falls over again, this time from my knocking the table while laughing. It is clear that Tiger is more interesting in private than he believes he can afford to be in public. Would the shoot-from-the-hip Tiger make his sponsors a little nervous? Absolutely. And in doing so, he would attract a mass of golf fans who desperately want to like him, but remain unsure of who he really is.

ROUND TWO

I arrive at the course for day 2 by 8:30 a.m. The players aren't teeing off for almost three hours, but I want to see Tiger's home course as he sees it, early in the morning, so I decide to take a walk. A worker is mowing the 12th fairway. Another is on the green. When they stop, there are no other sounds to be heard. A swan is swimming across Hourglass Lake. A pelican circles above, then dives beak first into the water in search of breakfast. It is almost too perfect, as if behind a hedge I might find a worker with different joysticks to control the various wildlife for maximum serenity.

Between holes, Isleworth's massive open spaces are occupied by eclectic works of art. The current display includes twenty-five different steel sculptures by Bernar Venet, a French artist who claims on the club's Web site that his goal with the collection is "to take the principles of minimalist art and push it to the limits." That seems sort of contradictory to me.

I turn right and walk down Payne Stewart Drive, past the 89,000-square-foot Mediterranean-style clubhouse (almost 70 percent bigger than the White House), and start the long walk to the driving range. The range sits on the far south finger of the property and is surrounded on all sides by water. It's easily fifteen degrees colder down at this end, dipping into the forties and windy. Except for the two people polishing yet another black Escalade, I'm the only one here.

11:00 AM • In a completely surreal moment, an hour and five minutes before his tee time, I watch Tiger open his front door with Stevie and make the walk across the street to the driving range. It's Tiger's shortest commute of the year.

There are many opulent pieces of property around Isleworth. Some estates stretch for a hundred yards. By comparison, Tiger's house is modest: a two-story stucco home that backs up to the water. He could have bought the one that looked like Monticello, but he didn't. Yes, there are the twelve acres on Jupiter Island, but he's in no rush to move there. If he never does, it will be the most expensive case of buyer's remorse in real estate history. But Earl was the same way. When Tiger purchased his mom a new house in the

Orange County suburb of Tustin, his dad chose to stay behind in the family's longtime Cypress home. Success, not stuff, is Tiger's definition of greatness.

11:03 AM • On the range, Tiger is chatty, sharing stories with teammate Craig Parry about all sorts of memories from tournaments over the years. Parry laughs when Tiger tells him of a caddy he once had overseas who didn't refer to pin positions as "front" and "back" but "near" and "far." It's another peek into the true gameface-free Tiger.

He is so detached from the event that he calls across to teammate Charles Howell III and asks, "Hey, Chuck, who we playing today?" They'll be facing off in their singles matches against that compost lover Justin Rose and South Africa's Retief Goosen.

12:00 PM • Gary McCord, CBS's handlebar-mustached announcer, stands on the first tee with a microphone, introducing the groups. Since I missed the first two holes yesterday, this is my first look at the opener, a 399-yard par 4 that ducks right. I glance down and see that the yardage markers for these back tees are called the "Tiger" tees. At more than 7,500 yards from the tips, it's the rare place that can push Tiger's limits in preparation for some of the long setups he'll see at majors throughout the year. Still, he could probably play this course in the dark. In fact, he probably has.

12:32 PM • After four pars on the 1st, we move to the 2nd, a 228-yard par 3 over Lake Chase and through a shoot of cypress trees. There's no wind at the tee, but when Charles Howell III's ball clears the trees, a gust pushes the ball hard right and into the big bunker near the lake. Tiger sees what happened and makes an adjustment, flighting his iron even lower. His ball hits the same breeze and gets thrown into the trap anyway. No one else gets any closer. Under these circumstances from these tees, this may be the most difficult par 3 I have ever seen.

1:23 PM • While Tiger waits to play on the 4th green, he and Stevie (again sans bib) notice that the group in front of them is still waiting to hit on the 5th tee. "This is going to be a six-hour day," he says, worried. But he's lucky; he only has to walk down the street when this is over. I wasn't able to change my departure city and have to drive all the way back to Miami tonight.

2:06 PM • With plenty of time to kill, Tiger, Justin Rose, and Chuck Howell stand around and talk about Isleworth's newest team member, J. B. Holmes, who hit a drive nearly 400 yards yesterday on the 18th hole. Tiger takes his driver and mimics J.B.'s abbreviated backswing, taking the club only three quarters of the way to the top, then asks, "How does a guy who only takes it to *there* hit it 350?" They all seem equally bewildered at the thought. Tiger may have beaten him in the first round at the Match Play, but a little bit of J.B. is still in Tiger's head.

4:19 PM • Tiger successfully keeps Lake Nona's Goosen and Rose a few shots back for most of the round, making the day feel all the more mellow. But on 13, his eagle putt from the front of the green to the back pin climbs only halfway up the tier, then turns around and rolls down and off the green altogether. It keeps going another thirty feet to the bottom of a collection area. The Bloody Mary crowd stops stirring long enough to gasp at the miscue. When it's all over, Tiger makes a bogey, Goosen makes par, and Rose makes a birdie. He seems not to want to care about what's going on this afternoon, but suddenly he has no choice.

He responds by hitting a 375-yard drive down the right center of the 14th fairway. When his easy wedge shot sucks back off the green, he helps break in his Tavistock bag by chucking his club at it. He saves par to stay in control of the match.

5:01 PM • Both of the matches are now Tiger's to lose, and he nearly does just that on the 16th, a short par 4 of just 349 yards. Tiger is hitting last and pushes his drive way right. Before even watching it land, he asks Stevie for another ball, thinking the first one is out of bounds. But the seventy-five fans down in the fairway assume that everyone has played and start crossing as Tiger unloads on drive number two. This one is straight down the middle and tracking on one unsuspecting gallery member holding a homemade cocktail. It looks as if it will take out the man, which will then create a domino effect, sending a dozen different fans to the ground in a straight line toward the hole. Instead, the ball whizzes right behind him and rolls up in front of the green. Tiger is too angry about the first drive to notice how close he was to killing one of his neighbors.

5:57 PM • His first drive on 16 ends up being in bounds after all, and his lead is never in jeopardy again. With the end in sight, the speed of play accelerates with every shot. The format is a drag at this point, just delaying the inevitable. Tiger seems ready to be done. For his second shot into 18, he doesn't take any practice swings or try to figure the wind. He hears the yardage, grabs a club, and hits it. It lands on the middle of the green anyway. From there it's a mindless par and a round of 2 under at a track that has been ranked as the hardest course in Florida.

Tiger's two points finishes off the Isleworth rout, with Mark O'Meara's team handing Ernie Els's Lake Nona squad a 19½-11½ smackdown. Tiger's cut of the purse is $210,000, just $75,000 less than he won at Doral with his fifth-place finish. He sticks around long enough for the trophy ceremony, but within fifteen minutes, he slips off the green and I lose him in a sea of red and blue shirts. The next time we meet will be inside the gates of the most exclusive golf tournament in the world. The Masters.

First, I just need to figure out how to get in.

A NATIONAL TRAVESTY

The Masters

Augusta National Golf Club
Augusta, Georgia
April 10–13, 2008

In the mid-1980s, there was rarely any change to my father's Sunday routine. He would play golf in the morning, then return home, change into a pair of beat-up shorts and a T-shirt, and get to work. My parents had bought a new house in 1984, and every weekend for the following two years, Dad was sanding, digging, or mixing something.

First, he cordoned off our side yard with railroad ties and planted alder trees. One of his summer jobs in college was with Davey Tree Expert Company, and as his alders started getting bigger, my thirty-nine-year-old white-collar father would shimmy up to the top and prune them as if he were still nineteen. From there he moved on to the backyard, where he was laying a brick patio all by himself, obsessively cutting hundreds of bricks into an intricate pattern. My sister and I started to wonder if the three hundred pounds of loose sand piled in front of our house was a permanent part of the landscape.

Then, one Sunday afternoon in April, I walked into the living room and found my father sitting five feet from the television.

"What are you watching?"

"The Masters."

That was all he said. I sat down next to him and watched as a plaidtrousered Jack Nicklaus made every single putt he saw. When it was over, my dad stood up calmly and ejected a videotape from the VCR. I had never seen him record a sporting event before. He carefully applied a white label and wrote with a red Sharpie, "1986 Masters." He then snapped off the little plastic tab on the front of the tape, ensuring that no one could ever accidentally record over it. I knew then, at age eight, that the first major of the year was not just another golf tournament.

I have been working on finding a way into Augusta National since February, and I have learned only one thing: I am starting a little late. Tournament badges are made available only to those on the official patron list. And that list has been closed since 1972, before either Tiger or I was even born.

But this is America, and if you can't get it for free, you can always buy it, right? Technically, yes. When I first looked into purchasing a black-market badge back in February, most of the ticket brokers were asking for well over $3,000 for all four days. So I revisited my connections. I talked to friends at the Golf Channel, CBS, ESPN, *Sports Illustrated* . . . nothing. One friend said he knew of a way in: "Parachute." The most creative solution came from a buddy who said I should tape pink flowers to my body and sneak in as an azalea bush.

And now that I am back home from Florida, with Tiger having won four of his first five events and the Vegas line on him winning the Grand Slam holding steady at nine-to-one, the ticket broker price has climbed to more than $5,000, twice what I spent on my honeymoon and equivalent to what I've paid for all my previous trips this season—combined.

But again, it isn't an ordinary golf tournament. It's the Masters. Two weeks after returning home from Florida, I leave for Augusta with a few leads, but only one confirmed ticket. For a Tuesday practice round. I have a thousand dollars stuffed in my wallet and the understanding that I will probably need a lot more.

MONDAY NIGHT • My last leg of the three-part journey is a commuter flight out of Charlotte. I expect it to be sold out and full of golf fans. But there are only a few of us scattered about, easily identifiable by our childlike giddiness. Two such fans sit behind me and work closely together on a crossword puzzle.

"Five down could be wrong," the first one says.

"Well, I'm not real comfortable with this whole area!" They give each other a pep talk and refocus. It's amazing the things men will do on a golf trip that they rarely do with their own wives. They're still working as the plane touches down. Rolling to Augusta's colonial-style terminal, I see thirty to forty private jets parked in the dark near some distant hangars, each of their owners hoping they won't be needed again until late Sunday night.

Outside of the actual Masters badges, the most expensive thing about a trip to Augusta is the hotel room. The Days Inn has a normal rack rate of only $69 a night. This week it's charging $305, and it's been sold out for months. Frankly, it could afford to spend a few dollars and buy an *S* for the sign out front, which currently reads, "We welcome our new and returning guest."

Though I do not have a badge, I am very fortunate to have a free place to stay. A stranger named Joe read a piece I wrote for ESPN about driving to the Tavistock Cup and e-mailed me to offer his couch in Augusta if I wanted it. For the money I would save, I didn't even ask him if he was creepy. I call him around ten o'clock at night when my plane lands. He's a few beers into his evening and tells me to "hurry up and get here—we're watching the coverage!" I follow my GPS through the empty Georgia freeways and exit at Washington Road. Even though it is now pushing eleven, some scalpers sit in lawn chairs near the end of the off-ramp with signs offering to buy any and all badges. Joe had told me to "just turn left at the Hooters" to get to his place, but I can't. I have to keep driving.

I've never been here before, but when I pass Berckmans Road, my heart rate picks up, as if my golf-centric soul instinctively knows where I'm taking it. On my right, a twenty-foot hedge blocks any views from the street. I drive along slowly in the right lane as cars pass me on the left. With no warning, the hedge gives way to a modest white guard shack. Beyond it is a long dark road and, at the very end, lit up in soft yellow light, the unmistakable clubhouse of the Augusta National Golf Club. I react as any mature fan of the game of golf would and should. "Holy crap."

TUESDAY • By 7:30 a.m., I have already passed through security and am standing at the front of the low wooden fence that is separating Masters patrons from the course itself. In front of us is an expanse of perfect grass. The only people on the course are a few volunteers, security guards, and—who else—Luau Larry, using his press credential for an early-morning hula around the sacred grounds.

In 1934, one year after Augusta National formally opened, its cofounder Clifford Roberts suggested calling his new club's tournament "the Masters." The other cofounder, retired golf legend Bobby Jones, thought it was too pompous, especially in the midst of the Great Depression. Instead they named it the Augusta National Invitational Tournament. Five years later, Jones gave in to the (eventually) well-deserved title by which it's been known ever since.

Tiger is one of only three golfers, along with Nicklaus and Palmer, to have won here four times (1997, 2001, 2002, 2005). It's a course that rewards power, strategy, and fearless putting, and Tiger can deftly move among all three. In 2006, he finished third. Last year, he finished second. I'm hoping the trend continues.

All the fans around me already know where they're headed. Some will make for the first tee. Others are going to the bleachers at 16. The gate swings open exactly at eight, and they spread out like kids at Disneyland heading to their favorite ride. I have no plan. Anywhere is a good choice. I follow the slope down and across number 1 fairway, past number 9, then into a large stretch that isn't a hole at all. It turns out that Augusta's original design called for not only a practice area right here but, even stranger, a 19th hole that would be used to settle any outstanding bets. When it was discovered that the hole would obstruct the view of the clubhouse from the 18th green, the idea was scrapped.

I continue in the same direction, in an increasing daze, passing number 8, 7 green, across 15, then 14, and I start to realize that I'm walking, without having really known it, right into the intersection of three of the most famous holes in American golf: Amen Corner. I wander through a grove of pine trees, still slipping downhill, and come to a clearing. There in front of me is the 12th. I can almost hear the voice of Jim Nantz softly purring the hole's botanical name in my ears . . . *Golden Bell* . . . If there was only a flag on the green, I might actually think it were a painting. The hundred fans in front of me start to rumble, and I turn my head to see why. It wasn't Amen Corner that was pulling me. Walking onto the tee from number 11, in black slacks and a black sweater is, of course, Tiger Woods.

Tiger teed off on the back nine before the gates opened and managed to finish only two holes before being discovered. He plays one ball to the left side of the par 3, then changes clubs and plays a second ball to the right. He and Stevie head down to the green and across the Hogan Bridge. It's strange to see them all alone. No other players. No security guards. No cameramen. As Tiger putts in different directions, an Augusta National worker appears from behind us with a yellow flag and speedwalks down the fairway and over the bridge to replace the pin for the four-time champion.

I could follow Tiger, but for once I let him go on without me. Instead I find a spot in the bleachers behind the 12th tee and soak in the view. The three holes that make up Amen Corner flow like Rae's Creek from left to right. The par-4 11th sweeps down through a grove of pines to a subtle, flat green. In the center is the 155-yard 12th, a hole so picturesque that when India's Jeev Milkha Singh comes through, he stops and has his caddy take a picture of him. Tucked behind the 12th green is the tee at the par-5 13th, the most secluded spot on the course. The only people within two hundred yards of it are a couple of officials, intentionally camouflaged by flowers and bushes so as not to spoil golf's perfect panorama.

WEDNESDAY • Already out of tickets, I had walked down Washington Road after Tuesday's practice round and taken down some scalpers' phone numbers. When I wake up this morning, I call them at random to see what the day will cost. The low price is Tony, asking $350. Yesterday, he was working the curb near Arby's. Today, he's set up on the south end of town, just off the Bobby Jones Expressway, and claims to have only one left. I am obviously losing a sense of what is too much to pay for a ticket and set out in my red Pontiac to find him.

On the way, I pass another scalper who offers me the same ticket for only $300. I call Tony to see if he can match the price. "What?!" He's angry. "You're killing me! I could have just sold your ticket to someone for *four* hundred!" He hems and haws as if he's getting ripped off on a ticket that has a face value of $36. His tough Boston accent is intimidating, but it's the first time I've had any leverage, and I let him wriggle. He finally agrees to match it, so I keep driving.

Tony is on the sidewalk with another scalper, working the long line of traffic headed to the course. I pull over, and he comes to the window, but he wants to make small talk first. I'm not sure why I mentioned that I was a TV writer, but he gets excited and decides to pitch me his life story, which he thinks would make a great movie. "It'd be called *Death Row to Front Row*," he says. "You were on death row?" I ask, quietly slipping the car from park into reverse. Tony explains that yes, technically he killed a guy, but eventually they proved it was self-defense and now he's free. "Awesome," I say. His buddy interjects that he thinks *his* life would make a great movie, too, but says it would have to be an adult film.

The conversation thankfully returns to my ticket. Tony's still not convinced that I actually found someone selling "a Wednesday" for $300. He turns to his pal and says, "Should we take a ride?" This is just what I want—to be driving around Augusta with these guys. The other scalper, the sixty-something leader of the gang, cools him off. "You got it for two seventy-five. You made twenty-five. Good." I give Tony the cash, he gives me the ticket. Never having taken the Pontiac out of reverse, I make a quick escape.

At the course I discover that Tiger isn't even going to play a practice round today, which means I just paid three hundred bucks to watch Tiger on the putting green. I can't conceive of being able to play Augusta National and choosing not to do so. But statistically, recent history points to the putting green as the place where Tiger needs to be. He hit more greens at Doral than he had hit any other week since the Buick Invitational. But the thirty-two putts he had in his third round was his worst number of the entire season. He is still easily the favorite, but the question in my mind is whether he has arrived in Georgia having fixed whatever was wrong in Florida. Based on a story I heard a few months earlier, I can only assume he had.

It was back in February, and my old boss Alan invited me to play Lakeside, a gorgeous, Hollywood-friendly club across the cement-bottomed Los Angeles River from Universal Studios. After our round he introduced me to Ernie, one of Lakeside's starters who had been there for thirty years. "You want a Tiger story? I got one." He told me about a time years ago when Earl Woods was in L.A. having bypass surgery. That day Ernie got a call from Kevin Costner, who told him "Tiger needs a place to hide out." Ernie said no problem, and later that day Tiger showed up. "I tell him, 'What do you want to do? You want to play, you want to hit balls?' " Tiger just held up his hands. In one hand was his putter and in the other were three golf balls. "This is the worst part of my game," Tiger explained.

He walked to Lakeside's putting green, dropped the three balls, and started putting around to the different flags. "An hour and forty minutes later—I timed it—and he's still putting," Ernie says. Finally, Tiger stopped going in circles and found the toughest putt on the green. Ernie stepped out from behind the starter window to show me. It was about twenty-five feet, broke four feet left to right, and was dead downhill. It was Tiger's winning Bay Hill putt on steroids. After another hour and fifty minutes, Ernie realized what the game was. Tiger wouldn't let himself leave until he had made the hardest putt on the putting green three times in a row. Tiger came back the next day and did the same thing. By Ernie's estimation, Tiger spent eight hours on the putting green those two days at Lakeside. It was early 1997. A few months later, Tiger won his first Masters by twelve shots.

FIRST ROUND

Wednesday night I hear from a sportswriter I had met in February. He has found me a badge that I can use for Thursday and Friday. For $1,800. I have prepared myself for this worst-case scenario and have already taken a $4,000 cash advance on my credit card. Amazingly, no one at the Augusta branch of Bank of America seemed thrown by the request. The manager said that for months people had come in and pulled out a few hundred dollars at a time so they would have enough for their black-market badge come April. I asked for so much cash the teller didn't even count it. She just slapped down two prewrapped bundles, each holding $2,000 apiece.

Surrounded by fog, I meet the writer early Thursday morning. I slip him the cash, and he hands me the most sought-after piece of plastic in sports. It is square and white, with a photo of the 12th hole and a hologram that says "Masters 2008." The back side is filled with small print from top to bottom, detailing all the rules I am breaking. The state of Georgia legalized ticket scalping a few years ago, but Augusta National still holds to the policy that the use of a resold badge is prohibited and subjects the user (and the original patron who sold it) to permanent loss of the credential. I pass through the metal detectors and arrive at the ticket scanner. The volunteer scans my badge. It beeps. She looks me in the eye for a moment, then smiles. "Enjoy your day."

11:06 AM • Tiger, wearing khaki slacks and a pink, white, and brown striped shirt, is nearing the end of his warm-up session. The range heads away from the clubhouse and dead-ends at the edge of Washington Road. From outside the gates pedestrians can hear the occasional clang as players hit the fourteen green poles that rise a hundred feet into the air and support the giant net. Yesterday, the short-hitting Tim Clark was having trouble reaching it. Tiger's drives are hitting about halfway up, then falling back to Earth.

This may be a major, but Tiger's routine is the same, and when he finishes on the range, he heads to the chipping green where Stevie has already left handfuls of balls in different places for Tiger to find. The all-white jumpsuit that Augusta makes caddies wear only adds to the Easter Bunny imagery. And of the roughly fifteen times I have watched Tiger practice these shots before a round, I have never *not* seen him make at least one. Today he starts with some soft, high pitch shots. His second effort bounces twice and rolls into the cup. After a few bump and runs, he moves to the sand. His first ball—*in*. After a couple more, he aims toward a different flag. *In*. He aims to the third flag, twenty-five yards away. It stops three inches from the cup. He is ready.

11:40 AM • There's nothing more quaint than the number 1 tee at Augusta National. A round patio umbrella and table sit near the back. Resting on the table is a wooden box filled with tees, Sharpies, and some extra copies of the day's hole positions. Other official paperwork is held in place by a couple of loose rocks. Two Augusta members in their trademark green jackets stand near the table as a pair of young men in blue blazers step onto a split log bench and slide Tiger's name into the metal green sign to the left of the tee. In one of the Masters programs, there is a picture of the first tee from the 1950s. Nothing has changed.

11:45 AM • The comforting southern accent of the starter rings out from the tee: "Fore, please. Tiger Woods driving." We applaud as Tiger touches the brim of his cap and begins his quest for the first single-season professional Grand Slam in the history of golf.

The 455-yard 1st at Augusta National is a hole I have seen on TV and considered flat—which it is, as long as a player carries his drive 290 yards over a deep valley to the top of the fairway where it levels off. Tiger tees up his ball the way I've learned he always does: Nike swoosh on the inside, face up. And pointing toward the hole, the word *Tiger* stamped on the other side. He mashes his drive, and we try to follow it, but it's lost against the gray sky. I figure that when it comes down, the fans near the fairway will clarify. Nothing. Silence. The lady in front of me gives her best guess, "To infinity . . . and beyond." He finds his ball just off the fairway and starts the 2008 Masters with a par.

12:15 PM • The fact that I have never heard anyone mention the beauty of the view from the 2nd tee is a testament to how spectacular the rest of the course is. A 575-yard par 5, it plays slightly downhill through the pines toward one massive, blindingly white bunker on the right side, just over three hundred yards away. From there players hit from what feels like a plateau toward a well-guarded shallow green.

Tiger lays short of the trap off the tee and then lays up again with a long iron. There's no question he could have reached it, but Augusta rewards intelligence more than might, and Tiger knows that the best chance for birdie will come from below the hole, not above.

Even so, he pitches eight feet long and has a downhill putt. His first birdie putt of the day is a poor effort from the moment he strokes it.

12:35 PM • The 3rd is another missed opportunity for Tiger. On this short, uphill par 4, the big decision for Tiger is always whether to hit driver near the base of the elevated green or lay up with an iron. In the final round of the 2003 Masters, Tiger came to the hole down by 3 shots. He wanted to hit an iron. Stevie convinced him to go with the driver. Tiger blocked the drive into some bushes, had to play out left-handed, and eventually made a double en route to a disappointing 75. The duo was overheard cursing at each other throughout the day, and Tiger would later have to release a statement saying that their relationship remained intact despite the public fight.

Feeling more confident about his game now than he was five years ago, Tiger hits driver again and flies it all the way to the upslope of the green but can only put his ball twenty feet away, settling for another par.

1:39 PM • In the pine straw to the right of seven, two camera assistants stay busy rebundling the extra cable into a perfect coil every time the cameraman adjusts his position. I'm sure this isn't done out of boredom. To say that Augusta National prefers things neat is like saying fish prefer being wet.

On Tuesday a number of workers walked through the fairways, whisking the dew off the early-morning grass. Others did the same around the greens, removing any sand that had been blown out of the traps. Neither of those sights shocked me more than when I grabbed a napkin from a dispenser and a worker promptly tucked the next one back inside so it wouldn't have that repulsive loose-napkin look to it. I actually admire the ambitiousness. If the goal of Augusta National is to present the world's greatest golf tournament on one of the world's greatest courses, why strive for anything less than obsessive perfection?

1:49 PM • Tiger leaves the 7th having made seven straight pars. The volunteers working the leaderboards are running low on zeros. The 570-

yard 8th hole plays back up the hill that number 2 played down. Tiger pummels a drive 320 yards past the hole's only sand trap and will face 225 yards up the hill.

I want to run around to the back of the green, but I can't. Running is another Masters no-no. The intent is to provide a relaxed environment for all. It's a hard adjustment for me, but I put my head down and speedwalk up the steep hill instead.

The second shot into the long, skinny, bunkerless 8th green is a blind shot. We can't see Tiger down below, but we can only assume it's his ball that we see sailing long and left of the green. It ricochets off the grandstands and kicks hard right, back over to the other side of the green. It's closer to the flag than he would have been, but it's left him an impossible chip that runs uphill to the fringe and then downhill to the flag. He makes only par and wanders away, still unsure about how his second shot ended up where it did. He mutters to the blond-headed Aussie, Stuart Appleby, "I thought it was long left . . ." Appleby might not be able to handle anyone else's problems at this point. While Tiger has parred eight in a row, Appleby has one par, three birdies, three bogeys, and a triple.

3:00 PM • The Masters isn't supposed to be boring. But here, as I watch Tiger miss a birdie putt on number 12, the heart of Amen Corner, I yawn. That makes twelve straight pars. But something is bound to change, since I just joined up with my college roommate, Rob. He has never been to the Masters either and, unlike me, actually has enough power and influence to find himself a free badge for the day.

The only reason we ended up roommates our freshman year was that someone in our school's housing department had a sense of humor. There were eight guys on our wing, two to a room. Their names: Mike and Ryan, Mark and Brian, Rob and Bob, and for good measure, Andrew and Tyler. That one didn't fit the mold until we discovered their last names were Fisher and Crabtree and they went by the nicknames Fish and Crab.

Rob had been recruited by Princeton to play golf, and convinced me to try out for the team sophomore year. I made it. During a team meeting that winter, the coach called me "the definition of dedication." The next day I quit. I just wasn't good enough to make the traveling team, and knew my time was better spent focusing on writing. But I did leave an indelible mark. That spring, the upperclassmen created a one-day team event called the Tiger Cup, named after our school's mascot. The team captain even bought a fancy glass with the Princeton crest on it from the university store and wrote on it in black Sharpie, "Tiger Cup." I was no longer on the team, but I was invited back to even out the numbers. I don't even remember the format, but the trophy was ceremoniously placed next to the first tee. While I watched another player hit, I was swinging my Ping putter around in my hand and heard a clink. I knew exactly what I had done without having to look down. "Smiley broke the Tiger Cup!" the captain screamed in disbelief. The hope was that it would be an annual event, but the tradition began and ended there.

3:30 PM ● Rob and I walk down the 13th fairway and look back toward the tee, a shot that demands that a player hit a sweeping draw around the trees to have a clear view of the green. A perfect drive will leave a sidehill lie to a rippling putting surface. Go short of the green, and the ball is in Rae's Creek. Go long, it's in a trap. Go really long, it's in a sea of azaleas. Tiger misses just over the green, and his ball settles into a swale. He decides to chip his third rather than putt it, but he misplays it and the ball rolls back off the green again. His fourth rolls past the hole, and he misses the par putt coming back. I was hoping Rob would change our luck for the better, not worse.

3:45 PM ● Unlike the unoriginal holes at Doral, there are no F7s at Augusta National. No two holes could ever be confused with each other. The 14th, for example, has no bunkers. Anywhere. Yet historically, it ranks as one of the course's hardest. It's 440 yards and tight between the pines, with a green that slopes severely left to right. Tiger pulls his drive left just inside the ropes. It's behind a tree and sitting on pine straw, still 200 yards to the hole. Rob and I speedwalk to the spot like a couple of senior citizens doing laps on a cruise ship and are rewarded with a second-row view.

Tiger sees what faces him and wants to go left of the tree. Stevie doesn't mince his words. I'm starting to realize that he never does. "Definitely can't get there." Tiger listens and decides to go low and hook it around the tree instead. He tries to get as stable a footing as he can on the pine needles and swings hard. And tops it. It is a full on, thin, ugly, piece of junk shot that bounces only ninety yards down the fairway. Tiger makes just enough blunders to never let anyone forget just how hard the game of golf truly is. It leads to his second straight bogey. Tiger is now 2-over par, and all since Rob joined me. But I don't need to point it out to him. "Do you want me to leave?" he asks earnestly.

"That's ridiculous," I tell him. "Not yet."

4:05 PM • Every hole at Augusta is named after a species of plant that was discovered on the land in the days before it was a golf course, when it was a rolling, 365-acre property called Fruitland Nurseries. The 530-yard 15th has the toughest-sounding name (Firethorn) but historically ranks as Augusta's easiest hole. A downhill, reachable par 5, it can yield low scores (Gene Sarazen made a double-eagle 2 in 1935), but the dark blue pond in front of the green and another pond behind it make it look like trying to land a plane on a grass-covered aircraft carrier.

Tiger finds himself in trouble again when his second shot misses over the green in two. From Rob's and my perspective, it's a nearly impossible pitch shot. The pin is cut near the back-right edge, and Tiger can only pop it up and hope it doesn't roll all the way to the front.

Tiger stalls before hitting the shot, perhaps in order to allow the grass on Augusta's slick greens to grow infinitesimally longer. While waiting, I try to figure out what I've done today that I haven't done any other. Right as Tiger brings his wedge back, it dawns on me that, this morning, I replaced my stained and faded red TW hat with a bright-green Masters cap. My hat! In one fluid motion, as Tiger's wedge returns to his ball, I pull off the green one, rip my old hat from my belt loop, and place it on my head just as Tiger makes contact. The ball hops up, lands on the edge of the green, and rolls into the cup for eagle.

The crowd roars for Tiger as Rob and I high-five. After the chip-in eagle, Tiger pars out to salvage a round of 72. It puts him 4 behind Justin Rose and South Africa's Trevor Immelman. I will never change hats again.

LANE'S TOUR • I never thought I'd like a couple of self-described "good ol' boys" as much as Joe and Lane, the two guys who have donated their couch for the week. Joe is a twenty-seven-year-old who works for a pest control company, and Lane is a twenty-nine-year-old motor repairman. While they've been friends for years, they have grown closer over the last few months since Lane started dating Joe's cousin. It's a relationship that provides endless opportunities for jokes depending on who is trying to insult whom.

Thursday night, I ask Lane if he'd be willing to give me a tour of his hometown. As we start to drive down Washington Road in his enormous black Ford pickup, I tell him I haven't seen a lot of Priuses here. "What's a Prius?" He isn't joking. I figure a couple of blue-collar guys would roll their eyes about the Masters and all its snobbery. But "the National," as they call it, is their pride and joy. Lane hasn't even been inside the gates for more than a decade, but says without a hint of sarcasm that being there felt like he was "touching God."

I can't disagree with the quasi-spiritual reason to love the Masters, but there's an economic reason to love it, too. The millions of dollars brought in over this one week help to sustain the city for the other fifty-one. And the hotels and restaurants aren't the only ones making out. Lane's girlfriend/Joe's cousin is spending the week working for a catering company. Joe is driving a hospitality van, shuttling businessmen from place to place. If the tips are decent, he'll clear $2,000 by Sunday night. Hundreds of other Augustans, even kids, are working the tournament itself. The school district doesn't try to fight the allure anymore. After years of dealing with students and teachers not showing up for class, now it's easy to know when spring break falls—Masters Week.

Lane has never been west of the Mississippi or north of the Mason-Dixon Line ("When they start playing bowl games up north, then we'll talk"), but he gladly takes me over the Savannah River and into South Carolina. Even though Augusta is only a 3-wood away, he and Joe consider anyone from the neighboring state to be a lower life form. He wheels the truck around and points out the Butt Bridge, named after Major Archibald Willingham Butt, an early-twentieth-century Augusta war hero who died on the *Titanic*. We pass through Augusta's half-seedy/half-gentrified downtown and head into the hills where the streets are lined with mansions built by Willis Irvin, the same 1930s architect who designed the clubhouse at the National.

Lane's whole tour builds to his final stop: Forest Hills Golf Course. It's too dark to see anything, but in front is a historical marker, and Lane, a true history buff, proudly rolls down my window so that I can read it. Forest Hills is the course where Bobby Jones won the first tournament of his season back in 1930, the year he won golf's only Grand Slam. The fact that few Masters fans will ever see this place is a reminder that winning tournaments like the Dubai Desert Classic is nice, but the legacy of Tiger and his 2008 rests squarely on how he performs in the year's four majors.

SECOND ROUND

Before Friday's round, I go shopping. Augusta National has a permanent gift shop on its property, a massive, forest-green warehouse of all things Masters. The items range from the obligatory shirts and hats to the obscure and the plain odd. I didn't know the Masters has a mascot, but it does. He looks like Mr. Met, the goofy ball-headed New York baseball icon, but wears a green hat instead of a blue one. Throwing a fancy dinner party? No problem. There is a variety of Masters stemware, including martini glasses and even crystal. Want to think about the Masters while you're transferring files? Pick up a logoed USB flash drive. Need something romantic for the wife you abandoned to follow Tiger Woods all year? How about a lovely set of Masters candles? Or maybe some soap imprinted with the Augusta National logo?

The National doesn't release any figures on how much it makes from its merchandise, but I spend $130 without even trying. Most people are walking out having spent not hundreds but thousands. As I see an endless line of credit cards being swiped, it's obvious that Augusta National could use its power to snuff out the secondary ticket market overnight. But it's never, ever going to do so. Without new people coming from different corners of the world to be here, who would buy a Masters mouse pad? Or Masters barbecue tools? Its best ploy is to do what it's been doing—tell people not to buy resold tickets and then make examples of the handful who are dumb enough to get caught. The net result is that the club has increased the allure of being inside its gates all the more.

1:52 PM • By the time Tiger starts his second round, first-round leader Trevor Immelman has already shot a second straight 68 and Tiger is starting round two a daunting 8 shots behind. He acts quickly, making a birdie on the 1st, and is under par for the first time this week.

But no one has much of a chance to enjoy that red "1" on the white scoreboards. On the par-5 2nd, Tiger tries to play a big flop shot to the tucked left pin and dumps it into the trap short of the green from only thirty yards out. He fails to get up and down, and stumbles right back to even par.

3:40 PM ● This is starting to feel eerily similar to Doral. Tiger misses a short birdie putt on 3, pars the difficult 4th and 5th, and misses a par putt from five feet on the 6th. He's now *over* par and 9 shots back. I refuse to believe that he hasn't fixed his stroke, so I flash back to a comment he made to reporters early in the week, when he said there was more grass on these greens than he has ever seen. In theory, the thicker and healthier the grass, the more the natural grain will play a role, which could make the greens harder to read. I guess. I have arrived at the point where my tortured justifications for Tiger's poor play no longer make sense even to me.

4:21 PM ● He has a chance to bounce back at the 8th, the uphill par 5 where he ricocheted his ball off the grandstands yesterday. Today his long second shot bounces off one of the big anthill-shaped mounds along the left side of the hole and kicks down toward the cup. He has just ten feet for eagle.

While waiting for Tiger to make the long walk, I meet Richard, a friendly-looking bloke in his early forties who speaks in an Australian accent and asks me, "Are you a golf tragic?" I'm not sure what that means, though the term might perfectly describe Tiger's last two rounds. He sees my confusion and translates—"a golf nut." Oh. Yes. Slightly.

Richard is a member of the Australian Parliament and is making his first trip to Augusta as an advocate for Golf Australia, his country's equivalent of the United States Golf Association or Great Britain's Royal & Ancient. The pairings for the first two days were a godsend for him. He receives credit for watching his friend Stuart Appleby while getting to see his hero, Tiger Woods. He's been following Tiger all day and knows that putts like this makeable eagle need to start falling. The ball only burns the edge, and he taps in for a disappointing birdie.

5:05 PM ● It's a good thing Richard is here, because enduring this by myself at a cost of $900 a day might make me punch a tree. And I assume that punching anything at Augusta National is grounds for removal and confiscation of my badge. Leaving the course yesterday, two men pushed by me, dragging their friend who had decided the Masters was the ideal place to get completely sloshed. These sorts of indiscretions could be expensive mistakes. Ticket brokers threaten customers with the promise to charge their credit card an additional $10,000 if they don't return their badges at the end of the day—the fear being that if the buyer doesn't have the badge, the National may have taken it and the original owner will have his name forever erased from the patron list.

I already received a warning myself yesterday. While sitting on the hillside near number 6, I stretched out on my elbows, then briefly lay on my back to take some notes. Within fifteen seconds, a uniformed security guard approached and said that elbows were okay, but lying on my back was not allowed. Then for good measure, he added, "And you have to leave your shoes on." My shoes *were* on. The Masters is stunning me with its beauty and perfection, while leaving me completely on edge and uncomfortable at the same time.

Richard and I arrive on the hillside near number 10 green. Tiger's thirty-foot putt for birdie starts six feet right of the cup but breaks only six inches. Tiger has played here every year since 1995, and he just misread a putt by five and a half feet. Even worse, he misses the putt for par and is again 1 over for the week.

5:17 PM ● Rather than confront the misery in front of us, Richard and I head down number 11 and talk about past misery, specifically his countryman Greg Norman's sudden-death loss to Larry Mize in the 1987 Masters. Norman's inability to win a green jacket is a national travesty in Australia, none of his losses more painful than when Mize, a local

Augustan, chipped in from forty-five yards on the very hole Richard and I are traversing. The shot was so scarring to an entire nation that everyone in Richard's Golf Australia group made a pilgrimage earlier in the week to the very spot just right of the green, where they each stood in silence and considered not what could have been but, in their minds, what should have been.

Despite Greg Norman being the number one player in the world for 331 weeks between the late 1980s and early '90s, the Shark's record when holding a fifty-four-hole lead in majors is a nightmarish one for six. Tiger, on the other hand, is thirteen for thirteen. Australia loves him for just that reason. Where Norman left his countrymen heartbroken time after time, Tiger reminds them that greatness is still possible. Or, as the forever wounded Richard says, Tiger "handles your emotions with care."

5:43 PM • Tiger pars the 11th and 12th. He is the only one on the ten-man leaderboard who is not under par for the tournament. On 13 green, he's so unsure of himself he actually asks Stevie for a read—something he hasn't done more than three times all season. The advice leads to a tap-in birdie and a return to even par. If this were June at the U.S. Open, bouncing around par like this might be just fine, but not when a half-dozen players are cruising between 4 and 8 under.

6:47 PM • Tiger's birdie effort at the 15th is so mediocre that it doesn't garner a single clap. After another ho-hum par on the 16th, my energy is starting to flatline. So is Tiger's, who until now hasn't given any clue that he is playing below his expectations. But as he arrives at the log bench next to the tee, he lets his driver fall with a clunk and drops his head.

7:06 PM • Tiger senses my growing ire and promptly birdies number 17 after sticking his second shot within a foot of the hole. That didn't seem so hard. If he can just finish at 1 under, his name will stay at the bottom of the leaderboard and provide some much-needed pressure on the twelve players ahead of him. I join the invigorated crowd and move to 18. "No running," a security guard reminds me.

7:10 PM • There are few golf fans who can't close their eyes and picture the 18th hole at Augusta National—the tee box pulled back like the end of a slingshot between two rows of pines, the dual fairway bunkers straight ahead as the hole turns right and uphill to the final sloping green. Tiger just needs to hit something short of the traps, play a mid-iron to the front of the green, and be happy with a 4.

I'm sure that was his plan, but as I watch his ball sail into the trees way right, a 4 looks unrealistic. There are no crosswalks on the 18th, so getting to the right side requires going all the way back to the tee and around, a distance that is impossible to cover no matter how fast a speedwalker I am becoming.

I watch from the left side as Tiger looks at his ball on the pine straw and then walks toward the adjoining 10th fairway. He's not pitching out. He's actually attempting to advance the ball up the wrong hole.

7:19 PM • I speedwalk up the left side of 18 like a wind-up toy, then back down the right side of number 10 where Tiger's ball has come to rest after weaving 170 yards through the forests of Georgia. Stevie is pacing the distance from the hole by foot since for some reason the shot from 10 fairway to 18 green isn't one they worked on during their practice rounds this week. To save par, Tiger must hit a lob wedge high and soft, carrying the right bunker but only by a few feet or else it will roll right off the other side. After hitting so many mediocre shots from around the green this week, his most difficult one of all is perfect. It lands just on the green and turns left, heading down toward the hole in the front-right corner. It picks up speed and looks as if it might even go in before hitting Stuart Appleby's unmarked ball, seven feet above the hole.

No front-runner should be experiencing the stress of a par putt on Friday, but there is the definite sense that if he makes this, it could alter the momentum of his entire week. His custom Scotty Cameron putter only moves backward an inch before nudging the ball forward, rolling it past Appleby's mark and into the hole.

It was torture from beginning to end, but Tiger has somehow squeaked out a 71 and should feel blessed to be only 7 back of Trevor Immelman.

THIRD ROUND

I was hoping that the writer who sold me the badge for Thursday and Friday would have heard about what a model patron I was and allow me to use it for the rest of the tournament for free. No such luck. The cost of a scalped weekend badge is even more—$2,000. Outside gate 3A, I pass a man holding a sign with flames around the edge that reads, "Ask me why you deserve hell." I don't need to ask. I just spent $4,100 to attend a golf tournament.

1:00 PM • The weather has been different every day. Thursday the fog was so heavy it delayed play for forty minutes. Friday was windy. Today, rain. Tiger is on the putting green in waterproof pants and a jacket. He's working on his long putts, trying to adjust to the slower speed of the wet greens in this weather. He rolls a forty-footer right at me. It's tracking toward the hole. If he makes it, it will be the longest putt I've seen him make since the 18th at Bay Hill. Right as it falls into the cup, the horns sound.

Tiger's coach, Hank Haney, steps out from the side of the green and Tiger slips under his umbrella. They walk off the putting green and into the clubhouse, where, for a brief moment as the door hangs open, I see members and guests laughing and sharing drinks around the fireplace. But $4,100 did not include a clubhouse pass. I met a ticket broker who dangled one in front of me, but he wanted a cool $10,000 for it. That was almost as much as Arnold Palmer took home in prize money when he won his first Masters in 1958.

1:51 PM • After a half-hour delay, Tiger is on the tee with Andrés Romero, the twenty-six-year-old Argentinean who finished third at last year's British Open. After he and Tiger shake hands, Tiger shows him his ball. "I'm playing Nike Ones," he tells him, information that is news to no one. Tiger hits his opening drive so perfectly that we give it two sets of applause, one when it's in the air and another when it stops at the top of the hill, three hundred yards away.

The crowd at the Masters is not as homogeneous as I'd expected. Young, old, black, white, each one feeling blessed to be here. All have their Masters story on how they came upon their badges. I meet a woman from the Midwest named Paula who came to a Masters practice round back in 1963. She asked how one procures a badge for the actual tournament and was told to just write and ask. So she did. *Thirty-one years later*, she received a letter from the National saying her name had reached the top of the waiting list. She hasn't missed a year since.

Not everyone is as aboveboard as Paula. While new badge holders are limited to two passes a year, the oldest patrons have many more, some as many as eight. Upon their death, they can will them, but again, no more than two. The result is that some families haven't told the National that great-grandpa has actually been dead for years.

2:15 PM • After a par on 1, Tiger hits his standard drive on the par-5 2nd to the edge of the plateau. The pin today is all the way on the green's left side. Tiger knows that if he can get something near the middle, he'll have a real chance at eagle. He takes his 5-wood and draws it around the pine trees. He jogs to the right for a better look (the "no running" rule is apparently limited to patrons). His ball lands softly between the bunkers and on the green, twenty feet away. As his eagle putt rolls toward the hole, Tiger tries to will it in by bending his knees, but it doesn't fall. The tap-in birdie takes him to 2 under.

3:29 PM ● Tiger's third-round putter is no warmer than it was on Friday. After the encouraging start, he misses the following chances to move up the leaderboard:

> Hole 3, 20 feet
> Hole 5, 12 feet
> Hole 6, 20 feet
> Hole 7, 12 feet
> Hole 8, 8 feet

Expecting him to make all of them is greedy, but two? At least. The only thing that helps is that I again run into Richard from Australia. When he sees me, he says somberly, "Hi, Bob." "Hello," I answer, as if we're attending the same funeral. As we did yesterday, we walk along and talk about anything except how Tiger is playing.

I was surprised that a proper Aussie would actually want to hang around an American golf fan who had slipped someone a wad of cash to be here. But Richard's personality matches the golf world he has described back home. Australia is not a place dominated with stuffy country club types. At its core, the golf scene is blue-collar. Sometimes too blue-collar. He tells me the story of when Peter Dawson, the secretary of the prestigious R&A, came from Scotland to see the country and was taken to play Inverleigh, a track Richard calls the "the worst course in Australia." Its greens aren't even grass; they're "sand scrape"—a mixture of oil and sand where a player must rake his line before he putts. When Richard heard that the head of golf's oldest governing body had played there, he was mortified. But in the eyes of Dawson's hosts, Inverleigh was real Aussie golf.

3:50 PM ● Of all the famous holes at Augusta National, the 10th looks more different in person than any other. First is how steep it is from the tee to the low point in the fairway. It fills in the blanks of my early Masters memories of watching players hit drives that seemed to roll for a hundred yards. With the lengthening of the National over the last ten years, most of those shots have, sadly, disappeared. The 10th is the exception, insulated from most of the change by the putting green, which sits just thirty feet behind it. Most drives still can't make it to the bottom, leaving players to face a downhill lie to an elevated green, a mean combination that causes even pros to hook and even shank their approach shots.

The other sight that is lost between the camera and the TV, no matter how hi-def it may be, is the sheer scale of the hole. The 10th is the home of Augusta National's oldest and tallest pines, and they loom over the green, casting shadows on it the entire day.

As he has been doing all week, Tiger finds the fairway and hits his second to the middle of the green, fifteen feet away. He finally makes one. When he is confident, his putts drop right in the middle of the cup. This one slips in the right side. Still, it's progress. He's down to 3 under.

4:45 PM ● After pars on 11 and 12, Tiger draws an iron onto 13 green and two-putts for another birdie. Amazingly, he is within 4 shots of the lead without having solved his putting woes.

5:45 PM ● The mini-charge slows as Tiger manages only to par the 14th, 15th, and 16th, leaving him 5 down on 18 tee. Just as he had the day before, he overcuts his drive into the pine trees. Yesterday, his only shot was up number 10. I don't even think he can do that today. He's between tree trunks. Big tree trunks. The Georgia pines down the right side of 18 are a good thirty to forty feet high, and he has at least 175 yards to the flag. Tiger looks up through the grove in front of him and is convinced that he sees a gap no one else does.

As he whips his hips through the shot, he purposefully falls backwards, sending the ball high and out of sight. We hear it clip some needles on the way out and wait for a response from the crowd. After a quiet second, the distant gallery roars. Tiger slams his iron back into the pine straw in celebration.

He has managed to hit the front of the green from nowhere. He lags the birdie short and makes a nervy five-footer for par and a 4-under 68. Although it's hard to believe considering how poorly he putted, it's Tiger's best round at the Masters since 2005. Still leading are Immelman, the shaggy-haired Brandt Snedeker, Steve Flesch, and Paul Casey. The only hope now is that the posting of Tiger's 5-under total will create a Saturday meltdown that rivals the collective collapse at Bay Hill.

6:12 PM • Tiger signs his scorecard and tells CBS's Bill Macatee that he has put himself right back into the tournament. But his problem remains the same. He returns to the practice green and putts by himself as Hank Haney and Stevie whisper on the far side of the green. After a few minutes, Tiger calls out, "Haney!" His coach crosses to him and watches as he strokes one straight eight-footer after another. Haney is watching only one thing—the blade of his student's putter. With each stroke, he tells Tiger exactly how open the face is. "Half a degree," Haney says after a stroke that looks just fine to me. I chuckle at the notion that such a precise calculation can be eyeballed. Even crazier is the idea that Tiger can take that information and translate it into a physical correction.

Haney's style is reserved; he serves mostly as an extra set of highly trained eyes. On the range, he rarely speaks unless Tiger looks to him for an explanation of what he did wrong. He's much closer to my original assessment of him than I thought: "Good one." *Smack.* "Good one." *Smack.* "*Really* good one." At thirty-two, Tiger is beyond hand-holding. Six years ago, Tiger left his longtime coach Butch Harmon in order to fix a swing that no one, especially Butch, thought needed fixing. After all, Tiger had just won six majors over the previous three seasons. But Tiger was adamant his swing was not as consistent as he felt it could be. Following the split, Tiger failed to win in his next ten majors. He endured plenty of media criticism and even Harmon's own well-publicized comments that his longtime student was "in denial" about his game. Tiger stood his ground. After he connected with Haney in the spring of 2004, the pair quickly silenced the critics. Over the last three years, Tiger has tacked on five more majors.

Back on the Augusta practice green, Tiger is still putting and Haney is still watching. He putts two more that roll dead center. "Perfect," Hank says. After eight more minutes in which he makes almost every one, Tiger looks back up at his coach. Hank just nods. "Good," Tiger says. He picks up the balls, and they head for the clubhouse.

FINAL ROUND

Tiger's 68 didn't have the effect on everyone else that I had hoped. By sundown on Saturday, he had actually fallen from 4 strokes behind to 6—two more than Nicklaus overcame to win the '86 Masters. After skipping church on Easter Sunday for the CA Championship, I decide not to make the same mistake twice.

National Hills Baptist sits kitty-corner from Augusta National, right on Washington Road. Thirty-seven-year-old Pastor Kevin Steele stands at the front in a perfectly pressed mint green shirt, a tie, and, on top, a navy blue sleeveless sweater with the Masters logo on the front. "Happy Masters Sunday to all of you," he begins, "but *every* Sunday is the Master's Sunday."

I grew up going to church every week, even while on vacation, and was expecting the usual stares from locals who knew that I didn't belong. But these folks don't do that. They go out of their way to shake my hand and wish me a good morning. What I really need is a good afternoon, and I take the second song as a sign that today I might just witness a miracle.

> God will make a way,
> Where there seems to be no way.
> He works in ways we cannot see,
> He will make a way . . . for Tiger.

Fine, the Baptists didn't tweak the lyrics like that. But if God has followed any part of this season, how could He not resist bestowing a little divine help on Tiger? As I cross Washington Road, the hymns mix in my head with another hopeful refrain golf fans hear every year on this day—that the Masters doesn't really start until the back nine on Sunday.

2:05 PM • When I grab the pairing sheet and see that Tiger is playing with Stewart Cink, I let out a little yelp. Not a big yelp—I'm not sure where Augusta National stands on those. If there's one player Tiger has pummeled with regularity this season, it's Cink. Between the Buick and the Match Play, they've spent 75 holes together, and Tiger has a fourteen-shot advantage.

Adding to the positive vibe, I've reconnected with Mark, a Masters patron whom I met in line for the taxis in Dubai, of all places. Now I just need some nematodes from Bay Hill and I'll have Tiger surrounded with something from all four of his previous wins.

2:59 PM • Three holes in, there's no sign of a miracle. Tiger pars 1, is unable to get up and down for birdie on 2, and, for the fourth consecutive day, doesn't make birdie on 3 despite being just short of the green with his drive. To play that hole in even par for the week is nothing less than dreadful.

With Tiger still sputtering, I tell Mark one of my favorite Augusta National stories of the week. Each of the gallery guards (or marshals, as they're called everywhere else) is issued a bright yellow hard hat for the week. The helmets have the Masters logo on the front, and on both sides in red is the number of the hole to which the marshal has been assigned. When I asked one of the guards if he was allowed to keep the hat when the week is over, he said, "Oh no . . ." On the contrary, every night before he leaves, he has to check the hat back in. "And if you don't?" He smirks and tells me about a dentist from Atlanta who decided one year to quit on a Wednesday and just go home. With his hard hat. That night, there was a knock on his door. It was a sheriff from Augusta, 150 miles to the east.

"Are you Dr. White?"

"Yes."

"Sir, I believe you have some property that belongs to Augusta National."

"I don't know what you're talking about."

"Sir, you can either give it to me now, or at seven a.m. tomorrow I will return with a warrant for your arrest." The dentist excused himself and came back thirty seconds later with the hat. I didn't need to ask the gallery guard if Dr. White was ever invited back. Besides losing his inside the ropes access, he lost the best perk in golf—every May, the National says thank you to the gallery guards by inviting them back for a round of golf and lunch in the clubhouse.

3:19 PM • Up at the 5th, Tiger faces a forty-foot putt from the front of the green to the back. It's so steep that as Stevie tends the flag, his feet appear even with Tiger's head. The putt starts left and climbs, then nearly stops at the top before picking up speed and rolling right to the hole. It looks as if he has made his first extreme putt of the week, when it stops only a half inch short. Tiger drops his putter and throws his hat down with both hands in frustration. He stands there for a while, unable to bring himself to tap it in. When he does, he uses the toe of his putter, not giving the blade side the satisfaction of finishing the job.

5:15 PM • With Tiger standing on the 11th green, now six strokes back, he is about to butt up against the Wall. Art Wall, the 1959 Masters Champion. Forty-nine years ago, Wall arrived at the 12th tee five shots behind and caught fire. He birdied five of his last six holes, passed twelve players along the way (including defending champ Arnold Palmer), and won by a stroke. No one since has come back from as many shots in as few holes. If Tiger doesn't pick up a shot here, his only route to victory will be by breaking Wall's record.

It starts with this putt. It doesn't have any of the elevation change like the putt on 5, but it's at least twice as long, roughly eighty feet from beginning to end. In front of me is a member of the golf course staff who has sneaked away to watch a bit of the action. He knows the course as well as anyone and tells me that this is a putt that Tiger can make. Who knows, perhaps Tiger's money range is inside three feet and outside seventy-five.

The putt starts out five feet right, then slowly makes its way to the back of the green, eventually sliding left and dropping into the heart of the cup. The worker next to me turns and shakes my hand while we cheer. The back of the Masters badge has a message from Augusta National cofounder Bobby Jones that reads, "It is appropriate for spectators to applaud successful strokes in proportion to difficulty, but excessive demonstrations by a player or his partisans are not proper because of the possible effect on other competitors." But seeing as Tiger hadn't given the crowd anything to roar about since his chip-in eagle on Thursday, I think Bobby would forgive us for the applause that carries Tiger all the way from the 11th green to the 12th tee. Just like Art Wall, Tiger is down 5 with 7 to go.

5:44 PM • Tiger wants to keep the momentum but can't, straining as his birdie effort on the 12th just misses. He follows it by missing the fairway on the 13th for the first time all week. It's a crucial error. From a crummy pine straw lie, he can only pitch out to about a hundred yards, meaning eagle is out of the question when he needs it most. Back behind us, in the middle of Amen Corner, Immelman has just bogeyed the 12th. A birdie here would pull Tiger within only three. His wedge to the back-right pin along Rae's Creek shows that he is not interested in second place. It hits and stops six feet from the hole.

This is his last chance. Church hasn't worked. Mark from Dubai hasn't worked. Stewart Cink has been completely worthless. All that is left is gritting my teeth and talking to Tiger under my breath. I sound like a high-strung parent at a T-ball game, but I don't care. *Come on, Tiger. You're better than this. Forget technical stuff. Forget Hank saying "Half a degree . . ." You're eleven years old again. You're playing with Pops. If you make this, you beat him for the first time. Just make it.*

When Tiger's putt skirts the hole, I don't gasp. And neither does anyone else. His misses have stopped being surprising. Somewhere between Thursday and Sunday, the exception to the rule has in fact become the rule. And as Tiger and I leave the 14th tee, the crowds that have followed him all week stay behind.

I don't understand. At the beginning of the season, I thought Tiger was ridiculous for thinking that he liked his chances of winning the Grand Slam. But after winning his first four events, I truly believed he could make a legitimate run at history. Yet at no point this week did Tiger even come close to the lead. By the time he made the turn on Thursday, his victory was already dependent on his ability to make a birdie run on a course that doesn't surrender them with the ease it did in 1997. If I could talk to him, I'm not even sure what I would say. "What's wrong with you?" seems like a good place to start.

6:54 PM • The only thing that would ease the pain would be if Trevor Immelman wins by a lot. Like 7 or 8. If he eagles in, that will be perfect. Then I could spend my flight home telling myself and the disinterested people around me that Tiger couldn't have caught him even if he wanted to. But Tiger birdies 18 to finish at 5 under. When his putt falls in, he rolls his eyes and dismisses the ball with a wave of his hand. While he's in the scorer's hut checking his card, the leaderboard flashes the update that Immelman has double-bogeyed 16 to fall back to 8 under. And that's where Immelman finishes, only 3 measly shots ahead of second-place finisher Tiger Woods.

It's the second straight year he's been the runner-up at the Masters, but last season he didn't start the year by saying that winning the Grand Slam was "easily within reason." The press doesn't let him pass without bringing up his statement from January. "I learned my lesson," Tiger admits. "I'm not going to say anything." At least he didn't backpedal on the notion that he still believes it's possible. As for the putting: "I wasn't releasing it, wasn't getting the overspin like I normally do." Despite his Saturday-afternoon putting session with Haney, he never could close his putter blade that last "half a degree." That's all it took to lose the major he seemed most due to win.

AUGUSTA TO CHARLOTTE • CHARLOTTE TO LAS VEGAS • LAS VEGAS TO L.A. • Every summer my hometown of Ventura has a fair. Ventura is a beach town sixty miles north of L.A., and as much as we try to be cosmopolitan, the fair always reveals our true country soul. There is the Arts and Crafts tent, the rodeo, and plenty of 4-H kids displaying their prized sows. Over the years, the fair has been sanitized, but when I was really young, there was still a circus freak element to it. The carny that always intrigued me most was the one advertised as "The Wild Woman." Her greasy assistant stood next to the concealed viewing area and talked about just how wild she was. She came straight from the Amazon and hadn't adjusted to contemporary society. She was raised by reptiles. She was dangerous. She was seductive. And in case we missed it, she was "wiiiiild"! My parents' judgment was so impaired by deep-fried food that they gave in to my nine-year-old curiosity and ripped off two tickets for me to see for myself exactly what a Wild Woman looked like.

I steadied myself with a breath, then climbed the five steps of the metal staircase and arrived at the platform and the window into her world. She sat on the floor, barefoot. Her hair was dark and tousled, and the only thing she wore was a tattered top and a flimsy loincloth. Around her neck was a snake whose tongue flapped in and out. She had spotted me by this point, and when I looked her in the eyes, she snarled. She was everything I hoped for and more in a Wild Woman. Since I felt fairly protected by the glass, I took another minute to take in her surroundings, the cruel pen into which she had been thrown when she was pulled from the jungle just weeks ago. There were leaves and vines and even more snakes. Big ones, little ones, some coiled, some stretched out. But none of them was moving. I pressed my nose against the glass to confirm my suspicions. All of them were completely fake.

My dad met me at the bottom of the stairs. "How was it, pal?" I shook my head, having finally put the pieces together. "She wasn't real." He put his arm around me, and we headed for the giant carpet slide. I was too young to know the word "disillusionment," but I had just experienced it for the first time. It's safe to say that Tiger Woods has never been compared to a trashy woman in a loincloth, but after what I witnessed over the last six days, I feel similarly duped.

PERISCOPE DOWN

Rehab

April 15–June 11, 2008

When I arrive home from Augusta on Monday, I have no desire to visit tigerwoods.com to see how he has spun the defeat. No need to restock my supply of Tigerade. Might as well delete the Sunday coverage off TiVo. My irrational behavior lasts just over twenty-four hours. Before dinner on Tuesday I receive an e-mail with some breaking news. There is no burying the lead: "Woods Has Knee Surgery, Will Miss a Month."

Tiger's first surgery on his left knee was in 1994, while he was still at Stanford. A benign tumor was discovered and removed. Eight years later, in December 2002, doctors revisited the knee to drain a cyst that was found on the surface of his anterior cruciate ligament (ACL), the main ligament that connects the femur to the tibia. He was out for two months. After pain returned in his knee last summer, the same doctor who performed the '02 procedure went back in, discovered damaged meniscus cartilage, and repaired it.

Meniscus cartilage is the spongy tissue attached to the inside of the knee joint and acts as a shock absorber between the two bones. When it's torn, it means the bone is now rubbing against bone, which is as painful as it sounds. Once repaired, the tissue remains swollen and takes a month or two to shrink to its normal size and allow the joint to flex and accept the full weight of the body without discomfort.

Within a minute I'm back to tigerwoods.com to confirm that this is not a joke. From there I salvage Sunday's final round from our Recently Deleted folder on TiVo. Hillary pops her head out of the kitchen.

"What are you watching?"

"The Masters." Unlike me with my dad back in 1986, she does not join me in front of the television. She groans and returns to the laundry.

I'm looking for evidence. I'm not convinced that Tiger had to do this now. It seems more likely that once he had blown the Grand Slam, he decided to go under the knife and try again next year. And if so, what a jerk. That would far more disappointing than the Wild Woman. That would be as if I had bought two tickets for the Wild Woman, climbed up the stairs, and found Margaret Thatcher drinking tea. I grow angrier until Tiger reaches the 4th hole. Then I see it. After hitting his bunker shot, the cameras cut to him stepping out of the trap. He plants his left leg and tries to climb out. He can't do it. He stops, pulls his left leg back, and steps out with his right instead, using his sand wedge to support himself. David Feherty notices it and says that Tiger looks "weary."

He wasn't weary. He was injured.

Suddenly I'm the detective at the end of *The Usual Suspects* who starts piecing all the clues together long after Kevin Spacey has limped out of the precinct. I remember the shots that Tiger seemed to like, but landed short. I flash to the pitches on 2 and 3 that Tiger couldn't put any closer than twenty feet. I think about the drives at the 18th on Friday and Saturday that he wanted to cut and ended up flaring into the pine straw. And most obvious to me now is the fact that he played only nine holes on Tuesday and no holes on Wednesday.

He wasn't playing like Tiger Woods because he *wasn't* Tiger Woods. He was Lance Armstrong with a flat. He was Michael Jordan with a baseball glove. A banged-up knee doesn't account for poor putting, but if the injury had affected just three full shots over the course of the week, that could be the difference. It had taken 72 holes to push me away and just one failed attempt to step out of a sand trap to bring me back. Shoot, we really are out of Tigerade.

Four weeks. A month wouldn't be enough time for Tiger to make it back for the Players Championship in early May. Fine. He hadn't won there since 2001 anyway. So that would put him on target for the next event he typically plays, the Memorial, six weeks out. What in the world do I do for six weeks?

The desire to follow Tiger had started with the idea of wanting to see what I could learn along the way. But the painful reality is that most of what Tiger has displayed aren't things anyone can just wake up and do. They aren't even things he could always do. In Tom Callahan's book *In Search of Tiger*, he tells a story about a Tour event Tiger played while still an amateur where he looked up and realized that he was hitting balls between Greg Norman and Zimbabwe's Nick Price, two of the game's top players at the time. He turned to his coach Butch Harmon and quietly asked, "How far away am I, Butchie? When will I be that good?"

There are few quick fixes. But with six weeks, I have a window. It's not much, but if Tiger is going to use that time to rehab and return to normal, maybe I should use it to *stop* being normal and finally try to improve.

42 DAYS UNTIL THE MEMORIAL • Over the last ten years, I have transitioned from a scrappy-looking kid who ate anything he wanted without recourse into a man who continues to eat anything he wants but looks worse and worse every day. Three months of following Tiger up and down hills, and my health is comparable to that of a first-century shepherd. Cardiowise, I am pretty solid, but my body is wasting away on a diet consisting of stale granola bars and bottled water. Since I didn't like paying five bucks for a hot dog, most days on the course I would eat almost nothing; then, when Tiger was done, I'd stop and have one gigantic meal before going to bed. As it now stands, my face is tan and full but everything else is gaunt and pasty.

So, just two days after Tiger's surgery, I buy a used workout bench. It even comes with a bar and some weights. I demote my truck from the garage to the street and set up the bench in its place. I'm not using it today, though; I'm sore just from unloading it.

40 DAYS UNTIL THE MEMORIAL • I've got to believe I have a little head start on Tiger. Tonight he is at Tiger Jam XI, his foundation's annual fundraiser in Las Vegas. The pictures show him hobbling around on crutches. I, on the other hand, have just benchpressed *forty-five pounds*. Or at least that is what someone told me the empty bar weighs. I'm well aware of how pathetic that is. The maximum weight one can lift should not be the minimum weight possible.

37 DAYS UNTIL THE MEMORIAL • Apparently I wasn't pushing myself enough with the forty-five-pound bar. Three days after I began, I am maxing out at 130 pounds. Most trainers would say that's too soon to see any results, but between sets I take off my shirt right as our fifty-year-old neighbor Sandy walks past our garage. She stops, then backs up to wave and say hello. Hey, if you've got it, flaunt it.

35 DAYS UNTIL THE MEMORIAL • I play a round of golf with John Ziegler, talk radio host and "Pastor of the First Church of Tiger Woods." The house of worship is his Web site, tigerwoodsisgod.com, where Ziegler chronicles everything Tiger does that can be interpreted as divine. The premise makes me laugh and I assume the whole thing is a joke, but after meeting Ziegler, I'm not so sure. "If it wasn't for Tiger Woods, I probably wouldn't be here," he says. He didn't mean playing golf with me, he meant alive. After a rocky 1995 in which he broke up with his girlfriend, lost his job and then his mom, it was his interest in seeing what the nineteen-year-old defending U.S. Amateur champ would do that kept him from taking his own life.

As a professional talker, Ziegler happily fills the void caused by my uncomfortable silence. And, eventually, he admits that he's an agnostic who is having a little fun with the idea that Tiger is God. It doesn't change the fact that his best reason for living was to watch Tiger. "What are you going to do when he retires?" I ask him. "What will you have to fall back on?" I don't know if it's a question that Ziegler has considered, but his response is distressing. "Nothing," he says. Maybe I'm wrong, but I don't think that keeping John Ziegler alive is a pressure that even Tiger Woods wants to bear.

30 DAYS UNTIL THE MEMORIAL • Even though I taped my Golf Channel interview back in March, it is airing for the first time only tonight. With Tiger having been out of action for more than two weeks now, I assume some producer went into the Tiger Vault and I was all that was left. The piece actually turned out pretty well, but I am aware as I watch it that I look chunky. I keep this to myself and then receive an e-mail from someone I met at Doral who says, "Man, you looked fat!" I was going to skip a day with the weights, but feel compelled to return to the garage.

28 DAYS UNTIL THE MEMORIAL • Tiger has his two-week checkup today and reports to GolfDigest.com that he is "right on schedule" to play again in four to six weeks but gives no further details. It convicts me of the fact that I have set no specific goal as to what I'm trying to achieve during my "rehab." I set two goals. (1) To bench press my body weight (160 pounds) before I leave for the Memorial in Ohio. For some reason, lifting one's own weight is the accepted measurement of masculinity, but I will have to push myself a little more if I am to have any chance at reaching it. (2) To play golf and break 80 before Tiger's return. I used to do this about half the time I played. But I look up my handicap and see that I haven't shot in the 70s in almost a year.

26 DAYS UNTIL THE MEMORIAL • Having goals is definitely making a difference. I am consistently working out every other day, plus I have been to the driving range three days in a row. I don't think this was the "new Bob" my wife was envisioning when I told her she was going to see some real changes over the next six weeks.

I decide to play golf with my dad, believing my daily practice sessions have finally revealed what is wrong with my swing. I shoot a 39 on the front to confirm everything I have been working on and a 49 on the back to make me question all I've ever known.

22 DAYS UNTIL THE MEMORIAL • With my own analysis worthless, it is time to call Keith. Keith is the pro who gave me the last golf lesson I paid for, three years ago. He fixed my swing then, and now I'm back. I ask him whether he wants me to tell him what I think I'm doing wrong. "Nope." He just wants to watch, like Hank Haney. I start to hit some balls, and he quickly says, "Oh yeah . . . uh-huh." Within five minutes, he has unraveled everything, showing me that I am burying my right elbow in my side on the way down, essentially "getting stuck" with every shot. I can get away with it on my short clubs, but it makes my long irons and driver impossible to start on line.

"That's Tiger's old swing problem."

"Yep," he answers. In my efforts to get better, the only thing I have successfully achieved is the one flaw Tiger has gotten rid of.

20 DAYS UNTIL THE MEMORIAL • It has been more than three weeks since Tiger's operation, and there are no new updates out of Isleworth. I feel desperate to fill the void, so I make a short trip to Stanford University. Outside the varsity golf office is a long wall covered with the plaques of every All-American golfer in Stanford's history. I don't think it's a coincidence that the two hanging directly over the office door belong to Eldrick "Tiger" Woods.

I pop my head in, and one of the assistants is watching the Players Championship on a giant flat-screen TV. The walls are coated with photos, flags, and scorecards. The biggest thing of all is a three-by-four-foot framed photo of Tiger, circa 1995. He is wearing a red Stanford hat, a red Stanford shirt, and shorts. He's squatting down to read a putt, and I notice that the elastic on his socks is shot, making them hang loose around his ankles. In two years, that kid with crummy socks would be the most sought after man in sports. The plaque beneath the picture provides the real evidence of his early greatness:

NCAA Individual Champion—1996

Jack Nicklaus National Player of the Year—1996

1st Team All-American—1995, 1996

Pac-10 Champion—1996

Pac-10 Player of the Year—1995, 1996

71.1 Stroke Average

10 Tournament Victories

22 Top-tens in 27 Tournaments

Ten wins in 27 events. That's a 37 percent winning percentage as only a freshman and sophomore. It makes me wish he had stayed in school, just to see how much higher he could have pushed that number before graduation.

Inspired by Tiger's record and using the swing fix that Keith taught me yesterday, I head out for eighteen holes on the Stanford Golf Course. By number 6, I have already ruined my chances of breaking 80. Late in the back nine, I have to look at my scorecard to make sure I will actually break 100. I shoot a 94. At least I hear some Tiger stories. I'm paired with a local contractor, a Stanford professor of ancient religion, and the professor's forty-year-old son, Andrew. Andrew makes sure that I've heard the tale that has become part of the Tiger/Stanford lore. It was the middle of the night during a torrential downpour, and the football team was returning from an away game. As the bus drove by the driving range, a player noticed that the lights were on and told the driver to pull over. A few of them hopped out and found Tiger, soaking wet, pounding balls into the distance. Knowing him from the gym, they called out, "Tiger! What the heck are you doing?" Tiger looked up and said, "Working on my rain game."

There have been no Tiger sightings at Stanford of late, but the assistant coach tells me that earlier in the year when the team traveled to Florida for a tournament, Tiger invited everyone over to his house in Isleworth for a BBQ. A college dropout flipping burgers is usually a cautionary tale. For the Stanford golf team, it's their most powerful recruiting tool.

17 DAYS UNTIL THE MEMORIAL • Tiger appears via satellite at a press conference for the BMW Championship, an event that isn't played until September. When asked for an update on his rehab, he says he is still only chipping and putting and "just trying to get the leg organized." By saying "the leg" and not "my leg," it's as if he refuses to personally associate with his own body part until it's performing up to his standards.

12 DAYS UNTIL THE MEMORIAL • Since I started trying to salvage my golf game a month ago, I have tried to emulate Tiger's work ethic and willingness to change. The results have not been encouraging. Since the Masters I have played four rounds of golf, and my scores in chronological order have been 83, 85, 88, 94.

Today my buddy Paul invites me out to Encino Municipal for a round. I start off by trying one last time to force my elbow in front of my body like Keith had instructed. After four holes, I'm already 3 over par.

While the other guys in the group tee off on the 5th, I move off to the side and thinking about Captain Jay Brunza. Brunza was the Navy psychologist Earl Woods brought home to meet Tiger at age thirteen. The first night, he taught Tiger a few mind tricks. When they went out the next day to play, Tiger birdied five of his first seven holes. The legend only becomes nuttier. In Tim Rosaforte's 1997 book *Tiger Woods: The Makings of a Champion*, Rosaforte says Brunza could soon hypnotize Tiger in less than a minute and that Tiger would stick out his arm and have Earl hang on it without being able to bend it. Tiger had Brunza caddy for him during the 1991 U.S. Junior Amateur, and together they won five straight USGA titles between 1991 and 1995. Then, just as Tiger left the hands-on Butch, he moved on from Brunza, having acquired all the tools he needed.

I'm not ready to be hypnotized or ask my friend Paul to hang on my arm, but it's becoming clear that if my "getting stuck" on the downswing were just a physical correction, I'd be seeing some progress at least. Even when Tiger was failing to win during 2003–2004, he always said "I'm close" and "It's getting better." I'm not getting better. I'm *mentally* stuck, too.

For the first time in years, I decide to forget about my score and just enjoy the round no matter where I hit it. Something basic that I had lost over the years is that golf, after all, is a game. And why play a game if it's not any fun? When I putt out on 18, I have no idea what I shot. As we walk back to the parking lot, Paul finishes adding up our scores.

"Seventy-eight?" he says.

"What? Are you sure?"

"Yeah." Turns out I played the last fourteen holes just 3 over par.

"Nice round," Paul says.

"Wow. Thanks. That was fun." For once, I wasn't lying.

6 DAYS UNTIL THE MEMORIAL • The high of breaking 80 carries me through the final stretch of Tiger's rehab. But there is still one goal left. Today is my big workout. The day I go for that magic number: 160 pounds. I do my first set at 125, then my second at 150, then add the final five pounds on either side. I look at the weights, now using almost everything that came with the bench, and decide I shouldn't be doing this without adult supervision.

Hillary is busy blending baby food. When I ask her if she can spot me, she grimaces and says, "I'm scared," as if she's the one who will be lifting the barbell. I tell her she will have to do something only if I can't, which won't happen.

I lie down on the bench and start to take deep breaths. I have no idea if this helps, but the magician David Blaine did it a lot before he held his breath for seventeen minutes in front of Oprah a few weeks ago, so it must be good for something. I lift the bar off the stand and feel its weight on my hands. I refuse to make eye contact with my wife, since I'm sure her look won't be one brimming with confidence. I drop the bar slowly to my chest, inhaling one last time, then push. To my surprise, it pops up rather easily. I did it! With a little discipline, a goal that was completely unrealistic only five weeks ago is one I have actually achieved. And I've still got a week to spare.

Then, of course, I get greedy. Rather than move the bar to the stand and accept the accolades, I drop it a second time down to my chest. This time it doesn't pop up so easily. Thirty percent of the way up, my muscles revolt. Hillary and I probably should have discussed a signal in case I'm in trouble. Hoping not to scare her, I say as calmly as I can, "Help." She reaches down and pulls up, and together we plop the bar back on the stand.

It's rare in our marriage that I am able to do anything that classifies as particularly macho, but this certainly is. Hillary congratulates me, gives me a kiss, then adds, "Don't ever make me do that again." In the history of human accomplishments, almost everything is more heroic than breaking 80 or lifting 160 pounds. But for me, it's a great start.

Three hours later, I find out that Tiger has decided to skip the Memorial. Which means that after eight weeks off, his first event back will be the hardest tournament of the year: the U.S. Open, June 12 at Torrey Pines.

THE MAN

· ·

The 108th U.S. Open

Torrey Pines Golf Course
La Jolla, California
June 12–16, 2008

When the United States Golf Association staged its first Open in 1895, it was only 36 holes. Horace Rawlins, an Englishman and one of only eleven men in the contest, shot a 91 and an 82. And won. From its beginning, it was the most difficult test in golf.

It will be no different for me. The Open is a golf fan's ultimate challenge. Whereas the Masters limits the number of badges to create an intimate experience among the patrons and the players, the USGA creates a different kind of intimacy by cramming in as many people as possible. Those numbers are sure to swell because of Tiger's return. Plus, the sadists at the USGA have decided to pair him with world number two, Phil Mickelson, and number three, Adam Scott, for Thursday and Friday. The predicted attendance is around 50,000 fans per day. For me to follow this group will be the equivalent of trying to watch a Major League Baseball game where, every half inning, the players and all the fans in the stadium migrate to a different field.

But I've done my homework. I pulled out my notes and the overhead map from the Buick Invitational and have refamiliarized myself with the course. I know where traffic will bunch. I know corners to flat-out avoid. And I know where I will have no choice but to sprint.

One part of this trip that is different than any other is that for the first time this year, I have brought the entire family with me. After two months at home, I didn't want to leave them again. They're not coming to the actual tournament, of course. If either of my kids were to scream in Tiger's backswing and cost him a major, I would feel such guilt that the four of us would move to Iceland and only return after Tiger surpasses Nicklaus's eighteen-major mark. Yesterday the four of us piled into the Camry and drove south. Unfortunately, after a half hour, I realized I had forgotten my periscope, so we drove home again. Going to the U.S. Open without it is like going off to slay Dracula without garlic and a wooden stake.

The U.S. Open is the only major that Tiger hasn't won since he overhauled his swing over the 2003–2004 seasons. But it's unfair to say he has struggled. In 2005 and 2007, he finished second. Last year at Oakmont, he had a curving downhill birdie putt on 18 to tie Angel Cabrera, a cigarette-puffing Argentinean, but couldn't pull off the miracle. In '05 at Pinehurst, he finished two shots behind Michael Campbell, a New Zealand–born player who spent the final round running to and from port-o-potties, where he would calm himself by privately doing eye exercises. As much as that seems like a foolproof formula for long-term success, Campbell hasn't won a tournament since.

In between those two runner-up finishes came the 2006 U.S. Open, which was the last time Tiger chose not to play between the Masters and the U.S. Open. His dad, Earl, had died in early May of that year after a long bout with prostate cancer, and Tiger was so distraught that he couldn't bring himself to touch a club. It was understandable.

When Tiger was only six months old, Earl dragged his high chair out to the garage, where Earl was busy hitting balls into a net, trying to make sense of a game he himself had only started playing a year before. After a few shots, he looked up and saw that his baby son was entranced.

As Tiger's passion for the game grew, Earl supported him, found the best local teachers, and taught him the importance of practice and hard work. "This game doesn't owe you anything," he told him. And when Tiger's interest waned as a teenager, Earl didn't fight it. He told him to go hang out with his friends. After a few days of video games, Tiger always returned to the sport he loved. As he began to dominate as an amateur and a pro, it was Earl's voice that Tiger heard, sometimes literally, encouraging him and reminding him of the lessons he'd been taught over the last thirty years.

After a month of mourning, Tiger finally did pick up a club and started to prepare for the 2006 Open at Winged Foot. When he showed up a few weeks later, he claimed he was ready. After shooting back-to-back 76s to miss his only professional cut in a major, he admitted that, indeed, he was not.

Tiger claims he is good to go this week and I believe him, mostly because I'm desperate to believe it's true. Over the last two months, watching tournaments without Tiger was thoroughly unsatisfying. Was Sergio Garcia's 5-under win at the Players Championship impressive? Beats me. If Tiger had been there and finished 10 under, then no. By being the best ever, he's also a gauge that tells every other player just how good they really are.

FIRST ROUND

I felt it was only appropriate to start the U.S. Open at Torrey Pines the same way I had ended the Buick Invitational at Torrey Pines—with Nelson, the periscope-loving father of four whom I met on the first hole back in January. He didn't need much convincing to slip away from his work as a financial planner and relive our past glory. Last time we teamed up, Tiger shot a final-round 71, his highest score of the week. But five months later, with the fairways harder and the greens faster, a 71 at Torrey Pines would be pretty good.

Early Thursday morning, as the seaside dew still blankets the course, I notice the most glaring change of all. The rough just inside the ropes is so long it actually has stalks growing on the ends of it. I didn't even know that grass had stalks. And when I put my foot out and try to drag it through the mixture of Kikuyu, rye, and poa annua grass, I can't do it. It's too thick. This is no dumpy municipal track anymore. It's a legitimate test of championship golf.

6:54 AM • I walk to the brick-walled putting green, and, for the first time since the 18th hole at Augusta, have found him. Blue shirt, gray slacks, white swoosh, no crutches. It's the real Tiger. Two months hasn't changed his routine. He's orbiting the putting green with three balls while Hank Haney and Stevie stand off to the side. Everything is as I hoped it would be—completely normal.

7:06 AM • His speed dialed in, Tiger picks up the two balls and makes for the range. For Open week, the traditional Torrey Pines driving range has been overrun by hospitality tents and the player parking lot. It was a low-rent range anyway, the net around it attached to weathered telephone poles. An expansive, three-tiered practice area has been created by mowing down all the grass on the 9th and 10th holes of what was Torrey Pines North.

If it weren't for Torrey Pines North, the USGA might never have entertained the idea of bringing the Open to Southern California for the first time in sixty years. Besides the range, the press tent is way down on top of number 2. Another set of corporate huts covers number 4. And somewhere beneath the concession stands and the 40,000-square-foot merchandise tent is the dead fairway on the North's 1st hole.

With Tiger on the move, half of the crowd begins running. I'm impressed. These aren't the lightweights I assumed they'd be. Some of them may be faster than I, but here's where my preparation will reap some rewards. As the other fans run to the near side of the range, I know from some advance scouting that so far this week Tiger has hit balls only from the far left side of the range. And he is undoubtedly a creature of habit. So as the lines build up for the grandstand closest to Tiger, I walk to the far one and easily find a seat. Tiger bypasses the first set of bleachers, and the crowds react with a disappointed "Ahhhhhh . . ." The second set of bleachers cheers, "Yaaay!" but I already know their fate. Tiger keeps walking. "Ahhh . . ." He arrives in front of me, and we all applaud his wise choice.

I won't feel truly relaxed until I see his first full swing. He finishes with his wedges and grabs what looks like a 9-iron. As Haney stands behind with arms crossed and Stevie polishes clubs that already look impeccable, Tiger hits a flawless, high draw that travels 150 yards and settles within ten feet of the flag. Perfect.

7:58 AM • Nelson and I have paired up directly behind the first tee, our periscopes already rising above the masses. We have no choice. The crowd around us is twenty deep and growing. To the right of the tee box is a full grandstand, and gathering in front is a formless pack of forty sportswriters. Lined up on both sides down the fairway are fifty photographers, their faces already hidden behind telephoto lenses.

Phil Mickelson arrives first, wearing a black collarless shirt and gray slacks, acknowledging his hometown fans with his favorite gesture, the nod. In this regard, Phil truly is the opposite of Tiger, wooing the crowd with his demeanor first and game second. I followed Phil for a round of the L.A. Open during a Tiger off-week back in February, just to compare the two experiences. After hitting a poor shot to the back fringe, Phil arrived and nodded his appreciation to all of us for the warm welcome. What made the whole thing strange was that not a single person had applauded the shot or his arrival. For better or worse, you don't need to work hard for Phil's love. It comes whether you want it or not.

8:05 AM • Adam's off first, then Phil, and finally Tiger. The driver is the only club he wasn't hitting well on the range. He had hooked a few and then tried to hit some low ones, which he missed right. Haney never said a thing. Twenty minutes before the U.S. Open is not the time to be offering swing tips. But maybe he should have said something. Tiger's drive on the 452-yard par 4 is another hook, clearing the left trap and disappearing into the deep rough. Nelson and I turn to leave, but we can't. Since we had arrived on the 1st tee, another twenty rows of people had packed in behind us. I tell Nelson to head to the right, and we force our way through the jam and down the fairway.

8:15 AM • Tiger hasn't made anything worse than a bogey all season. And the last time he made a double bogey at Torrey Pines South was six and a half *years* ago. So I'm a little numb as we walk to number 2 with Tiger starting his "comeback" with a 6. The only thing that was competent was the pitch out from the rough. Everything else was poor. The drive, obviously. The 75-yard wedge that flew the green. The pitch shot back to the hole that ran eight feet by. The final blow was the bogey putt that didn't even touch the lip.

I start to feel the warm pull of negative thoughts. *He's not ready. He's going to embarrass himself.* Somehow Tiger finds a way to be positive about things without sounding as if he's been programmed by a sports psychologist. When he lost the year's first major in April, he said, "I got three more." When he was 7 back after two rounds at Bay Hill, did he consider himself in striking distance? "Oh, yeah." And when his winning streak ended after the CA Championship, "You've just got to get ready for the next one." So what in the world is he thinking right now?

9:01 AM • He makes his first post-op birdie at the cliff-hugging 4th, the same spot he made his first birdie of 2008 back in January. And why not? It's only a 488-yard tight par 4 with death all down the left side. He's back to 1 over.

"What's your game plan?" Nelson immediately asks me after Tiger taps in from two feet. I may have made a mistake by telling him that he was paired with the most savvy fan at Torrey Pines today. It's the equivalent of announcing that the Grand Slam is easily within reason. I could think it, but I probably shouldn't have said it. I tell him to head to the hillside behind the 5th green. From there we will be ahead of the ten thousand fans who have congregated at this corner of the course, and we can zoom up the hill to the 6th ahead of them all.

When Tiger misses his birdie effort from the fringe on number 5, I turn to go and see that the marshals have already raised the ropes to create a passageway for the players. We've missed our chance, and the mob catches up, pressing us against the rope.

First through the chute come the caddies. Then the players. Next comes Officer Freymueller, the giant cop who took a stab at color commentary while doing crowd control at the Buick. I think he has grown another couple of inches since January. His head darts from side to side, looking for someone to Taser. After the cops come the USGA officials. Then the marshals. Then the photographers and TV crew. In all, the procession must number at least a hundred. Back at the CA Championship, Calypso Dave had dubbed them "da vultures" because of their tendency to stand right between he and Tiger and take away his perfect view.

Last are the sportswriters, led by Luau Larry, his calves resembling a pair of yams after six straight months in the sun. The writers receive the bulk of the fan's abuse since they slowly pull up the rear and are single-handedly keeping us from getting to the next hole. It also doesn't help that they look the least intimidating. Fans pepper them with sarcasm—"Hey, no rush!"—and honesty—"You're kidding, right?" The writers do seem as if they're at a class reunion more than at a major championship. They laugh and chat with friends they haven't seen in months, completely indifferent to the fact that thousands of us are standing two feet away, thinking terrible thoughts about each and every one of them.

By the time the ropes come down, even mild-mannered Nelson is cracking. We start to walk up the hill, and a volunteer tells us that because of all the people, they have blocked off the route and the only way to get to number 6 is by walking all the way down number 2 and back. "That's a real good idea," Nelson says, shaking his head. "It *is* a real good idea," the marshal responds aggressively. The U.S. Open is not where I want to take part in my first real fistfight, and we're already falling behind Tiger, so I take off running down number 2, and Nelson follows.

10:10 AM • Tiger continues to right the ship from his opening double with a five-foot birdie on the 8th and arrives at the 9th tee again even par. By getting back to where he started, he has passed Phil, who has slipped to 3 over. It's too early to look at the leaderboard, but I do anyway. The leader is 3 under, a player named Justin Hicks who has made a grand total of $8,464 this year. A player like Hicks is what makes the U.S. Open special. Any golfer with a handicap near scratch can pay the $150 entry fee and try to qualify. A fan next to me has a smuggled BlackBerry and is looking at the players' scorecards. I check out Hicks's opening nine. He's had six birdies and three bogeys. The U.S. Open is supposed to be about pars, and he hasn't made one yet.

11:45 AM • Five holes later, Tiger is back in contention. He birdied the 9th after bouncing a ball off a spectator and has made a bunch of clutch par saves to settle in at 1 under. His game is what I should have expected after a layoff where he couldn't hit balls for a month. His full swing shots are a little wild, but his putting appears as strong as it was at the beginning of the year.

After Tiger tees off on the 14th, Nelson and I jog down the right side. The closer we get to the clubhouse, the more suffocating the crowds become. The marshals see the wave of people coming behind us, and, just as they did between 5 and 6, they hold up a rope and tell us we can't keep going down 14. It's ridiculous. When I mapped out my strategy, it was based on how they had directed traffic at the Buick. I never considered that the USGA would simply not allow people to follow the marquee pairing that *they* created in the first place. Even the Masters wouldn't try something like this. "It's an infringement on our basic rights as sports fans!" I pronounce. Nelson has wisely tuned me out and heads down 15.

12:06 PM • We can't see what Tiger is doing back on 14, but it is taking forever and we haven't heard a single roar. Nelson walks to the scoreboard operator on 15 and asks what they know. "Double," they tell him flatly. "A *double*?" Nelson says, loudly enough to depress the thousand people gathered around the green. He turns around and stomps back to me. Tiger was only 2 off the lead before that. Now he has fallen 4 behind Hicks, who is done with a 68, and 3 behind Rocco Mediate, the cheery journeyman who has posted a 2-under round of 70.

12:51 PM • Tiger doesn't make any more mistakes after the 14th and comes to the par-5 18th 1 over. He still hasn't made any bogeys. He has two doubles, three birdies, and a half-dozen world-class par saves, the biggest being a sixteen-footer on 15 that stopped the bleeding after the mysterious disaster on 14.

Nelson and I have secured a prime spot behind the last tee. The hole can stretch all the way out to 570 yards, but it's not playing that far today. The USGA had considered turning the par 5 into a long par 4 for the Open but decided to keep it as is—a birdie hole. It's nice of them, but after the first 17, I'm not sure how much the players can actually enjoy it. It reminds me of my kids' pediatrician, who thinks that slapping on a Big Bird Band-Aid will take away the pain of the shots he's just given them.

Tiger has driver in hand and looks down the left side of the fairway. He is thinking about playing a cut, away from the two bunkers on the left. When he hits it, we applaud as he launches it high with the intended fade into the middle of the fairway. But when I look at him, I'm confused; from behind he's acting as though he hates it. Slumped shoulders, no twirling of the driver, no quick pickup of the tee. He is frozen, just standing in his follow-through position as the driver slowly slides through his hands, as if his body just had a power failure. It only takes me a second to diagnose what I'm seeing.

It's the knee.

Tiger turns and slowly walks back to Stevie. Most of the fans start to leave, but I can't pull myself away. I'm sure a lot of people see Tiger's expressionless face and confuse it with his typical on-course demeanor. No way. His normal look is intimidating and focused. This look is empty and—is it possible?—fragile. He doesn't limp, not even a little, but he wants to. It is taking every bit of strength to conceal it from Mickelson and Scott and the fifty different cameramen. Those ten awkward steps from the tee to his bag are the most revealing ten seconds of the entire season.

Nelson has seen his own son go through far worse than arthroscopic knee surgery but he recognizes the same look on Tiger's face.

"He's hurt," he says.

"I know."

Tiger has always moved in a cloud of impressive invincibility with which it is hard to identify. But here he is, right in front of us, looking broken. He's the furthest thing from omnipotent; he's a man with a lowercase *m*.

The crowds are so dense that they won't allow us to get much closer to the 18th green than a hundred yards without a fight. We watch from afar as Tiger summons the focus to clear the water of Devlin's Billabong in only two shots, but he still seems flattened by the painful drive. He leaves his uphill eagle putt fifteen feet short and misses the birdie. A three-putt for a par and a 1-over round of 72. Four shots back. Nelson and I were hoping for a day filled with fireworks, and we got only question marks.

SECOND ROUND

Today is June 13, my wife's birthday. For her, it couldn't have fallen on a worse day. When I tell her I have something planned, I lead with "Well, Tiger tees off around one o'clock . . ." Before I can finish, she says, "Oh, this already sounds so romantic." My plan is to take everyone to the beach in La Jolla for a few hours. But as Danny splashes around in the water, I keep finding myself preoccupied, thinking about yesterday.

The press didn't miss what I saw and asked Tiger about his drive on 18 when he finished his round. "It's a little sore," Tiger responded. I start to imagine the worst possible scenarios . . . that what I witnessed was the repaired cartilage coming loose, fluid pooling, infections, pus . . . Back in reality, the kite I'm supposed to be flying with my daughter crashes into the sand, nearly taking out a German family. I see the MetLife blimp heading north toward the course and check my watch. Both tell me it's time to go.

1:00 PM ● Tiger starts his day on the back nine, and the only painful thing I notice for the next three hours is the numbers on his scorecard. Four bogeys mixed in with one spectacular eagle, leaving him at 3 over par through twenty-seven holes.

If Tiger has been grimacing, I haven't seen it. But I'm not exactly standing in the front row either. The crowds are thicker today. Walking from the 11th tee to the green, there is no grass to be seen, just a rippling sea of heads, each of us going only as fast as the person in front of us.

My best looks have come from fans who are renting something called Championship Vision, a tiny handheld TV feeding NBC's live coverage. But it's not quite live. The three-second tape delay has left many spectators confused, and long after Tiger's shots are already in the air, a fan can often be heard announcing "Okay, he's about to hit . . ."

Yesterday, Rocco Mediate was one of many players in the mix. Right now, his lead on Tiger is seven. No fan in good conscience can hate Rocco. At forty-five years old, the only thing intimidating about him is his name. A native of Greensburg, Pennsylvania, just southeast of Pittsburgh, he wears his pants happily pulled up high like *I Love Lucy*'s Fred Mertz, and his scruffy-faced smile disappears only when he turns his head to spit.

But Rocco's career has been littered with just as many highs as lows. After winning at Doral in 1991 and Greensboro in 1993, a ruptured disk and the surgery that followed knocked him out for most of the 1994 season. He clawed his way back to his former level, won the 1999 Phoenix Open and the 2000 Buick Open, then traveled the following week to the PGA Championship, where he sat in a chair, only to have it collapse. Rocco bonked his head on a railing and injured his shoulder, neck, and wrist, ultimately having to withdraw. His most recent run at a major came at the 2006 Masters, where he was in contention on Sunday when his back problems flared up again. He hit three balls into the water on Augusta's 12th and finished with a round of 80.

He's always had the game to contend in a major, he's just never had the luck.

4:05 PM • Tiger has always had both. But that's not what the smashed guy next to me on number 1 thinks: "Tiger's *done!*" Besides the crowds being denser, they are also decidedly drunker, which I attribute to the fact that it's Friday. Most of these people don't have to work tomorrow. At this rate, this guy won't be able to walk tomorrow. But his assessment of Tiger's situation could be right. Seven shots is a lot of ground to make up, but still within the record Lou Graham set in 1975, when he came from 11 shots back after Friday to win his only U.S. Open.

If Tiger's knee is to blame, and if it's only getting worse, I don't really understand what he's doing here. He's right next to the clubhouse. There would be no shame in removing his cap, shaking hands with Mickelson and Scott, and slipping away. He's scheduled to play the Buick Open in two weeks and the British Open the week after that. To risk making his knee worse and then missing those events just so he can finish in a meaningless tie for 30th here is baffling.

But his hat stays on. He tees up the ball and promptly pushes it way right, over the bunkers and down near the cart path. The crowds have already swarmed the ball, so I raise my periscope as high as it goes and watch from afar. Turns out he's not near the path; he's actually on it, or at least his feet are. Flanking him on all three sides are beer-guzzling spectators. It looks as if he's hitting the shot out of a sports bar.

He takes his swing, and the metal cleats under his left foot slip. He immediately grits his teeth in agony. *This is stupid*, I think. But as usual, he hasn't asked my opinion. He's just watching the shot. The ball clears the greenside bunker and lands hole high, fifteen feet right of the pin. The crowd cheers; Tiger shakes off the pain and starts walking. He makes the birdie putt as Rocco bogeys the 10th. Tiger is back within 5 and never once looks at the clubhouse.

4:23 PM • I would have thought that the pain would make him take a more gentle approach to the course. Instead, he is now trying to over-power it. On the short par-4 2nd, he booms a drive 350 yards, then rams a twenty-five-foot putt into the cup. Stevie saddles over to him and gives him a frat boy, congratulatory shove. The push nearly knocks Tiger over, and he hops away on his right foot before reburying the in-jury. "What are you doing?!" he says. Despite Stevie's best efforts, Tiger is finding his rhythm. It's his first back-to-back birdies since the Tavis-tock Cup.

5:07 PM • After a par on the par-3 3rd, Tiger birdies the 4th hole for the second straight day, this one a twenty-foot putt with the Pacific making a blue backdrop behind his right-armed fist pump. He's still not done. On the 5th hole he makes *another* birdie. Phil pours one in on top of him, which the crowd loves, but there's no question about the story of the day. Tiger's front-nine scorecard now reads 3-3-3-3-3. He's played his opening five holes in 4 under par. I pass yet another drunk guy. "That's *sick*," he says, summing up Tiger's play. The stretch has taken him from 3 over to 1 under in just over an hour.

5:59 PM • After Tiger pars 5 and 6, I run down the downhill, dogleg-right par-4 7th and find a spot fifty yards up from the green. Tiger has put yet another approach shot within birdie range, fifteen feet left of the back-right pin. The combination of summer heat, heavy drinking, and Tiger's rediscovered game leads the tubby fan next to me to threaten, "If Tiger makes this, I might have to run across the hole naked." Considering the six empty beer cups nested in his hand, I think he's serious.

As Tiger takes his last practice stroke, I've never had a stranger motivation to want a putt to fall. The chance to see Officer Freymueller figure out how to arrest a fat naked man without actually touching him would be the perfect addition to an amazing nine holes. One person is definitely rooting *against* Tiger: the man sitting at waist level in front of the potential streaker, who says out loud as Tiger draws back his putter: "*Please* don't make this putt . . ." Tiger misreads it, and we groan in disappointment. The drunk guy takes another sip and stumbles away, adding, "You guys are soooo lucky."

6:29 PM • After another par at the 8th, Tiger has a five-foot putt on the 9th hole for a final birdie and a closing-nine score of 30. 30. It would be his lowest nine holes in a U.S. Open and only a stroke off the nine-hole U.S. Open record of 29. Stevie has his bib off again, finally free from that burdensome piece of weightless fabric. He circles the putt with Tiger, making sure his boss doesn't miss something obvious, and then steps away as Tiger steadies himself over his ball. He knocks it in the dead center. Five under on his second nine and 2 under for the tournament, just 1 shot off the lead.

Tiger waits next to the green, then shakes hands with Phil Mickelson and Adam Scott, both of whom look like they've seen a ghost. *If we can't beat Tiger this week, when can we?* Before he started his run, Mickelson and Scott were within a stroke of him. Tomorrow they'll be teeing off three hours before he does.

THE BEST SWING IN GOLF • Energized by Tiger's play, I head to the course early on Saturday to do all the various touristy things I haven't done yet. There's no Buick Clubhouse and the RV with the free skin screenings is nowhere to be found, but I do find a white tent called the U.S. Open Experience Presented by American Express. It's a terrible name, but inside is a giant glassed-in case containing what I thought was Iron Byron, the clunky metal machine that golf companies use to test the performance of new clubs. In fact, this is the hi-tech version that has long ago replaced Byron, and its name is even less catchy than the tent's. It's the Golf Laboratories Computer Controlled Robot.

I stand there for a long time just watching it swing back and through. With every swing, the rigid steel arm on the black metal base winds up and then unleashes, each time sending the ball into the same exact spot on the hanging target. The strangest job of the week goes to Justin, a guy in his early twenties who has two pockets full of Titleists. Every time the robot is done, he opens the door and places another one on a tee.

As Justin exits for the thousandth time, I ask him if this is the weirdest job he's ever had.

"I used to transfer bull sperm from place to place, so no." Balls are his thing, I guess.

Gene Parente, the CEO of Golf Laboratories, sits on a stool next to the robot, ready to answer all the questions golf nerds like me can think up. Turns out nearly every major clubmaker owns one of their robots, as well as the USGA and the R&A. It can duplicate any golfer's specific swing conditions: ball speed, head speed, launch angle, and spin rate. The advantage in this isn't just for companies making clubs for average golfers. Nike engineers can set up their robot to mimic Tiger's swing so they can tailor clubs for him without asking him to hit a single ball. The cost? $130,000.

Gene says the only way to improve the robot at this point is to work on the biomechanics of it, essentially to make it look more like a real person. "Why don't you just put a hat on it?" I ask. Thankfully, he has a sense of humor. Or at least he has found one after sitting on that stool twelve hours a day since Tuesday. He admits that he's not sure how much more patience he has and already has his Sunday afternoon explanation ready: "It's a robot. It hits golf balls. What more do you want to know?"

THIRD ROUND

It's colder today and breezy, sweater weather for the players. I refuse to change any of the clothes I wore yesterday, just in case the reason Tiger shot a 30 on one leg was that God was smitten by my teal shirt.

The other players around Tiger on the leaderboard aren't the ones who make me particularly nervous. In first by a shot is Stuart Appleby, the Aussie who started the year with five straight top tens, but hasn't done much since. Playing with Tiger is Robert Karlsson, a lanky Swede whom Tiger beat in the 2006 Ryder Cup. The only memorable thing about that match occurred on the 7th hole when Stevie dropped Tiger's 9-iron into a lake and couldn't get it back. The rest of the players with Tiger at 1 under include only one major winner, Davis Love III. But in the time since Love won his only major, the 1997 PGA Championship, Tiger has won twelve. Unless Tiger went breakdancing last night, I can only assume he will soon have his first lead of the week.

2:52 PM • As he did Thursday, Tiger pulls his drive off the first. I'm down in the fairway when the ball bonks against a tree and settles just inside the gallery ropes, almost exactly where I tried to drag my foot through the high grass a few days ago. Tiger hacks his way out, and it runs through the fairway into the rough near the green. From here he plays a full-swing flop shot and catches too much of the ball, sending it long and back into the rough. After a terrible chip and a missed putt, he has once again made an opening-hole double bogey.

When he did that on Thursday, I walked away in a daze. Today I spontaneously start clapping and urging him on. I even yell, "That's all right, Tiger," like a soccer coach when the ball rolls through the klutzy kid's legs. Now I understand the difference between cheering and rooting. I thought they were the same thing, but they're not. For most of the year, I have been merely cheering for Tiger, wanting to see exciting things happen because I enjoy good golf and he is the surest bet to provide some. I was like someone at a monster truck rally, just celebrating the spectacle. How much you cheer is inherently connected to how entertained you feel. And when it's over, there's no emotional attachment to whatever you just witnessed. But after seeing the way an injured Tiger is willing himself not only to compete but actually contend, I've begun rooting for him.

Rooting goes deeper. It doesn't ebb and flow when good things or bad things happen. Wins and losses can't change its strength. It's constant and selfless, and when your guy is hurting, it hurts you, too.

To Tiger's ears, cheering and rooting all probably sound the same: one unending chorus of affirmation. Then again, when he is at his best, he may not even hear us at all.

3:35 PM • On the 4th, Tiger's favorite birdie hole, he hits a 3-wood right and into the rough. The pin today is tucked on the back-left shelf, and even from way over here he'll have to carry the bunker to get to it. Tiger goes through his thoughts with Stevie. "I've got to hit it past that front edge to have any kind of angle." Stevie suggests an 8-iron. "Eight isn't enough. If I'm short, I have no shot." He takes a 7-iron, chokes down on it, and promptly hits it exactly where he was trying not to—short and left and into the trap. He makes a bogey to drop yet another shot.

4:02 PM • Tiger pars the 5th, and I head down the 6th to check on the leaderboard to see the damage from Tiger's poor start. No one is playing well, but no one is playing as poorly as Tiger:

	TOTAL	DAY
Rocco Mediate	−2	0
Stuart Appleby	−1	+2
Davis Love III	−1	+1
D. J. Trahan	−1	+1
Lee Westwood	−1	0
Tiger Woods	+1	+3

5:40 PM • After Tiger bogeys the 12th, Rocco's lead grows to 5 shots. I continue to clap and yell no matter what, but I'm exhausted.

The par-5 13th at Torrey Pines South is one of only two holes on the course with any legitimate elevation change. The first 400 yards play slightly downhill before the fairway completely drops away into a deep valley that collects any shots to the green that come up short. It's especially true today with the pin only five paces from the front edge.

I have gone ahead to the fairway and look back to see Tiger standing over his drive, still wearing the black sleeveless sweater he started with almost three hours ago. I'm starting to think he should have stuck with his same shirt from yesterday, too.

The tee is so far back, I never hear the sound when he hits the ball, but his now familiar body language says it's going right. I look into the air and I see it, high against the gray sky, *forty yards* right of the fairway. I take off running long before it lands. Since no one else sees it, I look like a crazy person being attacked by a swarm of invisible bees. The ball thuds on the yellow, trampled rough and rolls to within a few feet of a concession stand. I am almost there when an eleven-year-old kid throws me an elbow and boxes me out to claim the best spot.

As we stop, it creates a pileup behind us for all the fans who were running full speed without knowing where the ball was. For the next five seconds, I can hear people behind me colliding with one another. As one guy pulls up, he spills his beer all down the back of another fan. Gore-Tex has probably never been officially tested for its resistance to Budweiser, but I'm happy to report that it beaded right off the fan's back without his knowing.

5:53 PM • From an iffy lie in the trampled rough, Tiger skies his 5-iron onto the back of 13 green. I "excuse me" and "pardon" my way into the middle of the wide hill that rises behind it. Tiger's ball had landed only a few feet from the front hole position, but released all the way to the back fringe, leaving him a sixty-foot monster putt. This is not even a simple lag. Theoretically, if he misjudges the speed, he could roll the putt not only past the hole, but also off the green and down the sixty-yard slope in front of the green. Like most putts, when he hits it, it's followed by the inevitable "Get in the hole!" screams. But this putt is so long that there is time for all sorts of screams: the generic "Tiger!," "Come on!," and "Do it!" My favorite is the nonsensical "Just . . . Yeah!"

The first clue that the putt has a chance comes from the grand-stands. They are a source we can trust. These are fans who have been sitting in one spot all day. They have seen dozens of players come through, and they know this green better than anyone else. About twenty feet out, the most confident ones up there stand and start the slow-building "oohhhhHHH . . ." Everyone joins in, hoping for the impossible. Twelve feet out, the volume grows as the putt slows and swings to the left. *There's no way.* We keep yelling. The putt must be tracking, because Stevie is so mesmerized that he only now takes out the pin he's been tending. *There's no way!* Five feet out, the ball is still rolling and Stevie starts to pump his right fist in the air as if there is a real chance this putt could actually drop. It does. I close my eyes, lean my head back as far as I can, and release a primal scream, raising my arms and my periscope into the sky. Then I just start jumping. And jumping. And jumping. I look down as Tiger appears from the right side of my vantage point for the first time, doing what must be his third or fourth or tenth fist pump at this point. He looks as if he is screaming as loudly as I am, but there are no individual noises to be heard. It is just one sustained blast of complete and utter joy.

Supposedly, villagers three thousand miles across the Indian Ocean heard the blast from Krakatoa hours after it happened in 1883. If that's true, around ten o'clock tonight someone in Hawaii is going to look up from his poi and say, "What the heck was that?" The putt moves Tiger from 1 over par to 1 under and within three of Rocco, who just happens to be standing back in the fairway watching everything that just happened.

6:02 PM • I'm hyperventilating, but I have to move. I take off running up the hill. As I pass 14 tee, I see the sad fallen faces of fans, the look of people who know they were so close to history and missed it. "Thank goodness for DVRs," one of them says to his friends, but it doesn't make them feel any better.

As I continue to run, the looks change from chagrin to confusion as people down 14 don't even know what happened. I feel like Paul Revere riding through town. "Tiger made eagle! Tiger made eagle!"

6:04 PM • Down in the fairway, I reach the third type of fan: the rabid ones. These are the fans who have made peace with their loss but only by committing not to miss one more moment, no matter the cost. So when Tiger pushes his 3-wood right and into the crowd again, the rush to the ball is total chaos. I see husbands ditch their wives. Frat boys simply drop their beers and run. Two cops who have been put on advance crowd-control duties immediately dive into the scrum and start pushing people out of the way. A USGA official is next on the scene and plants one khaki-trousered leg on either side of Tiger's ball, shielding it from further threats. Someone I can't even see barks an order: "Take ten steps back!" No one moves. As the fragile pocket starts to shrink again, a marshal (who, mind you, *paid* $150 to work here this week) gets nervous that the whole thing might collapse altogether and crawls into the space on all fours, reaches between the official's legs, and plants a tiny fluorescent orange flag next to the ball. Entire countries have been liberated with less fanfare than the frenzy around Tiger's missed drive.

6:50 PM • By stringing together pars on 15 and 16, Tiger has climbed to within two of the leader, but the leader is no longer Rocco. Rocco has suffered a mini-collapse, playing those same two holes in 3 over par. The new leader is England's Lee Westwood, 2 under through 17. Of course it would be Westwood. He has spent his entire year as the entertained but uninvolved observer to Tiger's triumphs. It was Westwood who smirked at Tiger in the midst of the Sunday coup in Dubai. And it was Westwood who got a shrug in Tucson after Tiger dusted the desert with J. B. Holmes. Now it is Westwood standing in front of him.

The strangest stat in his career remains the fact that he has won thirteen majors and they have all come while holding the fifty-four-hole lead. Or the negative translation: he has never come from behind on Sunday to win a major. Tiger chalks it up as coincidence, but talking heads have called it the one flaw in an otherwise perfect record. As Tiger has done time and again, the only way to silence critics is to prove them wrong. As much as I'd love to witness it, I'd much rather see him make up two shots in these next two holes and head into Sunday with a piece of that lead.

6:55 PM • Tiger's second shot into the 17th settles on a tongue of grass near the left bunker, playing to a pin that sits in the dead center of the green. I'm squished on the small hill across the green from the ball and can see the hole only through my periscope. But even then I'm looking through other periscopes. My periscope needs a periscope. The flag is limp. The wind that was around for most of the day is gone. Tiger settles into the shot, his right leg straight and his left leg bent as he stands awkwardly on the slope. He takes a final peek at the hole and then chops at the ball in the rough. It pops up and someone screams, "One time!!!!" I follow it like a cameraman through my scope as it bounces once and then disappears. *Wait. What?* I search for a split second, thinking I've just lost it. When the crowd erupts, I stop looking. He just chipped it in.

The putt at 13 had seven or eight seconds to crescendo. This time, the crowd goes from silent to thunderous instantly. I start spontaneously high-fiving the strangers around me who break out in chants of "Tiger! Tiger! Tiger!" He covers his face with his black Nike hat, then scratches his head—happily embarrassed at the way he just tripped up the leaderboard and closed within 1 shot of Westwood.

6:58 PM • Tiger's knee hasn't been an issue for most of the round. But that quickly changed over the round's closing holes. On 15, Tiger toppled over after his drive and had to grab the ground to keep from falling. He hit a 3-wood off 17, but he couldn't hang with it and lost it right. Here at 18, he fights through the pain two more times, first off the tee and then with his 5-wood over the lake, leaving himself his third eagle putt in ten holes.

This one's easier than the bomb he dropped on 13. Forty feet and with less break. Stevie's bib is off, thank heavens, ridding himself of his polyester yoke. Karlsson has already tapped in for a birdie of his own and fled to the edge of the green, anxious to be outside Tiger's blast circle. Yes, a two-putt would give Tiger a share of the lead for the first time all week. Earlier in the year I thought the notion of *thinking birdie* was absurd. But now that bar seems low. No one is thinking birdie right now. We are all thinking eagle. It doesn't matter that he can barely stand up for the full length of his swing. Or that he has had only a few weeks of practice in the last two months. Over the last six holes, our Pavlovian response to seeing Tiger face something undoable is to believe it will be done. And this putt, like the putt at 13 and the chip at 17, is perfectly missable. So why shouldn't it go in too? No one waits twenty feet to start screaming. We are screaming the second the ball's last dimple separates from the face of his putter. It starts off softly, flowing down the green and sliding right. I can't see the hole from the right side of the green, just Tiger and the ball. He's watching it intently. Either he's not sure it's going in, or he's communicating with it telepathically. His gaze never changes and he never moves a step. Not even when it drops into the hole.

Ten minutes ago, Lee Westwood assumed he would have the Sunday lead all to himself. Now he doesn't even have it at all. For the 14th time, Tiger Woods will be starting the final day of a major championship in first place.

From behind the green at 18, I squeeze through the mob in time to catch Tiger disappearing inside the meshed-in grandstands. He travels up its internal staircase, underneath the still cheering fans who have no idea the object of their adoration is right underneath them. The stairs open to an overhead walkway fifteen feet above the ground. As Tiger walks across it, two fans on the ground literally fall to their knees and bow down in homage. They've completely missed the point. What makes every second of today impressive is that he's *not* a god.

He comes down on the other side and is about to walk right in front of me as he heads to sign his scorecard, a half smile on his face. I haven't attempted to speak to him since Dubai, where I was ignored. He's within a few feet now and moving fast. I don't know what to say, so I just stammer out, "Nice finish, buddy!" He looks down and keeps walking. It was lame, yes, but no regrets. And "buddy"? Man, have I come a long way.

UNDER THE BIG TOP • Even after my awkward compliment, I still don't want to leave. Earlier in the week I bumped into a writer I knew who said he was walking to the media tent and asked if I wanted to join him. When I told him I didn't have credentials, he said, "What? Have you seen how big that place is? They give *anyone* credentials." No, not anyone. During Tiger's rehab, I contacted the Tour about any help they could give me and was told that media passes are reserved for people covering golf for news purposes, not for self-help purposes.

But with Tiger having just produced the most gripping closing six holes in major championship history, I don't care what my badge does or does not say. The main entrance to the media tent is blocked by two uniformed guards, but the back entrance is wide open. The loudest noise inside is the air-conditioning, which whirs as hundreds of reporters from Asia to Europe sit at laptops and try to figure out where the heck to begin. On the far side of the tent is the interview room. I pretend to scribble in my notebook as I pass a cop. The periscope hanging off my belt is a dead giveaway, but nobody stops me.

A camera crew is set up and standing on a riser behind the ten rows of chairs. "He's the greatest long putter I've ever seen," one of them says. The sun is sinking low outside, and when the side door of the interview room opens a few minutes later, it casts a long shadow of someone limping up the stairs. Tiger sticks his head in, not wanting to interrupt someone else's interview, but the floor is his.

Joining Tiger at the head table in a blazer and tie is the bespectacled Rand Jerris, the moderator and director of the USGA Museum. Tiger sits down to total silence. *Where is everyone?* Forget media bias; reporters should have carried Tiger on their shoulders all the way from the 18th green. The writers finally converge, most of them standing near the back while a few dozen take seats.

Tiger hits the highlights first, saying that on 13 he was only trying to put his second shot in the back bunker, but it got lucky and stayed on the back of the green. On 17, he hit the pitch too hard, and it got lucky and went in the hole. As for the knee? "If pain hits, pain hits. So be it. It's just pain." This is no twenty-first-century mind-set. We construct our whole lives around avoiding things that hurt or make us uncomfortable. Let's not fight through something that might make us stronger; let's just be happy now. And then when we're not, we're thoroughly confused.

It's getting dark now, and I know the kids are asleep, so I walk the mile and a half out the back gates of Torrey Pines to the taxi stand. Along the way, I pass the 13th green, where the Golf Channel's Frank Nobilo is trying to make Tiger's eagle putt. He gives it a few shots, then gives up. He can't even get it within seven feet of the hole.

FINAL ROUND

Late into the evening on Saturday, I had not totally abandoned the idea that this entire thing just might be rigged. Tiger's part in it was easy— he only had to pretend his leg was hurt, and a remote-controlled golf ball would do the rest. The NBC brass were obviously in on it, as was the USGA, which was setting up the course according to IMG's strict instructions, allowing for maximum drama. I even had an explanation for why the other hundred and fifty players were going along with it. They know that the more Tiger wins, the more people watch golf. The more people watch golf, the larger the overall purse money and endorsement deals. The thing that ultimately brought me back to reality was the fact that the ornery Colin Montgomerie had missed the cut. I couldn't imagine that he would have agreed to the deal unless he were guaranteed a top-20 finish.

12:31 PM • I'm standing beside the range with Gilbert, an off-duty marshal who for years played Torrey Pines every Sunday. At 3 a.m. he would put his bag in line at the starter window and go sleep in his car until six.

We watch together as Tiger works through his irons. When he gets to his 5-wood, Gilbert asks, "What brand are those?" I pause before answering, in disbelief that he truly doesn't know the answer. "Nike," I say. "Nike makes metals?" Now he's just embarrassing himself. When Tiger's done with his 5-wood, Gilbert gets excited. "Here it comes!" He thinks Tiger is about to hit driver. "Three-wood," I say, trying to be nice. "Three-wood? With the monkey on it?" This is almost too much for me to handle. "It's a bird," I say. I should just let Gilbert be, but after a few more shots, curiosity compels me to ask:

"You watch much golf, Gilbert?" And then one final, amazing answer.

"A *lot*. If it's on, I'm watching."

1:30 PM • On Saturday morning there were fourteen different players within four shots of the lead. Today there are only four: Lee Westwood (1 back), Rocco Mediate (2 back), Geoff Ogilvy and D. J. Trahan (each 4 back). With the extra breeze that has picked up today and the number of tough pin positions expected for the final round, it's hard to imagine anyone outside these four being able to put any pressure on Tiger.

I move down the 1st hole as the crowd back on the tee applauds Tiger's name. What I would give now for that 8-shot lead he had at the Buick Invitational. How I would love to spend my day picking up pinecones and sketching pictures of holes in my notebook. I don't want drama, I want an easy victory. It's the least I can ask for on Father's Day.

1:35 PM • It is wishful thinking. The calm lasts a grand total of six seconds, the amount of time that Tiger's ball is in the air. As it comes down among us along the left side, chaos ensues. "Out of the tree!" a gritty female cop yells at a fan who's trying for a better view. A giggly girl in a push-up bra barrels past me with her boyfriend, saying "This is so exciting!" while giving him kisses. It's a disaster, actually. It takes Tiger three shots just to get inside the ropes. He doesn't find the fairway until his fourth. Five minutes later, he has made his third double bogey of the week on number 1. Tiger didn't have the lead until the 54th hole of the tournament. By the 55th hole, he has already lost it.

For the third time this week, the new leader is Rocco Mediate. Back on the 9th hole yesterday, a fan saw the leaderboard and said, "Rocco is going to be 72 over par tomorrow. I wouldn't consider him a factor at this point." I didn't peg Rocco for quite that bad a round, but based on his fragile back, I assumed his best golf of the week was behind him.

1:50 PM • Tiger looked weaker on the range today than he did the rest of the week during warm-ups. Out of his thirteen drives, he hit only five of them on line and moved in slow motion after each one. My fear that he may not have the stamina of the past three days is confirmed on the 2nd, when, after hitting his drive long and right, he grabs his left knee. Yesterday he lasted fourteen holes before there were any real signs of pain. Today, he makes it through only one. We all try to root him on and he tries to walk but he stops again and bends all the way over at the waist, closing his eyes. The cheering abruptly stops. Some women even cover their mouths, fearing that that swing, as mighty as it was, may have been his last.

Tiger always cites how important it is for him to draw upon past experiences, believing there are almost no situations in which he can find himself that after twelve years on Tour he hasn't faced. He has never played through so much pain, but his dad did. When Tiger was a kid, he was supposed to play in a golf tournament with Earl when his dog accidentally bit most of the way through his dad's middle finger. Earl cleaned it out the best he could, wrapped a bandage around it, and continued to get ready to go to the course. "How are you going to play?" Tiger asked. "When the going gets tough, the tough get going," Earl answered. He played the whole round holding his middle finger off the club. And when the bandage became too bloody, Tiger would swap out the dressing for him so they could keep going.

Earl taught Tiger countless lessons from the driver's seat of a golf cart, but, today, none is as essential as that one. For the umpteenth time this week, Tiger straightens up, pushes off with his driver—and hobbles toward the fairway. He may lose, but he won't stop trying.

2:08 PM • Tiger struggles through number 2 and follows his 6 at the first with a bogey to fall back to just even par and now 2 shots behind Rocco. I'm having my own less painful but equally debilitating issue: my periscope just broke. I noticed earlier in the week that the center metal tube had become loose from all the abuse it had taken. So yesterday morning I went to see my friend A.J., the mechanical engineer with top secret clearance, and asked him if he could fix it. He carried it into his garage like a zoologist holding a baby condor, at which point he took it apart and dropped one of its screws on the ground. We were never able to find it and he assured me that the device would work the same without it, but as I raise the extendable arm to watch Tiger gimp down number 3, the bracket that he promised wouldn't budge has completely fallen off. I jimmy it back together and start questioning our country's national security.

3:10 PM • Tiger scratches out pars on 3 through 7 to stay at even par. Rocco has slipped back with Tiger, and now they're both behind Westwood, who's at 1 under.

There's nothing fun about today. Of course, there wasn't anything fun about yesterday either until the 13th.

Tiger lifts our spirits with a two-putt birdie on the 9th. He shares the lead for almost thirty whole seconds before Westwood birdies it as well and stays a shot in front. But Westwood falters at the 10th when he skulls a shot into the base of the grandstands, joining Tiger and Rocco at 1 under par. The other onetime contenders have all wilted, and so as Tiger and Westwood move to the 11th, the U.S. Open is down to a three-man race.

3:50 PM • The par-3 11th is a hole Tiger has owned in 2008. He birdied it every round during the Buick, the most memorable being the birdie putt that was so long and complicated he had to read it in sections. The hole is in a similar spot today, on the front-left corner, 217 yards from the tee. I'm against the ropes when Tiger passes by, and I spur him on with an inane "Keep chugging!" He chugs, landing his shot fifteen feet past the hole and then sucking it back off the hill and down within five feet. Tiger goes to 2 under and, despite his nightmare start, once again has the lead all to himself.

He seems to have figured it out again. This has become the routine this week: start off with a disaster, make some adjustment, and carry on. Yesterday in the media room he explained that because his swing was so off, he had intentionally been "overshaping" shots during the round. He didn't feel confident hitting his normal little draws or fades, so instead he played what he referred to as "big hooks or big fades" to at least gain some sense of predictability. Tiger likes to say he's stubborn, but what he's showing this week is the willingness to adapt minute by minute.

4:10 PM • He has an easy par on the week's hardest hole, number 12, and walks to the 13th tee holding a 1-shot lead over Rocco and 2 over Westwood, who missed the fairway on the 12th and made bogey. Of all the changes to Torrey Pines since January, none is as startling to me as the optional tee box on the 13th hole. During the Buick, the par 5 played a friendly 541 yards. Since then, a patch of land that seems to dangle over the Pacific has been flattened and covered in grass, 614 yards from the center of the green. They used the front part of it on Friday, and Tiger made it in two with a 5-wood. He didn't think he could reach from the full distance, and today we'll find out. The tees are all the way back.

But I'm not going. It's only seventy yards past the normal tees but another eighty to the left. Trekking there and back would be like adding another hole to my day. When I did venture back there on Friday, only a few dozen people were there, and most of them hadn't made it anywhere else. It was like a golf fan outpost. I felt guilty for not bringing them provisions. As I walked up, they all nodded in my direction, as if to congratulate me on a safe journey. It was a shame that most people who come to the Open never make it there. The ocean sits below, and looking north across the deep canyon is the green at the faraway par-3 3rd. It's the prettiest spot on the whole course.

4:15 PM ● Instead I arrive early on the hillside behind the green, where fans have packed themselves in, hoping what Tiger does today will match the miracle of his sixty-foot eagle putt from yesterday. His drive from the back tee finds the left edge of the fairway, a perfect angle for the hole cut on the far right side of the green. While we wait for him to make the hike back to civilization, I discover that I am standing next to a Tiger hater.

"He has a lot to learn from Jack and Arnie," he's telling his friends. I insert myself into their conversation.

"Really. Like what?"

"Well, for one thing he doesn't wave enough." He doesn't *wave* enough? That is Tiger's big crime? I couldn't believe it. What sort of an insecure person is upset that he hasn't been waved to? This guy is a complete joke. It takes me a few seconds of rolling my eyes before I remember that that's pretty much how I felt for most of the last twelve years. What I had failed to appreciate during that time was the significance of Tiger's focus. I thought it was a pseudo act allowing him to be rude. In reality that's the only way he can perform at the level he does. A more gallery-friendly version of Tiger would, without a doubt, not be as dominating or effective at pulling off the unbelievable with such regularity. I'm willing to sacrifice a Miss America wave for two eagles in a six-hole span.

Tiger is so far away down 13 fairway that he has to be hitting his

3-wood. The moment the ball is airborne, he immediately hates it and slashes his club back through the grass. It starts left and turns left, vanishing over the far corner of the green and out of sight. It's the same spot where Westwood went just a minute earlier. Since we can't see it, we're not sure how to react. If the two of them missed a little left, they're in the rough. If they went even farther, there are only bushes, canyons, and penalty strokes. The photographers run en masse and disappear below.

A few minutes after Tiger arrives, a ball flies up from the mystery location and lands on the back of the green, thirty feet above the hole. Okay, but not great. Off in the distance, I hear a roar. Tiger two-putts for par to hang on to his 1-shot lead.

The far-off roar was from the 14th green, where Rocco had made birdie to move to 2 under and into a tie with Tiger. But the standard-bearer for Tiger's group shows something worse. It says Tiger is only 1 under par, not 2. A photographer fills in the blanks. "In the hazard." Out of sight, Tiger had made a bogey and not a par. With only five holes left, his 1-shot cushion has just become a 1-shot deficit.

4:30 PM • Thankfully, the 14th is a definite birdie hole, but only today. Mike Davis, the USGA's senior director of Rules and Competitions, has successfully convinced his bosses to let him do something a little unorthodox for a U.S. Open. He has moved the tees 170 yards closer to the hole and made it a reachable par 4. The switch had been rumored all week and finally happened today. At just 267 yards, it's the shortest par 4 at a U.S. Open since 1955.

It's a fabulous idea, forcing every player who walks up to that tee to think. There will be no automatic club pulling here today. With Tiger and Stevie talking through their options, I squish in closer to hear what they're saying. Tiger asks Stevie what he thinks about trying to get there with a wood. "I wouldn't," Stevie says. They go back and forth, and

Stevie just keeps shaking his head. Stevie never says it, but if Tiger hits the same 3-wood that he just hit from the fairway on the last hole, he'll be in the canyon and with it will go any chance of victory.

Tiger takes an iron. There are scattered boos from those who have waited an hour in the hope that Tiger might knock it on and make an eagle. Instead, he lays up to 100 yards and walks away with only a par. Westwood, being 3 back of Rocco, has no choice but to rip a 3-wood straight at the pin. He knocks it on and two-putts for birdie to pull himself right back into contention.

5:03 PM • Tiger doesn't take advantage of a Rocco bogey on 15 when he blows his drive off the planet right and into the crowd, leading to his second bogey in three holes. Westwood makes a routine par. With three holes left, I double-check the leaderboard:

Mediate	−1
Woods	E
Westwood	E

I turn around and walk to the far left tee on 16, where reality begins to set in. *One down with three to go.* Rocco is already through the tough 16th, and I can see him walking toward the green on 17, dressed in all black but the most colorful player on the course. Tiger can't assume that Rocco will finish any worse than 1 under. It means he needs to pick up one stroke somewhere in the next three holes.

I had first seen the pin on the par-3 16th when I walked in this morning from the back gates. I started laughing, thinking maybe it had been put there as an overnight joke. The USGA's pin sheet says the hole is five paces from the back left corner. But from the tee box, the flag looks as if it's dangling off the edge of Torrey Pines State Park. It's the sucker pin to end all sucker pins, and any shots left of it have no chance of staying on the green or even on the property. The smart shot is to the middle of the green, which is where Westwood puts it to guarantee a par. Tiger's shot from 200 yards across the canyon starts right at the flag. *He's cracked.* He has overdone his pain medications and thinks this is the last hole and he has to make birdie. It lands exactly on line but a yard short in the rough and stops dead. Another foot, and it would have been absolutely perfect. Behind me at 17, the crowd lets an out an "Ohhhhh!" which tells me that Rocco had a look at birdie but missed.

Up at the green, Tiger takes the pin out. I guess if he was trying to make it from 200 yards, there is no reason to question whether he thinks he can make it from only eight. His pitch comes out too hard and doesn't check up, sliding six feet past the cup. By going for birdie he may not even make a par.

A friend once rode a roller coaster that had such a sharp turn that it temporarily shrunk his field of vision. It's the same thing that happens to fighter pilots. And it's happening to me a little right now. For Tiger to put his body through this week, to sacrifice who knows how many more events this year only to lose this one, is a crippling thought. If Tiger misses this putt, he can't win. He's just not as strong as he was yesterday to make up 2 shots in two holes. I'm 150 yards away, standing on the cart path, and I have to sit down. I set my scope on the ground and bury my head. I know Tiger has hit the putt when the murmurs build. The fan to my left is watching through binoculars: "He missed it . . ." *No.* ". . . he made it!!!" I peel myself off the pavement. Two holes left and still 1 down.

5:31 PM • Next to the 17th green, a long line of naive fans waits for a spot in the grandstands. The marshal in charge says, "In about five minutes, I can seat you all." Behind me a few hundred other fans are walking down 15 and heading home. *Home.* It's like watching the Moon landing and then turning off the TV right as Neil Armstrong steps out of the capsule. I don't know who they are or what good reasons they think they have for leaving, but they should never, ever refer to themselves as golf fans.

Tiger's approach shot from the fairway comes up thirty feet short of the hole. Up ahead are cheers on 18. Par cheers, not birdie cheers. It means that Rocco has finished the day 1 under. Tiger's putt for a three is never close on 17. And why should it be? In a week where he can't escape drama, it only makes sense that the U.S. Open would have to come down to the final hole.

5:36 PM • Tiger walks to 18. He doesn't look beaten, just old. This week has erased whatever remained of that twenty-four-year-old kid who won the 2000 U.S. Open by 15 strokes. He's a grown man pushed to his limits. Tiger and Westwood face the same challenge: a birdie to tie. Westwood has the honors and misses his drive right into the right bunker. Tiger's drive starts down the left side and stays there, one-hopping into the left bunker. They both just took the easy birdie out of the equation. Each will have to lay up and make a putt.

5:41 PM • The farther I move down 18, the less I see. Tiger becomes visible only in flashes as I rush behind rows and rows of fans. His layup from the trap misses the fairway right. It's a tired sort of shot. All day he has been using his clubs to help him into and out of bunkers, but this one he chucks at the side of his golf bag. Tiger needs to get up and down from one hundred yards out of U.S. Open rough to tie Rocco.

5:45 PM • If I wanted a guaranteed view of his putt at 18, I should have arrived six hours ago. As it is, I am twenty-five people back on the right side, parallel with the front of the green, and can see only by using my periscope and standing on my tiptoes. Behind me are another five rows of people. And beyond that is the Lodge, where fans are lined up at every possible balcony. Tiger's wedge hits fifteen feet right of the front right pin and sucks back to twelve. The crowd reacts as if it's a gimme, an instant roar mixed with piercing whistles. I'm not so confident.

Westwood's third lands fifteen feet behind the pin and receives a more tepid response. It's not just that his shot is three feet farther away, it's that every moment of this week feels like an over-the-top sports movie, and I don't think any of us sees how Westwood possibly fits into the plot. He's stuck between the legend and the journeyman. Westwood misses his putt short and right and makes way for the most pressurized moment of Tiger's career.

5:52 PM • My view of the putt is dependent entirely on the man in the third row wearing the floppy hat. I will never meet him or even know what he looks like, but every time he moves his head an inch, it creates a domino effect as the twenty-plus people behind him all adjust their own heads to see. Next to me is a small group of middle-aged friends. Two of them are standing on chairs. The third one is standing on the ground and can't see a thing. From above comes the question "What are the odds he makes this?" "Sixty-forty he makes it," responds the man without a chair. In spite of all I've seen, I don't go as high. "Fifty-fifty," I say.

There are only so many victories in every man's life. At some point, Tiger will miss a putt that he must make, and everyone will instantly realize how we have taken his greatness for granted. Tiger's preshot routine is normal until the moment he usually steps into the putt. Rather than taking one last glance, he stops and stares down the line for what has to be an extra ten seconds. He runs through his mental checklist: line—two inches right to left. Grain—down. Speed—firm. Ten seconds is a long time to make thirty thousand people wait in wretched silence. And it was more than thirty thousand. It's 3:52 a.m. in Kenya. I picture Njaaga kneeling in front of the TV, wearing his hat from the Greater Milwaukee Open. It's almost nine in Fort Lauderdale. Craig could only be pacing back and forth yelling obscenities, falling another day behind on his book. Even Cheryl in Tucson has to know what is happening, watching the coverage while a thin line of incense wafts up from the hearth.

Tiger steps forward and into the putt, now with his back to me. I begin to pray. It's not a complicated prayer. *Please, Lord . . . Please, Lord . . . Please . . .* The stroke is compact and the ball appears from behind Tiger, rolling left toward the hole. Four feet out, he takes one step back. It means he hit it exactly as he wanted to, but then he holds his position. He's not sure if he has made it. His back scrunches down as he tracks it the last ten inches. If this goes in, it won't be in the center. It dives into the right side of the cup. What follows is the sound of thirty thousand prayers being answered at the exact same moment. Our joy collides with the screams from the grandstands and engulfs Tiger in the middle. He could have turned in any direction, but he pivots on his bad knee and faces me with both hands clenched, then roars as he leans back with his face toward the sky. As the communal blast echoes back and forth in waves across the green, I turn and hug the man next to me. Someday Tiger will lose, but not today. Five minutes later, back behind the 18th green, NBC's on-course commentator Mark Rolfing hurries by. A fan calls out, "Another day, Mark!" Mark stops and smiles. "Why not?"

MONDAY PLAYOFF

7:10 AM • I practically float through the metal detectors. "Have a marvelous day," I say to the lone woman scanning tickets this early in the morning. I can't stop grinning. I just can't believe I'm back again. This must be what it feels like to survive a near-death experience. I'm acting like George Bailey at the end of *It's a Wonderful Life*. Hello, putting green! Hello, cart barn! And look at those grandstands. Have these always been such a beautiful shade of green?

7:55 AM • I take my now traditional spot at the far left side of the driving range but notice that the USGA has decided to set up Tiger and Rocco together on the far *right* side of the range. They even have their name placards waiting for them and their range balls of choice sitting in perfect pyramids.

No, no, no, no . . . *Tiger is not going to like this*, I think. I nervously move to the right grandstands and wait. A few minutes later, Tiger strides in from the putting green and walks right past his USGA-assigned spot, says nothing, and just points the grip of his putter toward his old spot on the far end. I love this guy. Two range workers spring into action, one grabbing the placard and the other trying to pick up the pyramid without all the balls toppling. It doesn't matter. Stevie is already crossing in with his own plastic bucket of balls. This isn't Shell's Wonderful World of Golf. It's the U.S. frickin' Open.

8:01 AM • Rocco makes his appearance, happy to hit balls wherever they want him to. In his hand is what looks to be an iced coffee from McDonald's. Only Rocco would want a beverage that makes him even more jittery. Tiger is the man. Rocco is the *every*man. He's the player who shows up at my local golf shop every February to sign autographs and give out door prizes. That's not an analogy—Rocco really does that. The only prize I have seen Tiger personally give away was in Dubai, where, in the middle of the trophy ceremony, officials somehow convinced him to stick his hand into a giant drum of raffle tickets and pull out a winning number. But the prize there wasn't a sleeve of Top-Flites, it was an all-expenses-paid trip to South Africa.

Rocco's the perfect foil to Tiger Woods. When Tiger scowls, Rocco smirks. In the press room last night, he was midsentence when Tiger walked in the side entrance. "You better watch yourself tomorrow, pal," Rocco said. Tiger backed off his red Tigerade and grinned.

Rocco appears harmless, but three years ago he put down $10,000 to play in the World Series of Poker and finished 600th out of almost six thousand players. He may do everything with a smile, but nothing is accidental, right down to the fact that out of all the shirts he could have worn today, he chose red, Tiger's patented Sunday (and now Monday) color.

As giddy as I am to be here, I can't get past the feeling in my gut that Rocco might make this closer than anyone probably thinks. Last night, as I received and made the now-daily round of phone calls from the friends I have made along the way, I floated Rocco's real chances to Craig from Florida. He almost hung up on me for even suggesting it. "Rocco is playing out of his mind!" he argued. "There's no way he keeps it up." As I have learned so many times over the years, nice guys don't beat Tiger. Except maybe this one.

8:58 AM • The crowds are still light this morning, and I have no problem stepping right up near the ropes on the 1st tee in time for the players' introductions. "From Naples, Florida, Rocco Mediate." The crowd cheers, and Rocco turns and waves a friendly, flitty wave to the crowd. If only that Tiger hater from yesterday were here, he would feel so affirmed right now. "And from Windermere, Florida, Tiger Woods." The crowd roars its praise as Tiger tugs at the brim of his black cap. "Mr. Mediate has the honor. Play away, please." When Rocco tees up his ball, he doesn't let one leg stretch out behind him gracefully like every other guy on Tour. He straddles the spot where he wants to put the tee and then bends over at the waist like an old man picking a newspaper off his driveway.

It doesn't matter how it looks; he finds the left side of the 1st fairway and in play, which is more than Tiger can say this week. There may be other more memorable shots played today, but none can make Tiger as nervous as his tee shot here. Four tries. No fairways. Three double bogeys. He draws the club back and bends his left knee, then fires it toward the target as his hands drop into the slot and release the club down the line with a blast. His ball is past Rocco's in about three seconds, but the marshal behind the tee is signaling *right* to the volunteers in the fairway. Somehow the ball hits in the rough and takes one giant hop left and back into the fairway. Fifth time's the charm. Tiger hits the green and two-putts, while Rocco misses a six-footer to save par. I wonder if Craig is right. This could be over very quickly.

9:29 AM • After four holes, the 1-shot lead has flip-flopped. Rocco is now a stroke up on Tiger after nearly holing his shot to the par-3 3rd. But out of the fairway bunker on the 5th, Rocco pulls his approach. "Fore left!" I'm above the green as the ball bounces once on the cart path, bounds thirty feet down the hole, and hits the cart path a second time. When it finally stops, it's resting twenty yards left on the steep, burnt-out downslope way left of the green. I look at the shot he has to play and decide there is zero chance he will pull this off. When he walks up, a USGA official reminds us that we need to stand still and be quiet. Rocco shrugs his shoulders and says, "Or you can talk." He nearly saves par, but the bogey brings him back to even with Tiger.

11:14 AM • For the morning's first ten holes, the crowd seems legitimately torn. They can't for the life of them figure out which player is the underdog. At first glance, it's Rocco, the 158th-ranked player in the world, who two weeks ago was in a sectional qualifying tournament just to earn a spot to be here. But then there's Tiger, the fallen hero who has at times looked like he might have to swap out two of his fourteen clubs for crutches just to get through the week. In the middle of the back-and-forth over the front nine, I hear one overwrought fan say that she just wishes *both* players could win.

But after Rocco misses short par putts on the 8th and 9th holes to fall 3 shots behind, they have found their hero. I notice the change right away when Tiger's shot into the par-3 11th disappears into the sand, and the crowd begins to cheer. Not a cheer against Tiger, but a cheer of encouragement for Rocco. He answers the call with an iron to the middle of the green and closes the gap to 2.

11:27 AM • I sprint ahead and all the way down the left side of the 505-yard 12th and see that the grandstands way out here are not actually full, so I sit down like a normal spectator. What a concept. Rocco continues to apply pressure by putting his tee shots in the fairway, while Tiger is starting to get sloppy. Another Rocco par on 12 paired with a Tiger bogey, and the lead is down to just 1.

11:53 AM • With a pair of birdies on the par-5 13th, Tiger and Rocco move to the 14th, which, for the second day in a row, the USGA's Mike Davis has set up at the forward reachable tees. The crowd around the tee greets their man with a cheer: "Let's go, Rocco! *Clap, clap, clap-clap-clap.*" Tiger has completely lost his grip on the fans' affections. I'm worried how falling out of favor affects him, but he is buried in Stevie's yardage book. The advantage of making the crowds invisible is that he doesn't notice them when they're for *or* against him.

Yesterday, Tiger said the tees were so far forward here that it put him right between hitting a 3-wood and a 5-wood, so he had no choice but to play safe and lay up with an iron. In a move that the poker-playing Rocco must appreciate, the USGA is calling Tiger's bluff because it has moved the tees back an extra five steps. It doesn't change Rocco's plan. He puts his 3-wood right on line and just short of the green. Tiger doesn't hesitate. He reaches for the kiwi bird head cover (or monkey, if you're Gilbert) and uncovers his 3-wood. The crowd cheers his bravado. He hits it down near Rocco and just into the rough. The bad lie hurts him, and he can make only a par while Rocco taps in for his second straight birdie. With eighty-six holes now played in the U.S. Open, Tiger and Rocco are once again tied.

12:10 PM • Out of fourteen holes, Rocco and Tiger have only had the same score three times. They both parred 2, they both parred 4, and they both birdied 13. Other than that, one of them has drawn blood every time. It's an all-out battle. Sprinting from 14 green down 15 fairway, I'm joined by seven other fans as we fly in and out of cross-traffic. The 15th at Torrey Pines is a tight, 478-yard par 4 with a towering line of eucalyptus trees down the left side. Off the tee, Rocco is in the fairway again, and Tiger is so far right that, from my spot near the green, I can't even tell exactly where he is.

"Is his ball on the cart path?"

"He's in the sand," a fan tells me.

"The sand?" I'm confused. One of the other features of the 15th is that it's the only hole at Torrey Pines without a fairway bunker. "There's no trap over there," I say. There isn't one on 15, but there is one on number 9. Tiger is forty yards off line.

Even so, Rocco is *still* farther from the hole and has to play first. He lifts the club over his head with his two hands, a clumsy stretch to just keep everything loose. He addresses the ball in his typical fashion, a series of nervous twitches and false starts before drawing the club back and then flailing at it in a way that no one would copy, but that he can repeat with unbelievable accuracy. The approach hits just past the front pin and stops twenty feet long. There is no choke in this guy today.

Back on number 9, Tiger is finalizing his attack. Besides the fact that he is on the downslope of a bunker on the wrong hole and behind a tree, it's a fairly routine shot. Tiger digs his feet in, takes a last look, and goes with a flailing swing of his own, wrapping his arms around his body and trying to will the ball left around the tree and over the green-side bunker. We all lose sight of it in the air and wait. It lands on the front part of the green, releases, and rolls inside Rocco's ball by at least ten feet—it's the best shot out of trouble that I've ever witnessed.

12:20 PM • Rocco is away. A downhill putt, left to right. It's still accelerating when it flies into the hole. As the crowd erupts, Rocco braces himself with his putter, as if waiting for the cup to cough it back up, having realized the ball is not a Nike One. All I can do is stand in stunned silence. Rocco shrugs and waves, then walks off to the side of the green, where he immediately turns his back on the 15th green and faces 16, already thinking about his next shot and what the wind is doing above the trees.

Unlike Rocco, Tiger's killer instinct is always on the surface, and when Rocco's birdie drops, Tiger's expression never changes. He's only looking at his own birdie putt—a downhiller as well, but ten feet closer. When Tiger knocked his second shot stiff, he must have thought he would be putting to take the lead. Now he needs it just to stay even. His birdie putt starts three inches right, and never comes back. Now everyone is shocked, twelve thousand people all telling one another, "I can't believe this." Rocco's birdie has already deadened my senses. Just like yesterday, Tiger is 1 down with three to go.

The inside-the-ropes mob must be two hundred people at this point, and at the front of the procession headed to 16 is Rocco. Seeing him go, the irony hits me. What I am witnessing is exactly the scenario I have been dreaming of since 1996: the unheralded, likable everyman challenging Tiger shot for shot on the biggest of stages and actually pulling it off. For twelve years it was just this possibility that kept me tuning in even when every bookie in the world said there was no chance Tiger could lose. And now that it's happening, I can't imagine anything less enjoyable.

In 1986, when Tiger was ten, Tiger and Earl came down as they did every summer for the Junior World Golf Championships. Tiger's age division always played at Presidio Hills, a pitch-and-putt course near SeaWorld. But with Tiger having turned ten, Earl told him he was a big boy now, and he would treat Tiger to eighteen holes anywhere he wanted. Tiger said Torrey Pines South. For him to let the Open slip through his grasp at a course he's cherished for more than twenty years may come as close as anything ever could to crushing his spirit.

12:32 PM • On 16, both Rocco and Tiger try to hole their forty-foot birdie putts from the front of the green. Rocco's misses right. Tiger's heads for the center of the cup and comes up one inch short. He never leaves important putts short. The putter drops from his left hand in disbelief. One stroke down with two to play.

12:46 PM • On 17, Tiger hits his first fairway since the 9th hole. Rocco hits the green and two-putts. So does Tiger, again leaving his birdie effort on line but short. They pass through the ropes from 17 to 18. For the third straight day, Tiger needs to make up a stroke on the last hole. If he can't, it's over. From the middle of the crowd, someone says, "Order your DVD today!" In time I may grow to acknowledge that is a pretty funny line, but not right now.

Rocco uses the big towel on his golf bag to wipe down his face. He's nervous. One more good hole and he will be the oldest winner ever of the U.S. Open. And a legend. After bogeying the 10th, Rocco has played the back nine 3 under par. And hasn't missed a single fairway . . . until now. The second Rocco sees where he's hit his tee shot, he growls, mad at himself. I can't follow the ball, but I don't need to. With his big draw, his only misses are left. Rocco will have to lay up.

Tiger doesn't need any more motivation to hit the fairway. He just has to erase any memories of his blocked drive on the 15th, the last time he used this club. If there's one thing Tiger has done well this week, it's forget. The double bogeys, the lost leads, the pain . . . His driver stops just short of parallel and rockets back down through the ball. It's high, fading, and perfect. He can go for the green.

12:53 PM • It's a Monday afternoon, and there are more people here today than yesterday. By seventy-five yards out, the only open gap through which to move is a single-file line with fans pressing in on both sides. The top speed of this line is roughly one inch every other second. I get into the queue just as Tiger's iron from the fairway clears the lake and lands on the front of the green. He will have a long putt for eagle to a back-right pin. When Rocco's third shot lands on the green, the crowd cheers again. I can't see a thing. My view is blocked by the back side of the scoreboard. I pull up my scope and do the very complicated maneuver of walking while using a periscope. My left eye looks through the sight, waiting for a clear shot. My right eye watches the woman in front of me and tries to keep the number of times I bump into her under a hundred.

I have to use the sounds and my imagination to guess what's happening. From watching 602 holes so far, this comes easily to me. I can still hear some scattered conversations. It means that Tiger has stopped halfway between his ball and the hole, swinging the putter through with only his left hand while looking at the cup. Rocco is moving manically, keeping busy with his towel, drying things that probably aren't even wet. When the chatter stops, it means that Tiger is over the ball, the hand-drawn black line on top aimed right down his line. Stevie is off to the side. Is he wearing his bib? He has to be. This is the rare time when he doesn't want the round to end.

I clear the end of the scoreboard just as Tiger's forty-foot eagle putt leaves the putter. If he makes it, Rocco can't catch him. Right away, the grandstands tell us he's missed it. It's a foot right and slides four feet long. He has avoided the worse sin of not even giving himself a chance, but he's given Rocco Mediate a birdie putt to win the U.S. Open. Tiger walks straight-faced to the ball and marks it, hoping he'll need to make it.

Rocco is in the middle of the green and has less than twenty-five feet to the hole. After working with his caddy on finding the right line, he fidgets one last time and hits it. The moment he does, everyone screams. Some are hoping to will it in, others trying to keep it out. His comes closer than Tiger's but rolls by on the high side and settles three feet away. People hoot and clap, knowing that if they both make their short ones, the most-watched Monday playoff in U.S. Open history will keep going.

Tiger summons Stevie to take a look at the putt. Stevie looks at it from both sides twice and then shrugs. If there's any break in it, he doesn't see it. Tiger is satisfied and starts to pull the trigger on what is usually a gimme when a seagull dive-bombs the green. Even the animal kingdom is making him work for this. He backs off, starts over, and putts it firm, dead center. Stevie was right and it rolls right into the heart of the hole. Rocco makes his par, and both men shoot an even-par 71. They remove their caps and shake hands. Seventy-two holes wasn't enough. And neither is ninety.

1:11 PM • The good news is that it's not 1946. Back then, when Lloyd Mangrum, Byron Nelson, and Victor Ghezzi tied after the first eighteen-hole playoff, the USGA made them play a *second* eighteen holes. In 1954, it changed to "hole by hole," a format that really just means sudden death. With Rocco plopped on the 18th green double-checking his scorecard, an announcement from a speaker informs us the playoff will continue at the 460-yard 7th, then move to the 8th, then back to 18. I've decided that they will do this in perpetuity for thirty to forty years, until either Rocco or Tiger dies.

1:20 PM • Tiger hasn't missed a drive on the 7th all week; it's just one of those holes that sets up well for his eye. He finds the right edge of the fairway. By contrast, it's a terrible hole for Rocco, a left-to-right hole for a right-to-left player. He misses his drive left and into the fairway bunker. It was out of the fairway bunker on 5 this morning where Rocco pulled his approach and bounced it off the cart path twice. He pulls it again, up against the grandstands.

Tiger's ball is only 150 yards from the hole. He and Stevie dissect the wind as they have all week, throwing grass into the air, looking at the tops of the trees and the row of flags behind them on the grandstands at 18. When ESPN.com did a feature on Stevie in April, Tiger joked, "Good luck trying to make him sound intelligent." Stevie does the occasional goony thing, but he has worked his tail off this week. It's hard to quantify who is the best caddy in golf, but he is undoubtedly the best caddy for Tiger—a perfect balance of everything Tiger needs at his side during the course of a round. He can be a jock, a jerk, a cheerleader, and, right now, a meteorologist.

It's only a short iron from this distance. The pin is cut left of the green's one bunker. Tiger swings at it hard, one last brutal twist of the knee as the club compresses the ball for a millisecond before it soars above the pines and lands safely on the front of the green, thirty feet from the hole.

1:24 PM • Rocco takes a free drop away from the bleachers and pitches it long, twenty feet away for par. All weekend Tiger has had putts he needed to make just to stay alive. Now he has one to win. As on 16, it's on line and stops an inch short. Tiger falls onto his knees. He has nothing left. He uses his putter for leverage as he stands back up, then uses it again to tap in for par on the 91st hole. Rocco must make his left-to-righter or it's over. Nothing seems impossible at this point. Way off in the distance, at least two holes away, I hear one last fading chant by a single fan: "Let's go, Rocco . . . Let's go, Rocco . . ."

Tiger and Stevie retreat to the right side of the green. Even now, Tiger is stoic, never flinching, never dropping his guard at the risk of losing. He watches the hole with the same death glare he gave me that first morning at the Buick Invitational. Rocco's putt heads down the hill. The pace is right, the line looks good, but it never breaks. Tiger Woods has just won the 108th U.S. Open.

I've cried three times in my life while watching professional sports. The first was after Kirk Gibson's ninth-inning home run to win Game 1 of the 1988 World Series. I was eleven. It was an L.A. kid's dream—the injured outfielder (oddly enough, also a left knee) coming off the bench to play hero one last time. The second was during the 1999 U.S. Open at Pinehurst: Payne Stewart's winning par putt on the last hole to beat Phil Mickelson. At the time, Phil was waiting for word from his wife, Amy, who was due with their first child any moment. He was crushed by the loss. Payne came over to him, grabbed his somber face with both hands, and said between tears, "There's nothing like being a father." I wouldn't have kids for six years, but I knew then that this was a man with the right priorities. The third time is right now, on number 7 at Torrey Pines after watching a broken Tiger Woods summon the will to win his fourteenth major championship.

His Saturday chip-in on 17 gave us embarrassed delight. The Sunday birdie to stay alive on the 18th triggered a scream toward the heavens. But as Rocco's putt misses on the high side of the hole, for a moment Tiger Woods has no reaction at all. He stands on the fringe of the 7th green with his hands on his hips, his mind focused on only one thing—the 8th tee. He won't relent, even when it's over.

Stevie turns and hugs him, and he's caught off guard. Cautiously, he returns the embrace, coming out of his daze little by little. Eventually, a smile appears. Rocco crosses over, and Tiger removes his cap, his hair matted and thinning. As he extends his right hand, Rocco brushes it aside. For the second time in less than a minute, Tiger's surprised by a hug.

The trophy ceremony is back on the 18th green. Since the bleachers have been full since late this morning, security lets us stream under the ropes and form a line in front of the lake. Tiger beat me to the green and is already there with his mom, Tida, his wife, Elin, and holding his daughter, Sam. She doesn't want him to leave, but he has to. The U.S. Open trophy is waiting to be claimed.

Jim Vernon, the USGA president, tries to introduce himself, but the microphone balks at the idea, sending feedback through every speaker. "How about that?" he says. If he weren't planning on cutting to the chase, he is now. "Please join me in welcoming our 108th U.S. Open Champion . . . Tiger Woods." Tiger takes the silver trophy, kisses it, and raises it high above his head. We all have one more true roar left in us, and now is the perfect time to use it.

48 HOURS LATER • I usually love hearing from Miller, the Iowa student who drove twenty hours from Texas to go to the CA Championship in March. He always seems to know interesting news about Tiger Woods long before I do. Miller is the one who told me Tiger had bought a $65 million estate in the Hamptons. It turned out to be a mistake, but I told him to keep the hearsay coming, because every once in a while, rumors turn out to be true. Unfortunately, the rumor he delivers today has already been confirmed by the Associated Press: Tiger Woods is done for the season.

Tiger tore his ACL, the ligament that connects the bones in the knee. And he didn't do it during the U.S. Open; he did it last July while on a run around Isleworth. In between, he had merely won ten of thirteen events. But the stress of playing on a weakened knee led to the cartilage damage, which in turn led to the surgery after the Masters. The hope was that the knee would be strong enough to carry him through the rest of the season.

When the rehab in April and May proved slower than Tiger expected, he kept working anyway and two weeks before the Open was told that he had fractured his tibia in two places. The fractures would heal as long as he spent three weeks on crutches and three more weeks of rest. According to Hank Haney, Tiger looked at the doctor and said, "I'm playing the U.S. Open, and I'm going to win."

The news explains why I swore I heard Haney's voice crack Monday afternoon in the press tent. At that point, Rocco had already come and gone, defeated but not discouraged. It had to be the first press conference a moderator ended by saying "Congratulations" to someone who had just lost. Rocco left behind his black Callaway hat covered in three collectible Open pins. It would be in Rand Jerris's carry-on the next day and on display at the USGA Museum by Wednesday morning.

Tiger was gone, too, off to film various sit-down interviews on the cliff behind the tent. In his place he left Hank. With the exception of when Hank told Tiger his putter blade was open "half a degree" at Augusta, I had never heard him speak. He was thoughtful and sensitive, the anti-Stevie. Whereas Stevie is happiest behind the wheel of a racecar, Haney appeared perfectly content just standing in the corner, his hands in his pockets. Reporters gathered around him, including Luau Larry. For the first time all year, he and I were getting the scoop at the same time.

There wasn't a flurry of questions. It was mostly just Hank talking. He explained how Tiger had prepared for this week, if one can call it preparing. "It was limp to the balls, hit five, then limp back to the cart." When he had hit fifty, he was done. *For the day.* That wasn't even half the number of balls Tiger had hit Monday morning on the range. When he tried to talk about how much this Open meant to Tiger, that's when I thought I caught him stifling tears. He knew then what I wouldn't know until today—that Tiger had given up the chance to play good golf for the rest of the year in order to play his best golf for just one glorious week.

AFTERWORD

The night that Tiger won his second U.S. Amateur in 1995, Earl Woods made a prediction. "Before he's through, my son will win fourteen major championships." At the time, the crowd around him cheered, but also laughed. Earl was prone to over-the-top statements. Thirteen summers later, I hope that number was a lowball estimate, because now Tiger is there. Fourteen. Four short of Jack Nicklaus's record. And injured.

When the news of his season-ending surgery filtered down to people who don't follow golf, a period of time that took less than three hours, I received a lot of phone calls from friends treating the situation as if there had been a death in the family. "I . . . I just heard," most of the calls began.

But assuming he returns stronger than ever, as doctors predict, there was no need to mourn. In 2008, Tiger Woods played in seven official events worldwide. He won five of them, all with a torn ACL and the last one with two stress fractures. That's not a bad season. In fact, as I write this, two and a half months after the U.S. Open and with all the majors now over, Tiger remains in first place on the 2008 PGA Tour money list with almost $5.8 million earned. Trailing him, by over a half-million, is Vijay Singh, who has now played in fourteen more Tour events this season than Tiger.

This is what my dad finds so amazing about Tiger. He was convinced that Jack Nicklaus would be the last player to ever dominate the sport. By the early 1980s, the talent pool was deeper than it had ever been, and the end result was parity. The top players, almost all of which were country-club bred, blended together in a haze of shaggy hair and polyester pants. The fact that the person who would threaten all of Nicklaus's records was an African-American who grew up playing on a military golf course was mind-boggling. And fantastic.

It was never Tiger's talent I questioned. I was stubborn, but I wasn't dumb. It was his attitude that always left me scratching my head. I couldn't understand how so many fans could happily root for someone who seemed to go to great pains to ignore each and every one of them. It appeared that America was drinking the Kool-Aid, or more appropriately, Tiger Gatorade, and the only reason to adore him was that Buick and Nike and TLC Laser Eye Center told them to do it.

Few of the fans I met felt his coldness. And like Gilbert, the fan I met on the driving range who didn't know Nike made "metals," not everyone even connected Tiger to his various endorsements. Only I was looking at Tiger and seeing an unhealthy obsession with winning. Most people just looked at him and saw a man who was determined to succeed and refused to apologize for it.

It's an out-of-fashion idea. In fact, the kind of man Tiger Woods represents is out of fashion. He's direct and disciplined. He rarely switches his opinion. He holds a grudge like a back-nine lead on Sunday. And the things that he can't control he treats with the same repeated thought: *It is what it is.* Over the course of his interviews and press conferences with reporters in 2008, he used that phrase a total of eighteen times. The noise of fighter jets near Torrey Pines: "It is what it is." The diseased greens at Bay Hill: "It is what it is." The rain delays at the CA Championship: "It is what it is." His troubled knee: "It is what it is."

Our modern-day heroes tend to be conflicted and sensitive, which eventually leads them to be bumbling and then, most deflating, apologetic. Any honest person knows Tiger Woods makes mistakes. He swears too much. He probably shouldn't have skipped his daughter's baptism. And perhaps he should have waited until his ball was actually in the hole before taking off his hat to shake Aaron Baddeley's hand at the Match Play.

But dwelling on Tiger's flaws seems like a misuse of resources. There are plenty of professional athletes who already fill that role quite nicely, doing far worse things with impressive regularity. His strengths are what deserve our attention.

And yet when you mash all those strengths together, the God-given and the learned, there's still no guarantee of greatness. It all hinges on something ultimately quite simple: a passion for improvement. Tiger Woods never did acknowledge me. For all I know, we'll never even meet. But that doesn't mean I don't know him. And with every tournament he wins, he reminds me of what can be achieved when someone does what he loves the best that he possibly can.

MONDAY, U.S. OPEN, 3:30 PM ● After Hank Haney's impromptu interview, I take my broken periscope and my notebook and walk back through Torrey Pines. Workers are already soaking the hard and dry Open greens. Inside the Lodge, there are no signs of Tiger's unforgettable victory ninety minutes earlier. The gift shop is empty, its one worker lost in thought. A few couples are eating a late lunch in the grill. At the bar are plenty of empty seats, where Open highlights play to low volume in the background. The little hint of what has happened comes when I step outside and Tiger Woods walks right past me, gripping the

U.S. Open trophy tightly against his chest. After everything that happened this week, he is not about to let it go.

I walk out to Torrey Pines Road and wait at the curb. A few minutes later, a gray Camry pulls up with a wife and two kids inside who are anxious to have me back. "I'll drive," I say. I click my seat belt, and we head home.

ACKNOWLEDGMENTS

Above all else, I must thank my wife, Hillary, for (1) encouraging me to follow Tiger Woods at the Target World Challenge and (2) showing great patience when what she thought was a harmless idea overtook our lives.

It's impossible to forget the day in January when David Hirshey at HarperCollins asked what would happen to the book if Tiger became injured—we shared a laugh over the absurdity of the thought. Thanks to David for his faith in Tiger (and me) from the beginning. I'm also indebted to Kate Hamill, my editor at HarperCollins, whose lack of obsession with golf made the finished product far better as a result. Assisting both of them was George Schlesinger, the lone golfer in Harper's office, who undoubtedly spent weeks defending my obscure golf terms without me knowing.

Scott Miller diligently served as my research and stats guru . . . all between his freshman and sophomore years in college. I made it clear that he would be receiving no summer credits from this, but he didn't stop until every last question was answered.

Thanks to my TV agent, Tom Wellington at Endeavor, for introducing me to my book agent, Shawn Coyne. Both made getting something published appear easy. But I would not have even had an idea to pitch if it weren't for Jason Sobel at ESPN.com, and his willingness to let an unemployed TV writer take a crack at golf humor.

Without the wisdom of the following writers and readers, I'd still be agonizing over my introduction: WFB, Grant Nieporte, Alan Kirschenbaum, Greg Garcia, Bob Pease, Bob Sandberg, Jamie Rhonheimer, Sharon Sampson, Jeremy Blachman, James Melcher, Pink Smiley, Mom, and Dad.

Since I couldn't pay them, I have to mention all those who made the adventure just that: Craig Nelson, Jay, Kelly and Dan, Craig and Katie, Joe and Lane, Grant Geckler, Matthew, Howard Wolf, Joe Buti, Doug Austin, Dr. Marc Lederman, Mike Werle, Dan and Mary Pennington, Drew and Jerry Leamon, Rob and Jim Hays, Scott Verplank, Bob Tway, and my kids, Danny and Katie.

And, of course, thanks to the great Tiger Woods himself. Hurry back.

Finally, to all true Tiger fans, who have the highest expectations in sports, I hope this book makes you feel that you were right there alongside me. And based on the size of the crowds I've traveled with this year, maybe you were.